FOUR YEARS' CAMPAIGN

IN INDIA

D1830129

Owing to the antiquity and rarity of this book, certain pages are regrettably absent, and readability is compromised due to the blurring of the original text. If you possess any insights regarding the availability of these missing sections, kindly inform us. Your assistance is crucial in ensuring the completion of this significant work for the benefit of future generations.

FOUR YEARS' CAMPAIGN

IN INDIA

WILLIAM TAYLOR

GYAN

Published by

GYAN

Gyan Publishing House
5, Ansari Road
Daryaganj, New Delhi-110002
Phone: 011-47034999, 9811692060
E-mail: books@gyanbooks.com

Distribution Network
gyanbooks.com
India, USA, Canada, UK, Australia

© Publisher
All rights reserved. No part of this work may be reproduced, stored, adapted, or transmitted in any form or by any means, electronic, mechanical, photocopying, micro-filming, recording or otherwise, or translated in any language, without the prior written permission of the copyright owner and the publisher.

ISBN: 978-93-7014-146-9 (PB)

First Published, 1880

2nd Impression 2025

Printed at: Gyan Press, Delhi.

The book is sold subject to the condition that it shall not, by way of trade or otherwise, be lent, resold, hired out, or otherwise circulated without the prior publisher's written consent.

FOUR YEARS' CAMPAIGN IN INDIA
Arthur WILLIAM TAYLOR

FOUR YEARS' CAMPAIGN IN INDIA.

1. 2. 3. 4.

KRISHNĀ, HIS WIFE AND COUSINS.

[FRONTISPIECE.

FOUR YEARS' CAMPAIGN IN INDIA.

BY

WILLIAM TAYLOR,

AUTHOR OF

"California Life Illustrated," "Christian Adventures in South Africa," "Reconciliation: or, How to be Saved," "Infancy and Manhood of Christian Life," "Election of Grace," "Model Preacher," etc., etc.

London:

HODDER AND STOUGHTON,

27, PATERNOSTER ROW.

NEW YORK:

NELSON & PHILLIPS, 805, BROADWAY,

1875.

PREFACE.

I HAVE not written a history of India, nor of its great Christian Missions, but simply a narrative of what I have felt and seen and done in the East, covering a period of four years and seven months.

As far as possible, I have avoided foreign words; but to assist the English reader in pronouncing Hindūstānī names, I will here explain that

"a" has the sound of short u, as in cut: "ā" the broad sound of ah: "ī" the sound of ee: and "ū" of oo.

This short, easy lesson, with its three accented letters illustrated in the word Hindūstānī, had better be learned at first sight, and then the reader can proceed with a correct pronunciation.

A "rupee" is equivalent to two shillings, or forty-eight cents; an "anna" is the sixteenth of a rupee; a "pice" is the fourth, and a "pie" the twelfth, of an anna.

"It is too soon to write a history of your campaign in India."

Philosophic deductions from history are held long in suspense; but without the current facts of history, what could the annalist do? Facts of value should be recorded fresh from the memory of those who know them. The delineation of individual character cannot be completed even when the individual is dead; for the current of his influence will run on in the great stream of life for ever; it is nevertheless proper to record facts about the man as he is passing—such as his birth, his baptism, his conversion to God, his business, etc. So I may be allowed to tell of the birth of a new soul-saving Mission in a great heathen country, and record specimen facts, incidents, and illustrations of the first three years of its eventful life. I am not writing merely for the historian, but giving the first published report of this new Mission to the churches at large, that they may thank God for its existence, and prayerfully sympathize with it in its great work, and in its struggles, defeats, victories, and prospects.

Some writers have a great dread of mentioning names. There are two classes of persons whose names I should always prefer to leave out: first, such as would be shocked or injured in any way by the insertion of their names; and, second, such as are anxious to see their names in print.

"But suppose some whose names are given as promising converts should turn out badly?"

Yes,—like Simon Magus, Demas, Hymenæus, Alexander, and many others, whose names were recorded by inspired authors. A writer who waits till the subjects of his narrative are all dead, and then (if he does not, meantime, die himself) gives only the good cases, does not, after all, give a true exhibit of history.

"Cooked" accounts in business, and "cooked" historical facts, are alike misleading. There are, to be sure, cases pending which cannot be judiciously stated till the evidence and the issue are known; but let us have a fair statement of the leading facts, in all their varieties and bearings.

With very limited opportunities for writing, this is what I have endeavoured to do in the narrative I now respectfully submit to my readers.

WM. TAYLOR.

LONDON, *July 6th*, 1875.

CONTENTS.

CHAPTER I.

PREPARATIONS.

CHAPTER II.

LUCKNOW.

CHAPTER III.

CAWNPORE.

CHAPTER IV.

CONFERENCE TIME IN LUCKNOW.

CHAPTER V.

PANAHPORE.

CHAPTER IX.

BOMBAY.

CHAPTER X.

THE MARATTI MISSION.

CHAPTER XI.

ENGLISH WORK IN THE INSTITUTION HALL.

CHAPTER XII.

MAZAGON MEETINGS.

[CHAPTER XIII.

NEW OUTPOSTS.

CHAPTER XVII.

INVITATION TO POONA.

CHAPTER XVIII.

THE SIEGE OF POONA.

CHAPTER XIX.

MISSIONARY RECRUITS.

CHAPTER XX.

PROGRESS OF NATIVE CONVERTS.

CHAPTER XXI.

CALCUTTA.

CHAPTER XXV.

BANGALORE AND ONWARD.

CHAPTER XXVI.

LIGHT IN DARKNESS.

CHAPTER XXVII.

SUMMARY REVIEW.

CHAPTER XXVIII.

THE OUTLOOK.

FOUR YEARS' CAMPAIGN IN INDIA.

CHAPTER I.

PREPARATIONS.

IT may be interesting to note some of the providential leadings to this campaign. As early as 1863 an old India missionary, Rev. J. Smith, now of the Baptist Mission in Delhi, attended my services in Melbourne, Australia, and begged me to make an evangelistic tour in India. The year following, in New South Wales, a Church missionary from Madras made a similar request. The impression thus made on my mind deepened, until I resolved (D.V.) to spend a year or two in India on my return from Australia. In December 1865 my family from California joined me in Sydney: I had not seen them for over three years, and should not have known my dear boys had I met them in the street. I embraced them and wept, and said to one of them, "Ross, do you know me?"

"Yes, papa."

"How do you know me?"

"My mother told me it was you."

So he received me by faith, based on his mother's testimony. "Faith cometh by hearing." Then the great wheel of tribulation passed over us. Our dear Stuart, a pious youth of nineteen years, was laid down by a dangerous illness; and after weary weeks of watching, we were told by his physicians that a voyage to the Cape of Good Hope might, by the mercy of God, save his life. Hence my African campaign, resulting in the professed conversion to God of twelve hundred colonists and seven thousand Kaffirs, as reported in detail in "Christian Adventures in South Africa." That work, I am glad to learn from missionaries there, has been gradually extending ever since. Thence we sailed for London, and in the early part of 1867 I laboured in sixteen chapels in that great city. From thirty to eighty persons in each short series of services (of about a week) professed to find the pardon of their sins; but the time was too limited for a signal result. I spent about eleven months in England and Scotland on that occasion, labouring principally among the Wesleyans, and a few weeks for the Free Church in Edinburgh. At the request of my family, who had spent the summer of that year in Switzerland, it was arranged that they should return to California—all except Stuart, who remained in Lausanne to pursue his studies.

Wesleyan missionaries from the West Indies repeatedly urged me to consider the need of those islands. The missions there, formerly very prosperous, had been declining, so that their reports in six years showed a decrease in membership of over 6600. I accordingly sailed for the West Indies by the Royal packet line in October 1867. We reached St. Thomas just after the great hurricane, tidal wave, and earthquake, which had done so great damage to the town, and sent to the bottom every ship in her beautiful harbour. I commenced work in the island of Barbadoes, and had a glorious work of God there under the superintendency of Rev. Henry Hurd. I went thence in a twenty-five-ton schooner (500 miles) to British Guiana in South America, where we had a still greater work. Then, owing to the relapse and severe illness of our dear Stuart in Switzerland, I was obliged to stop short and return to Europe. I found him more dead than alive, and took him by short stages to Great Malvern, in England, where in three months, under Dr. Grindrod's hydropathic treatment, he recovered. Meantime I laboured in contiguous towns, and visited the Irish Conference in Dublin. To confirm Stuart's health, I took him on a tour through the Highlands of Scotland, spending, on our way, a few days at the session of the Wesleyan Conference in Liverpool. In September 1868 he sailed for America, and soon after I resumed my labours in the West Indies.

When I went first to the West Indies I expected to go thence to California, but before my return-trip I received a letter from Rev. J. M. Thoburn of India, entreating me to go and help them there. Through this, with a variety of providential indications, I worked out the following programme for an evangelistic tour:—Tobago, Trinidad, Grenada, St. Vincent, Nevis, St. Catharine's, and Jamaica—West India Islands; thence by the Panama and New Zealand line of steamers to New Zealand, for a re-visit there, and on to the Australian colonies, and thence to India. I wrote my plan of appointments to my friend Dr. A. Moffitt, M.D., of Sydney, and that I would (D.V.) be at his house by the 15th of May 1869.

We had a grand work of God in all the said West India Islands, except Jamaica. The two months I planned for that island had to be spent at sea, on account of the suspension of the New Zealand and Panama line of steamers—which obliged me, by an extra ten thousand miles of travelling and an extra cost of one hundred pounds, to return to England, and proceed to Australia by the Peninsular and Oriental Company's line of steamers, by which I reached Sydney the 17th of May, only two days beyond the time set a year before.

On the voyage out I spent three days at Galle, Ceylon, and made the acquaintance of Rev. John Scott, chairman of the Wesleyan Missions of South Ceylon, and a number of his ministers. He begged me to put their missions on my plan, and I consented to do so. I spent fourteen months on this revisit to the Australian colonies and Tasmania, reached Galle again on the 6th of August 1870, and the following November came on to India.

The details covered by this meagre outline would fill volumes with facts of marvellous interest, but my present limits preclude them, except to state that in the West Indies the Wesleyans had that year a net increase in members and probationers of upwards of five thousand souls.

The review of the work in Australia was upon the whole most gratifying. During my former campaign in those colonies, of two years and eight months, the ministers, on personal profession and record by name, reported over six thousand converts at my meetings; and the work so widely extended that the aggregate net increase of members, not including probationers, in the returns of the Australasian Conference for the three years inclusive, amounted to over eleven thousand. Then, according to their Annual Minutes, instead of a shrinkage, the first year after I left they had a net increase of over three thousand more, the next, two thousand, the next, one thousand, the next, fifteen hundred, and the year of my return over three thousand—making a net increase for the seven years of over twenty-one thousand members. Other churches also shared in the blessing more or less, according as they co-operated in the work. Of course I am not claiming the credit of this work of God, being but one of unnumbered efficient agents used by the Holy Spirit; but I give these index facts for what they are worth. Sixteen of the young men who had been saved during my first tour in the Australian colonies, I found, on my return, engaged in the work of the ministry, besides scores of local preachers.

The work in Ceylon was glorious, both among the Wesleyans, and also the Church missionaries in Badagam and Kandy,—amounting to an aggregate, according to the record of the missionaries, of one thousand converts. Most of these were Singhalese, about one-tenth of whom were fresh from Buddhism—the remaining larger proportion from the ranks of nominal Christians, who had before received Christianity, but now received Christ and salvation in Him.

ARRIVAL IN INDIA.

THE Peninsular and Oriental Company's steamship "Malacca," on which I came from Ceylon, cast anchor at half-past eight a.m. on Sabbath the 20th of November 1870, in the harbour of Bombay.

On deck stood Bishop Milman of Calcutta, his chaplain and two servants, beside a small cartload of luggage, waiting for the first boat to take them ashore. The Bishop seeing me sitting quietly, book in hand, said,—

"Are you not going ashore?"

"Yes, Bishop; but breakfast here will be ready in half an hour, and I don't think it advisable to leave a good breakfast behind and go hungry into a strange city."

He replied that he was in haste, and could not wait, and soon after they descended the ship's ladder. Now two fair, tall, slender natives came aboard, wearing each a curious-looking, flattened stove-pipe turban.

"Steward," said I, "what sort of fellows are these?"

"They are Parsees."

I was at once carried back to Cyrus, Zoroaster, and other "wise men of the east," and was just beginning to live in the past ages, when one of them addressed me in good English, and asked me to become his guest in the Byculla Hotel; adding, "We have a boat alongside, and a carriage waitingon shore."

I replied, "If you will wait till I get my breakfast, I will go with you."

"All right; we'll wait: show us your luggage, and we will put it into the boat."

My small leather trunk and carpet-bag were soon passed down the ship's ladder. Braced up with a good breakfast, and safely seated in the Parsees' boat, I said to one of them, "Are there any Methodists in this city?"

"Metodist! what is that? I never heard that word before."

They took me through a shoal of sharks—boatmen and 'longshoremen—and I did not get a bite; and as we drove off in our carriage and pair in good style, we passed a clamorous crowd, and lo! in the midst of it, and its principal attraction, was a one-horse cab containing the Bishop and his chaplain, brought to a standstill by an extortionary lot of 'longshore coolies demanding pay. Any stranger, not having run such a gauntlet, can form but a very inadequate idea of the annoyance attending it. What a time the Bishop must have had! With a good breakfast aboard, I drive on in comfort, and leave the hungry Bishop and his "one-horse concern" hard aground. I had no pleasure in his discomfort, for he was very genial and kind to me on the voyage; but I thanked God for His good providence in giving me a smooth sail into India. It brought clearly to my mind one of the Lord's innumerable acts of tender care of His unworthy servant, which I experienced on my arrival in the West Indies. At one o'clock in the night our ship anchored a mile off from Bridgetown, Barbadoes, to discharge mails and passengers and proceed on her voyage in an hour. My departure for the West Indies followed my purpose to go so closely that I had no time to write; so no one was expecting me, and there I was a stranger in those dark waters. Mr. B——, a sugar planter from that island, and his two dancing daughters, were just returning home from a visit to England. He seemed to be much interested in my preaching on the voyage, and I thought I might tie to him. "What hotel are you going to, Mr. B——?"

He gave me the name, but did not invite me to go with him. Two boats came alongside, and Mr. B—— engaged one of them. When he had taken in his daughters and luggage, I said, "Have you room for me?"

"No."

The other boat was taking in some army officers; so I said to them, "Can you give me a passage ashore?"

"No; we're full up."

No other boat was in sight, and the ship steaming up for departure. Presently up the ladder came a big black man, saying, "Do you want to go ashore?"

"Yes, here is my luggage"; and in a few minutes we were under weigh. We had with us a couple of young men who had come with him from the shore. I enquired, "Which is the best hotel here for a stranger?"

They told me of one close to the landing.

Then I named the one to which Mr. B—— was going.

"Oh, that is not a good house; and, moreover, they have a fancy ball on hand, and there will be no sleeping done there by anybody to-night."

I then said to my big boatman, "Do you know Rev. Henry Hurd?"

"O yes; he my minister, and dis is de Methodist boat dat brings all de Methodists ashore!"

"Tell Mr. Hurd that California Taylor will be found at this hotel in the morning."

"Ay, ay, sir."

I soon got the only vacant bed in the hotel, and took refuge behind its curtains from hungry swarms of mosquitoes. Very soon Mr. B—— and his daughters and the said officers came in, having failed to get quarters where the dance was going on. To their earnest enquiries about beds, I heard the host reply, "We are full; a gentleman came in a few minutes ago, and got the only remaining bed we had."

I got a good sleep, and was waked up by the Wesleyan ministers, who had come to welcome me to their island mission. Mr. B—— and Co. passed a miserable night among the mosquitoes, and I was sorry for them, they looked so unhappy. Mr. B—— said to me that morning, "How much did your boatman charge you last night?"

"Five shillings."

"Indeed!—my boatman extortioned on me outrageously."

I don't pray to God for smooth voyaging, but He

gives me love-tokens in small matters without asking. I only recognize His hand of mercy and thank Him.

This is a geographical digression, but a part of the inner life I lived on my way to the Byculla Hotel with my two Parsee friends. I was conducted to room No. 26, on the second storey. It is a three-storey building, 230 ft. front, and about 150 ft. deep, and well kept; tariff seven rupees per day.

Suffering from the exhausting effects of excessive labours in Ceylon, and an attack of bodily indisposition on the voyage, I lay in bed nearly all day. In the evening I heard singing in the neighbourhood, and going along a narrow back street near the hotel, I found a congregation of about eighty well-dressed people. The minister was reading a number of parallel passages of the Scriptures, with short comments, "preparatory," he said, "to the ordination of a native brother to the ministry, as an evangelist,—a carrier of good news." Close to the door, near me, sat a young lady attired as a bride, and a young man who appeared to be the bridegroom. The minister, having finished the lesson, came and conducted the said young man to the platform to preach. He is a dark, modest-looking man, apparently about thirty years old,—I suppose of Portuguese descent. He preached about the "law of sin," (Romans vii.): sound in doctrine, brief, clear, and forcible in statement. It would have done credit to a bishop, though lacking illustration and incisiveness of application. Then the pastor, a short, thickset man, about thirty-five or forty in appearance, followed with a few remarks, striking out hard against the

Pope and the Bishop of Bombay; but he lacked the logical force of the man who preached.

"Now," said he, "we will sing one verse, and not detain the congregation." Then he announced the hymn, and said, "We'll sing two verses." Then read the hymn, and added, "We'll sing the last three verses." The singing was spirited, and I enjoyed it. Then the native was called, and came to the platform, and fell down on his knees before the preacher. The minister said, "It is usual publicly to question candidates on the doctrines they are going to preach, but as this brother has long been a preacher among us, and as the time is so short (a quarter to eight p.m.), we'll dispense with all that." He however read a few passages more on the subject of ordination, and gave the Plymouth Brethren a rap. He then told the native to stand up, and putting his hands on his head, offered extemporary prayer for him, and the scene closed with the benediction. That was my first night in India.

Monday, 21st.—Kept indoors, and wrote letters, till in the evening I dragged my weary limbs up Balassas Road as far as the railway bridge, and back to the hotel.

Tuesday, 22nd.—Just before breakfast a German sailor, who was then, he said, "a city missionary," came with a message from Rev. C. Harding, inviting me to stop with him. The sailor seemed full of love to God, but needing instruction. Feeling anxious to do him good, and increase his power of usefulness, I talked to him till half-past eleven a.m.

The train for Lucknow was to leave at one p.m. Having to go three miles to the bank, to get a bill of exchange on London to send to my wife, I took a cab, and the German to show me the way, and went in haste. On our return we called for one minute at the Tract Society's building, to see Rev. George Bowen. He is a long, lean brother. I have heard that he is the most devoted man of God in India, and lives very abstemiously, that he may have the more to give to those who are in need. If the Roman Catholics had him, they would canonize him as a saint. He shook my hand, and said, "Can I do anything for you? Will you have any money?" I thanked him, and replied, "I am in need of nothing, my brother." He expressed regret that I could not tarry a season in Bombay. I said, "Perhaps the Lord may bring me back," and bade him a hurried good-bye. By the help of the kind German I got back to the hotel in time to get my luggage on to the train. I took a second-class ticket for Allahabad—830 miles (forty rupees, eight annas). I have always been in the habit of travelling first-class, as a matter of economy. My travelling time is my opportunity for rest. The recuperation of my over-taxed energies is more to be desired than money; but here in India I must economise closely: I have no resources but the sale of my books. I have brought none to India,—probably no demand for any here, as I shall be working among the natives,—yet having heavy travelling expenses to bear, and my family to support, I must make a little go a long way.

Zig-zag we ascend the mountains, over 3000 feet.

In the same carriage with myself was the preacher whom I had the pleasure of hearing on Sabbath night.

I said, "What young lady was that whom I saw with you at the meeting the other night?"

He blushed a little, and replied, "She is a young lady who has just come out from England to be my wife, and we were married Sabbath evening, before we went to the meeting where you saw us."

"And what has become of her?"

"Oh, she is in the ladies' carriage."

"I am a stranger in this country, but you see I have got your bearings pretty well."

He laughed, and after that we had much Christian communion, though I did not tell him who I was, as he did not ask me. He said he was a Frenchman, but was educated in England. I found out that though of French extraction, he was Indian born. He was a good man, and has since gone to heaven, and the said bride is now a widow.

I spent most of the night in trying to get fixed, and got but little sleep.

Wednesday, 23rd.—Travelled all day over a country nearly level, with small rivers, and, in the distance, ranges of mountains. Trains stop for meals twenty minutes; breakfast seventy-five cents, tiffin fifty cents, dinner at night, one dollar. Weather biting cold.

24th.—Arrived at Allahabad at a quarter-past five a.m. Left for Cawnpore, distant 117 miles, at seven a.m., and arrived at half-past two p.m. Lucknow is forty miles distant; no train till to-morrow; stopping at the Railway Hotel.

25th.—Took a cab and drove across the Ganges on a pontoon bridge at eight a.m., and took train for Lucknow; arrived at eleven a.m. Was met at the station by Revs. Thoburn, Waugh, and Parker, and put up with Brother Thoburn, whom I knew years before, and who had written me to come to India. At six p.m. we had a "thanksgiving dinner" at Brother Messmore's. I had not for ten years met so many American brethren and sisters; for besides those just named, who with Miss Bella Thoburn live here in Lucknow, we have with us Rev. E. W. Parker and wife, just returned from America, and Sister Thomas, wife of Rev. D. W. Thomas of Bareilly, and Brothers Craven and McMahon and their wives, and Brother Buck, and Miss Fanny Sparks: new missionaries just arrived. They were all cheerful and happy, and gave us many of the songs of Zion. I was not well, and could not contribute to the entertainment of the occasion.

26th.—Was introduced to Joel, one of our first native preachers, and tried to drill him into the art of interpreting; but he is not quite well enough up in English.

CHAPTER II.

LUCKNOW.

THE capital of the recent king of Oudh, the scene of so much suffering and slaughter during the Mutiny, and of daring deeds by so many of Queen Victoria's brave soldiers, and the final resting-place of many, including Sir Henry Lawrence and General Havelock, was the place for my first engagement in India. It was one of the principal centres selected for the missionary operations of the Methodist Episcopal Church, and where, as soon as the smoke of battle had cleared away, they opened their mission of peace in 1857. It is not, however, my design to write a history of this Mission, any more than a history of the great field it occupies, but rather a simple narrative of what I saw and felt and did in conjunction with its agents.

Sabbath, 27th.—Preached to a congregation of about 130 natives, from Acts i. 8. Joel interpreted into Hindūstānī. He hesitates, and speaks very slowly, but I believe he gave the meaning pretty clearly.

At four p.m. Brother Thoburn preached in Hindūstānī to about thirty in our house.

At six p.m. we had a congregation of over a

hundred English-speaking people, Europeans, and Eurasians or Indo-Britons—or, as they are often called, East Indians—for convenience I will in this work use the last-mentioned name. To these I preached in English, but it did not seem to affect them at all for good. Some stared at me as though I was there on exhibition, and others seemed disposed to have a jolly time among themselves. Our ministers commenced preaching here to the English-speaking people about ten years ago ; then after a few years they invited the Wesleyans to send a man to take up the English work, that they might devote all their time to the native work. For some years the Wesleyans occupied our place of worship, but more recently—they having built a chapel in the cantonments, two or three miles distant—Brother Thoburn resumed the English services, but had not as yet gone in to get them converted to God and utilized in our mission work. I took strong ground from the start in favour of getting these Europeans and East Indians saved and incorporated into our Mission working force. In their present state the mass of them make a false showing of Christianity, and are terribly obstructive to our great work of leading the heathen and Mohamedans to Jesus.

Every one we get truly saved from sin will be a double gain to our cause—first to remove a stumbling-block, and secondly to secure a living stone resting on "the foundation of the apostles and prophets," and thus becoming an integral part of the spiritual house into which we hope to gather the perishing nations of this great empire. This will not draw us from the native work, but draw them to it as a co-operative and ever-augmenting force. The brethren had a consultation, and consented to this change in their mission policy, wherever a sufficient English population could be found contiguous to our native work.

Monday, 28th.—At seven a.m. preached to about sixty natives. Joel interpreted, but not with a ready utterance. He prayed in his own language most fluently and vociferously. I conclude that he is naturally very slow till his feelings are aroused, and then too impetuous for a good interpreter. He is considered the best native man in the Mission, and I love him; but I fear that he will not be the man for me. At six p.m., English service, we had about sixty hearers. Text Romans v. 1. Had a prayer-meeting after preaching, and three brethren prayed, but no visible stir.

29th.—More natives out at seven a.m. than we had yesterday. Text Luke vii. 29. Brother Thoburn interpreted: short, and to the point, it went home well. Had a prayer-meeting, and a native preacher prayed as they say he never prayed before.

At six p.m. we had about eighty hearers: text Rom. viii. 3, 4. Called for witnesses, and Brothers Thoburn, Parker, Waugh, Craven, McMahon, and Buck gave their testimony for Christ. We then for the first time in the series called for seekers. Seven came forward, and five of them professed to obtain peace with God. At the close of the meeting a woman came to the front and said, "I have been in the service of God from my youth, but for three months past I have walked in dense darkness. Jesus seemed to have left me; but last night, there in my seat, I found Him again, and now I am unspeakably happy." Turning to a young woman who came forward as a seeker, she said, "This is my daughter: she has a good husband." Then the daughter embraced her mother and wept, and told her that her sins were all forgiven, and that she too was happy. They kissed each other, and wept aloud for joy, and thanked God. One of the seekers was a man deep down in the debasement of inebriation, and we did not get him up to-night, though he seems to be sincere. All this is producing a great flutter among the Pharisaic fashionables who come occasionally to our meetings.

30th.—Over eighty persons at seven a.m. meeting. Text Romans iii. 20. Brother Thoburn interpreted well. Twelve seekers came forward, and ten of them professed to find the pardon of their sins, and gave a clear testimony. I explained the way of salvation by faith, through Brother Thoburn, to all of them together, and then spoke to each one singly by Brother Joel, who interpreted readily and well to the seekers. There seems to be a great awakening. This is the first invitation to the natives to come out avowedly as seekers. I wanted first to get them well instructed and awakened. The seeking seemed earnest, and the testimony clear, but no great noise or excitement, as would be seen in an African audience. God has been long preparing for this, and we shall have a great work. Glory to His holy name!

At six p.m. preached to the English congregation; but no seekers came forward. The break last night has excited the opposition of the enemy's forces, and some good people are shocked by what seems to them a novelty. It will work right for all who abide in Jesus.

Thursday, December 1st, 1870.—Good native service. Thoburn interpreted: twenty seekers; thirteen professed to find peace with God. Brother and Sister Parker left to-day for Morādabād, and Sister Thomas for Bareilly. Brother Parker has been home two years, to try to shake off jungle fever, and seemed to have succeeded; but since his return he has been attacked again. He is a noble missionary, and his wife a true helper: God bless them, and prolong their days, to do good in this most needy field!

At six p.m., English audience; seven seekers forward, and three professed.

December 2nd.—As we went this morning to our native service, we saw a Mohamedan sprinkling flour over some ant-holes. Brother Thoburn in Hindūstānī said to him, "What are you doing?"

"Giving food to the ants."

"Is that a work of merit?"

"Yes."

"The ants can provide well for themselves: why not give food to your starving neighbours?"

"The rich can do that; I am too poor to help them, but I can feed the ants."

At our meeting this morning we had nine seekers, and five professed forgiveness of sins.

Saturday, 3rd.—Took a lamp-bath to break a heavy cold, and got a little greatly-needed sabbatic rest.

Sabbath, 4th.—Preached on holiness. Brother Thoburn interpreted, but he was not well. Had a season of silent prayer, but not time for a public prayer-meeting.

At six p.m., English service, house filled; great attention and awakening. Twenty-eight seekers came and kneeled at the communion-rail, to be instructed and led to Jesus. It was thought that eight or nine of them found peace, but they were not personally examined, and no names were noted. For years in my evangelistic work I did all I could in preaching, calling the seekers forward, and personally instructing them; but the pastors examined them on their profession of saving faith, to satisfy themselves, by questions and otherwise, as to the genuineness of the work, so far as possible to human fallibility, and write down the name and address of each one, so as to give them suitable pastoral care. It is therefore not my place to make this examination, and note the names. Brother Thoburn, being presiding elder of the district, did not like to interfere. The pastor is a dear brother, whom I love sincerely, but he appears to be frightened, or rather his faith seems to be paralyzed, at the time we require decisive advance action.

Monday, 5th.—At seven a.m., native service as usual. Brother Unis, a native school-teacher, interpreted. Half a dozen seekers of pardon, and two professed. About a dozen came forward as seekers of entire purity,—the presiding elder among them, and he gave a beautiful testimony afterwards.

At six p.m., English congregation, eighteen

seekers came forward; none examined, and no satisfactory result. A general feeling of distrust seems to have paralyzed the workers. There may be some frogs in the net,—I know not; but I do know that if there are any good fish among them, we shall not get them into the boat in this way. I thought we had a good haul last night, and certainly the most of them looked well; but it seemed as though the lines were dropped at both ends, and the net was not hauled at all. I am not prepared to give a judgment in the case, not knowing the people: I only know that the Gospel I preach is adapted to all people, but with a doubting, hesitating church it cannot succeed much with any. I am sure all my brethren and sisters here are anxious for a great work of God; but some are not strong in aggressive faith, and some are very busy with other things, and think my meetings too long. Brother Thoburn is working like a Trojan; and many others will yet, I hope, get on the whole armour of God.

Tuesday, 6th.—Unis interpreted; many seekers of pardon, and some seekers of purity. George Bailey received Christ this morning, and told his experience, and exhorted the people in Hindūstānī, weeping as he talked. As we came out of the church, dear Brother Waugh said, "I never but once or twice before heard such Hindūstānī as that—so clear, terse, and forcible."

One day last week, when Brother Thoburn returned home from a visiting tour, he said, "I was in a little hell to-day,—the house of a widow and her two sons, nominally Roman Catholics, but practically worse than the heathen ; but George, the elder son, says he will come to the meeting." That was George Bailey. His great-grandfather was a French Bourbon, but in some disturbance fled to the court of Persia, later to the court of Delhi, and became a general of the emperor of Delhi. His grandfather was a general of the king of Oudh, and his father a captain in the same service. Owing to English prejudice against the employment of French officers by the native rājahs, their French name was dropped, and the plain English name of Bailey given them instead. In the defence of Lucknow during the Mutiny, George was but a boy of sixteen years, but so distinguished himself as a soldier that the rank and pension of an ensign for life were given him. Now he has enlisted in the army of Jesus.

Rev. Brother Weatherbee and his wife arrived today, to attend our services.

I was quite below par to-night with headache from loss of sleep, partly from the burden of this work on my soul. God is assuring me of His gracious designs, but our faith is being severely tested. We had fifteen seekers forward, and I think some of them found peace—among whom was J. Douglass from Calcutta.

Wednesday, 7th.—Unis interpreted well: a few seekers, and two saved. Called a council of war this morning, and I submitted two questions—"1st, Shall we open the doors of our Church and gather up the fruits of our labour, or let them drift? 2ndly, Shall we continue the present order of special services?" Their reply to the first question was, "Yes."

In regard to the second, Brother Thoburn said, "The work seems to be waning : even you do not manifest the same confidence and incisiveness of effort as at the first." He is a sharp brother, and could read me like a book. The fact is, so much was said about long sermons and long after-meetings, and the inability of people in this climate to stand such work, that I partially yielded to the judgment of others, and was also somewhat disconcerted by the general feeling of distrust which seemed to mildew the whole concern. They are all as kind and confiding as possible, and I love every one of them dearly ; but they are familiar and outspoken, and as I am but a novice in India, I have been deferring to them perhaps more than was wise. I know what sort of effort is necessary to success in other countries, and I apprehend that India will require greater zeal, and a more bold, aggressive faith, than any other.

Same day, six p.m.—Good congregation ; over a dozen seekers, and a few professed to find Jesus. Brother Waugh had half a dozen hymns printed on sheets, and the singing to-night was much better than usual; and there is more concert of effort in the church than before. We'll throw off this incubus yet. O God, in mercy deliver us ! I am stopping this week with Brother Waugh. He told me his religious experience and difficulties to-night, and we prayed together. He is a loving, noble brother. Oh that he may receive Christ for a full baptism of the Holy Spirit !

Thursday, 8th.—Preached on Christian fellowship, and explained our policy and position as a Church, and invited candidates for membership. George Bailey was the first to present himself—which he did with characteristic promptness; seven others followed.

In the evening we did the same in the English congregation, and explained our rule on total abstinence from all intoxicating drinks. Only one, a woman, came forward as a candidate for membership. It was altogether a new thing to invite Europeans and East Indians to become members of our Church, but I am sure it is the right thing to do, for they are really not members of any church. They are nearly all traditionally Roman Catholic or Church of England; and to break away and join the despised Methodists, and give up the custom of wine-drinking, and parties of worldly pleasure, which they have hitherto regarded as very harmless, is what they will not do until their conscience on these things shall have been more fully enlightened and quickened.

Friday, 9th.—Fellowship-meeting at noon, conducted by Brother Weatherbee. Brothers Waugh, Weatherbee, Thoburn, and Messmore spoke well. George Bailey testified with great force and effect.

Isā Dās, a native preacher, said, "I came to these meetings an unsaved man. I determined to seek salvation, but I thought to go forward as a seeker would disgrace me. One who has been preaching the Gospel for years to go forward as a seeker! I could not do it. It was too much for my pride. I went three miles out of town, and kneeled down in the darkness of the night in a mango grove, and prayed earnestly to God for the pardon of my sins, but got no relief. But last Wednesday morning I kneeled down there at that rail as a seeker, and received Christ as my Saviour, and got all my sins forgiven." I remember at the time he accepted Christ, Brother Thoburn said to me, "He is one of the most truthful, manly fellows in the Mission, and there can be no mistake about his conversion.

Several others spoke to the point, but some were misty and vague. We had a general time of weeping over the low experience of some; and I was led to say, "Sisters and brothers, you know the difficulties peculiar to India—the paralyzing influence of heathenism, formalism, and caste. It seems to saturate and mildew your very souls; and then you talk about the enervating effect of the climate. God made the climate, and God made the Gospel. If His Gospel is not adapted to this climate, then we will ask Him to change the climate to suit His soul-saving purpose and plan. I tell you, God's Gospel is adapted to every climate, and every variety and condition of human kind. We must have faith in God, and faith in man—God's ability to save, and man's susceptibility of being saved. God will help us, and lead us on to victory. I was overcome with weeping—a very unusual thing in my experience,—the interpreter also; so we kneeled down in silent prayer for a season. Then I led in prayer, and seven others followed. It was a gracious meeting.

At six p.m., English congregation, we had but four seekers, two of whom professed.

Received a letter from Dr. Moffatt, M.D., of Cawnpore, inviting me to go and preach there.

Brother Thoburn goes there for next Sabbath service, in "Union Chapel"—a warehouse fitted up for services, and supplied occasionally by Baptist and Presbyterian missionaries from Allahabad, and sometimes by Brother Broadbent, the Wesleyan chaplain, and by Brother Thoburn, from Lucknow. The Wesleyans had put Cawnpore on their list "to be supplied," but were not prepared to man it, or to commence a mission there. I had no wish to go there, having so much work cut out for me in our Mission Conference.

Sabbath, 11th.—In the morning Unis interpreted, and we had a good seed-sowing.

Six p.m.—The largest crowd of Europeans and East Indians we have had. Thirteen seekers, and six professed.

12th.—Good service morning and evening; six professed to find Jesus.

13th.—Good meetings for the Church, and four saved.

Up to this time over one hundred persons have been forward as seekers, most of whom profess to have found remission of sins. Of these twenty-five have joined our church; about thirty were members before, nominally; as many more are connected with the English Church, and others not organized in Lucknow. God is with us, and doing the best thing possible under existing conditions. George Bailey's wife, a native woman of beautifully fair complexion, received Jesus to-day.

14th.—At noon to-day we had thirty-five Hindū boys from Brother Messmore's school. I preached to them from "Suffer little children to come unto me." Then I said, "I'll teach you to sing." I saw the missionaries start up and whisper to each other. It was a thing never tried there before; and as they told me after the meeting, they expected to see the boys bolt at once; but I sang a verse, and told them of the thousands of children of all lands who were singing these very words. I sang again, repeating the chorus many times, till one and then another of the boys began to repeat after me. "There now! I knew you could sing. You have got the 'sing' in you, and if you will open your mouths it will come out"; and so they did, and we got many to sing, and had a very good time with the boys. At that time we had one small Sunday School in Lucknow; but Brother Craven, being a grand Sunday School worker, took the matter in hand from that day, and before the lapse of four years their Sunday Schools in Lucknow numbered about a thousand scholars, eight hundred of whom at least are Hindū and Mohamedan children. Brother Craven says that this has been done mainly through the agency of Europeans and East Indians brought into our work under this change of our mission policy in regard to these classes.

In the evening preached to the church on witnessing and working for Christ. After the meeting I had a consultation with the missionaries in regard to Cawnpore. Brother Thoburn spent last Sabbath there, and Dr. Moffatt stirred him up to persuade me to go there; and he says that the Doctor knows me, and is most desirous to see me. The brethren expressed themselves freely—some for my going and others against it.

It was urged against it, that Cawnpore was outside of our Conference boundaries, and we had no right to go there; but that was met by Mr. Wesley's saying, "The world is my parish," and by the fact that Brother Thoburn had already preached there several times. One urged that if we should get converts there we had no money nor employment for them. I said, "I never heard of the like before"; and it was finally agreed that if I would not commit the Mission to any responsibility in regard to Cawnpore, I might go and see what the Lord had for us to do there. I laid the whole matter before God, and had every lingering doubt against it removed.

They gave me George Myall, a native teacher and helper, who on Tuesday night last received Jesus and got an assurance of pardon, to accompany me as interpreter. He is a slow, but trustworthy man, had for thirty years lived in Cawnpore, and lost everything he had there in the Mutiny, including 900 rupees in cash; but had been away from Cawnpore for the last five years.

Brother H—— opened his case fully to-day. His complications are too horrible to be penned. When he came forward as a seeker, one of our dear missionaries was horrified, saying, as he passed out of the chapel, "That is the greatest vagabond in the North-West; I have no faith in such a man as that. We are not getting hold of the right sort of stuff at all."

I replied, "He is a large, fine-looking man. He looks like a Scotchman."

"His parents are Scotch, but he is Indian born, and the most hopelessly licentious man I ever saw."

"Well, what could induce such a man to come forward among the seekers, trembling like old Belshazzar, and to struggle there in penitential tears for an hour? God has called the poor fellow by His Spirit, and I'll stick to him and get him saved, if possible."

He came forward many times, and was clearly saved. God afterwards marvellously helped him out of his wicked complications, and he at once became a quiet but earnest worker, speaking personally to all to whom he could get access, and telling them of God's marvellous mercy to him. For example, he met a Scotchman, a stranger to him, at the "Dāk Bungalow," and spoke to him about his soul. The Scotchman opened an infidel battery against him; and as with one learned fallacy after another he tried to demolish the strongholds of Christianity, poor H—— trembled with apprehension for his cause and for himself. He thought he had "waked up the wrong passenger."

When his turn came to reply, he said, "My dear friend, I see that you are a learned man; I am not: I went to school a few months, but I was such a bad boy they turned me out; and I cannot pretend to meet you in argument at all, but if you will allow me, I will tell you a little of my experience."

He then gave the details of his horrible wickedness in the past, of his awakening, and struggles with sin and its dreadful entanglements, and of his great deliverance by the powerful hand of Jesus, and the great peace and joy that filled his soul from that day.

Brother H—— had not the courage to look up till he had done; and then, to his surprise and joy, he saw that the Scotchman was weeping, and heard him exclaim, "Oh, sir, that is just what I need! Will you kindly take me to the place where you got your instructions?" So Brother H—— took him to our preaching-hall, and got him saved. This occurred some months after I left, and is but illustrative of the personal working, witnessing spirit which pervaded the church in Lucknow, of which Brother H—— is now a prominent member.

Friday, 16th.—Good meeting for believers at noon. At night two were saved—one of them a Roman Catholic.

A Christian marriage in the city to-day. To celebrate the occasion, they had a great dance in the Royal Park Hall, which lasted nearly all night. Except the "dancing girls" of India, who are the lowest of fallen women, the Mohamedan and Hindū women would not think of dancing with men. These great feasts to Bacchus, by people called Christians, are innovations on heathen morality, and scandalize the name of Christ.

Saturday, 17th.—Rambled an hour before breakfast among the ruins of the "Residency." The walls of all the buildings are pecked over with the bullet-marks of the mutineers of 1857: on one two-storey wall, twenty feet wide, I counted 300 of them. Passed the gate through which General Havelock's troops, by the mercy of God, brought deliverance to the besieged sufferers ; saw the room in which Sir Henry Lawrence died. The monument here erected in honour of him, and the brave fellows who fell with him, is on a beautiful mound in the Residency grounds. The pedestal at the base is thirty feet square, narrowed by steps to about ten feet square, on which stands an obelisk about thirty feet high.

Left for Cawnpore at one p.m., arrived at four p.m., and was kindly received by Dr. Moffatt.

CHAPTER III.

CAWNPORE.

NOW I see a chain of providential pointers centring in Cawnpore. At the earnest request of my dear friend Dr. A. Moffitt, of Sydney, New South Wales, I promised to visit his nephew, Dr. Moffitt, at the Netley Hospital. I could find no time to fulfil that promise till my second return from the West Indies. Our splendid ship, the "Tasmania," arrived in Southampton early on Tuesday morning, the 16th of March 1869; and I was to set sail again on Friday ensuing, in the steamship "Syria," for Alexandria, *en route* to Australia. I had much to do in London, and time was very precious. I put my luggage in the railway waiting-room, and took a cab to go in haste five miles to Netley Hospital, to see Dr. Moffitt. On arrival I was informed that the Doctor had gone to his residence. I took his address, and the cabman said he could drive me "to the very spot." "Very well," said I; "go ahead; I'm in a great hurry."

When he drove to "the very spot," he found that it was not the spot where the Doctor lived. After seeking in vain for half an hour, I said, "I must be at the train for its next departure for London; and can't waste any more time." Just then a man told us where Dr. Moffatt lived; so we drove to his door. Mrs. Moffatt, with a ruddy, open countenance, received me with true Irish-lady hospitality, as I told her that I had a salutation for her husband from his uncle, Dr. A. Moffitt of Sydney. She said, "My husband is suffering from a severe cold, and has laid down; but I will tell him that you are here." She returned, saying, "My husband says he has no uncle in Sydney; but another Dr. Moffitt, our neighbour, who has just come in to see my husband, says that he has an uncle there." So in the house I was not seeking I found the man I sought, and thus became known to the man I sought not,—the Dr. Moffatt who subsequently came to India as surgeon of Her Majesty's 14th Regt., and now had opened the way for our work in Cawnpore. I see more and more clearly that it is too late for me to begin to make plans for the Lord by which to work, when God has so long ago made plans for me. It is not mine to ask Him to endorse my plans and go with me, but by all available means to discern His plans and go with Him.

Sabbath, 18th.—Preached in the "Union Chapel," at seven a.m., to a congregation of twenty-three soldiers and thirteen civilians. At eleven a.m. I went to the English Church to hear Rev. Mr. M——, the chaplain; but instead, the prayers and a short sermon were read by "our colonel." The whole thing was over, and we were out and gone in less than an hour. It appears that the people here can't stand the worship of God for more than an hour at a time. Went to the chapel at two p.m., and preached to twenty-three persons; then again, at half-past five p.m., to a congregation of thirty soldiers and thirty civilians. Deep attention, but not ready for an advance, except to explain the situation and get the people to "search the Scriptures and see if these things are so." It was arranged that our English services should be held in "Dr. Moffatt's prayer-room." During this week visited the colonel, the chaplain, and many soldiers' families, and preached every night; but with no decisive results in the way of conversions. When Christmas holidays set in, the people were so taken up with excursions and home entertainments, that we suspended English services, except the regular meetings on Sabbath and Wednesday nights; while George Myall and I spent our time in the native city. We encountered difficulties too numerous and too unimportant for detail here; but we succeeded in establishing a daily preaching service in two East Indian families, about two miles apart, and preached daily also in the bazaars, to the heathen and Mohamedans. At our out-door services we had from two to four hundred hearers, and usually very attentive. At one of them a young Mohamedan pressed through the crowd, swinging his arms, and with loud vociferations challenged me for debate. I said to him, through my interpreter, "It is of no use for you to waste your strength on me; I've only been a month in this country, and don't know a word you say. You may as well go and talk to that post as to talk to me." He subsided, and I proceeded with my discourse.

I often said at the close, "Now if any of you wish to talk to me, invite me to your house, and I'll sit down in your verandah, and we can talk in a friendly way. An old Hindū replied, on one occasion, saying, "If you will stop here long enough for us to get acquainted with you, we will invite you to our houses." He came regularly to our meetings, and said one day, "I want to be a Christian," but had not the courage to come out and incur the scorn and opposition of his heathen neighbours.

Wednesday, January 4th, 1871.—I thought I would not give details of this work; but I will drop in a few, for illustration of the many not written. At preaching-place No. 2, poor old Phillis found the Lord this morning. Four now in that family have been saved at our meetings. 'Tis said the chaplain threatened that those who attended my meetings should suffer all sorts of disabilities in life, which he enumerated, and should not be allowed a burial when dead. Thomas Phillis, who received Christ a few days ago, replied, "Thank God, I've got my soul saved, and I don't care what they do with my body."

After meeting this morning I got George to accompany me to the "Memorial Gardens." The gatekeeper would not allow my bābū to go in, because he was a native; though his unswerving loyalty was attested here in the Mutiny, when he was robbed of all he had, and narrowly escaped with his life. It is an undeniable fact that the native Christians were almost invariably true to the Government during the Mutiny, and some of them did good service for their country. The gardens are beautifully laid out with walks, lawns, flower-beds and borders, and shrubbery—all kept in fine condition. Over the fatal well is the monument, on which stands the statue of a weeping angel. Around it is an octagon wall about ten feet high, square pillars with Gothic capitals at each angle of the wall. Passing through the great iron gate, I descend by five steps to the base of the monument, which bears this inscription: "Sacred to the memory of a great company of Christian people, chiefly women and children, who near this spot were cruelly massacred by the followers of the rebel Nana Dhaoodopunt of Bithoor; and they cast the dying with the dead into the well below, on the 15th day of July 1857." ["I stand over this tomb of near two hundred bodies of the slain, and note this inscription, January 4th, 1871."]

January 5th.—Received a letter from Brother Thoburn to-day, saying, "The Missionary Board has granted all our estimates for next year, and two new missionaries. Perhaps God intends one for Cawnpore!"

I said to-night to Dr. Moffatt, who is a Low-Church Episcopalian, and son of an old deceased minister of the Episcopal Church in Ireland, "We now have about twenty East Indian converts here, with two Hindūs (Mrs. B—— and her adopted daughter, who, fifteen years ago, was taken from the breast of a dead Hindū mother on the banks of the Jumnā). I have organized these converts into two bands, one at each of our preaching-places; and they want to know what we are going to do for them in the way of pastoral care. They are all poor, but self-supporting, and want no help in that way. I am pledged to the Lucknow brethren not to commit them for any responsibility; but from Thoburn's letter I see that he is thinking about Cawnpore, and he will be here for Sabbath, and we may as well look the matter full in the face. You have a leading agency in this work, and if it shall result in the establishment of a Methodist mission here, it will be a feather in your cap."

"Yes, and a star in my crown."

"But you have already got yourself into disgrace in the eyes of your chaplain and others; so you had better count the cost before we proceed farther."

"Oh, my shoulders are broad; I don't care for any of them, except to do them good. They shall never hinder me from doing the work God may give me to do."

Next day, Friday the 6th, I breakfasted with Mr. McLeavy, manager of the Bank of Upper India, and a friend of our work. I showed him Brother Thoburn's letter, and spoke of the two new missionaries coming to India.

He promptly replied, "I hope they will send one to Cawnpore. The Presbyterians don't intend to establish a permanent mission here: Mr. W—— told me so. I have tried in vain to get my own church" (the Baptist) "to send a teacher here, who could also hold religious services. There is no mission in this city of 150,000 population, except that of the Propagation Society; and they are doing but little to meet the spiritual wants of this people.

"A Methodist mission would absorb all the interest that the Presbyterians and others now share among them as transient visitors. I will give all my influence to it, and I am sure Mr Jahans, the Greenways and others, will do the same. If a school also could be established, with a competent teacher, it would realize three hundred rupees per month."

All this was spontaneous, and came in as another indication of Providence that we should plant a mission in Cawnpore.

Saturday, Jan. 7th.—Dr. Moffatt ordered an elephant from the Commissariat, and at eleven a.m. the huge monster kneeled down at our door, and lay flat on his breast. Then mounting a chair, and seizing a couple of ropes attached to the great cushion on his back, we climbed up his side like climbing up the side of a small schooner. Thus mounting the monster, we explored the city. We tried to see everything we could, and the people seemed as curious to see us; for though they may daily see elephants hereabouts, they probably never saw one thus mounted, and passing through so many narrow streets and gateways, as they saw to-day. In one narrow alley a cow was tied to a verandah, on the floor of which lay an old Hindū fast asleep. The cow was dreadfully frightened at the sight of our great elephant, and first threw herself back to the full length of her line, then dashing forward, by a tremendous leap cleared the verandah railing, and lighted down on the old sleeping Hindū. I need hardly add that she waked him up, and he seemed as badly scared as the cow; and she, poor creature, frightened again at the sudden bound of the man, fell backwards into a sewerage trench in front of the verandah, and we passed out of sight and left them to their reflections.

At half-past three p.m. the Doctor and I drove out to the railway bridge, to meet Brother Thoburn from Lucknow. Later in the afternoon, Rev. Henry Mansell, presiding elder of the Morādabād district, and his family, drove up. He was on his way to Conference, to meet next week in Lucknow, but was too late for the branch-line train; so, of the three presiding elders in the whole Conference, I shall have two to spend the Sabbath in my new Cawnpore Mission. Thus they can personally inspect the work here, and be prepared to represent it on the Conference floor.

Sabbath, 8th.—At half-past ten a.m. Brother Thoburn preached in Union Chapel, to twenty-three soldiers and twenty-five civilians: a clear, powerful sermon—about the young ruler who bowed at the feet of Jesus. I seldom hear preaching, and greatly enjoyed this discourse.

At twelve o'clock Brother Mansell preached in Hindūstānī at No. 2, to twenty hearers. At half-past five p.m. Brother Thoburn preached again in Union Chapel, on the handwriting on Belshazzar's wall: a searching, powerful sermon. Thence we went to No. 1 native preaching-place, and Brother Mansell preached in Hindūstānī to twenty hearers; after which we took tea with our host, who had so kindly given us the use of his house. At this meeting, by the advice of the two presiding elders, we proposed organizing a Methodist Episcopal Church: Brother Thoburn read our general rules in Hindūstānī, and several gave their names as candidates. Next morning these two dear brethren went to Lucknow, and left me to organize further, as the way might open.

Tuesday, 10th.—This morning I drew up the rough draft of a petition addressed to the India Mission Conference, praying them to put Cawnpore on the list of their missions, and appoint to it at their coming session a missionary. Mr. McLeavy copied it, and got the signatures of many of the leading men of the station, with a subscription of eighty rupees per month towards the support of the missionary—which he said could easily be increased to a hundred. With this petition and subscription, and the list of my candidates for membership organized into two classes—fourteen in one, and eight in the other—on Thursday morning, the 12th of January, I returned to Lucknow.

CHAPTER IV.

CONFERENCE TIME IN LUCKNOW.

THE India Mission Conference assembled here on Thursday the 12th. On Friday the Cawnpore petition was presented and freely discussed. Considerable opposition by some good conservatives. All admitted that the manifest work of God there, and the call for a missionary and pledge of about 100 rupees per month towards his support, were pretty clear indications that God would lead us into Cawnpore; but some thought they saw lions in the way. It was pleaded that we were bound by some sort of compact with other missions not to cross the Ganges, and that the Conference boundary, as laid down in the Discipline, was in accordance with that agreement, and shut us in on that side.

I demanded the proofs of these statements; and diligent enquiry brought out the following facts: 1st, that the Free Church of Scotland in Calcutta, which through Dr. Duff invited us to establish a mission in India, recommended Oudh and Rohilcund as unoccupied and important fields for our mission, but did not attempt to restrict us; 2ndly, that though Dr. Butler had agreed on a line of limitation, with the "Church" missionaries, the Bishop of Calcutta ignored it, and sent missionaries into the part assigned to us. Then Dr. Butler wrote them, that unless it limited the Bishop it should not limit us.

I said, "All who come to Lucknow from the north-west, or south, must stop at Cawnpore and enquire the way, and must stay there till the next day, waiting for a train on the branch line to Lucknow, as a worthy presiding elder had to do last Saturday; and, not being a Sabbath-breaker, while he was resting we got two good sermons from him in our new circuit. Cawnpore, therefore, is the gate to Lucknow; and you may just as well deny a man the right of way to his own farm or bungalow, as to refuse to admit Cawnpore. Providential lines and railway lines clearly put that city within the bounds of this Conference."

A query was then raised, whether or not our Presbyterian brethren would consider that an encroachment on their lines? There were present Rev. Wyncoop of Allahabad, Rev. Wm. Morrison of Amballa, and Rev. Woodside of Dheradoon, of the American Presbyterian Board; and Rev. Dr. Ballantyne of the Church of Scotland, from Rājpatānā. All these gave a deliverance in favour of our taking up Cawnpore. Then it was asked, whether or not we should consult the missionaries of the Propagation Society? Rev. Woodside made an earnest speech against it, saying, "They represent the High-Church party, and claim the exclusive right to occupy and hold the entire country; and it is no use to challenge their opposition in that way." The

Conference voted to put Cawnpore on the list, and recommend the Missionary Board to confirm their action and appoint a missionary to it.

On that night I preached, and we had the communion-rail crowded with seekers of purity, and eight or nine penitents also. That night Dennis Osborne went up and got a baptism of the Spirit, and soon after joined our Church; and is now the most effective, soul-saving preacher, I believe, in the North-West.

Tuesday, 17th.—I preached to-day, at one p.m., in the house of Brother George Bailey: text, "God so loved the world."—Brother P. Mūkūrjī, a converted Brāhman, who was admitted on trial into the Conference to-day, was my interpreter. Bengālī is his language, but he seems to be well up in Hindūstānī. Bailey prompted him whenever he seemed at a loss; from which it struck me that perhaps Bailey was my man for interpreter.

An old Hindū said to Bailey, "I like all that I have heard here to-day. It seems nice, and appears to be true; but it is very hard for us to believe it. It takes time for us to know that it is all true."

I replied, "True, my old friend; it is difficult at once to believe in a thing both strange and new. If I had come here ten years ago, and told you all about steam-engines, railroads, and telegraphs, and that such things in ten years would be sights in Lucknow as common as the sight of elephants and camels, you would have found it as hard to believe all that as what I have told you to-day."

"That is true," said the old man; and a smile and general expression of approval came from the crowd. The Holy Spirit evidently impressed the minds of many there to-day.

Wednesday, 18th.—The Conference closed with the Sacrament of the Lord's Supper. A solemn occasion.

Thursday, 19th.—Preached at Bailey's at twelve o'clock to about eighty persons. I counted forty Hindūs and Mohamedans. Brother Bailey interpreted, and did it well. After we had been preaching about half an hour, a Mohamedan Moulvy (a kind of priest) came in and sat down on a chair. Immediately seven of the best-looking, well-dressed Mohamedans got up abruptly, and left the house.

I said to Bailey, in an under-tone, "What's the matter with those fellows?"

"The Moulvy sat down on a chair above them;" and turning to him, Bailey said, "Sit down there on the carpet," and he did so.

Then, quick as a monkey, Bailey bolted downstairs and out into the street, and overtook the deserters, and brought them back, and demanded of them in the presence of the crowd an explanation of their conduct.

The oldest one of them replied, "We are all equals, and don't allow any of our people to take a higher seat than that of his brother."

Bailey pointed to the old Moulvy on the floor, and they nodded assent. Then an East Indian gentleman and his sister got up to select a seat on the carpet; but the old Mohamedan took hold of their hands and begged them to sit down on their chairs, as that was their custom.

We then proceeded with the discourse, and they all listened with great attention.

Friday, 20th.—Preached again at Bailey's, on the Prodigal Son. At the close the people seemed unwilling to leave, and Bailey overheard them saying one to another, "If that man would stop here he would win us all over to his side."

An old Hindū said to Bailey, as he passed out, "I'll think no more about my own religion, but I'll think about the Lord Jesus."

I wish I had time at command to follow up this grand opening among these dear people. The same old Moulvy, and his son, a well-educated young man, were here again to-day. They claim to be related to the late king of Oudh. They, and several other Mohamedans, followed me to Dr. Waugh's, and again at night called on me at Brother Thoburn's. I told them my experience, and preached to them for an hour. They expressed great regret that I was going to leave the city so soon. I asked Brothers Waugh and Thoburn if they could interpret the old Moulvy's motives. They replied that they could see nothing indicating an improper motive: no very deep conviction of sin, but an interest in the truth of God enkindled in their hearts, and a sincere personal friendship.

Saturday, 21st.—Called to see Mrs. Davis, who was dying. I saw her a number of times before, but now she bade adieu to all her friends. I sang "The Home in Heaven," and "All is Well," and prayed;

and soon after she died in the Lord. Brother Mūkūrjī having been appointed by the Conference to labour in native work at Cawnpore, I went with him to-day to introduce him, and smooth down the disappointment of my friends there in not getting a missionary. At the railway station I met the old Moulvy and his friends, who came to see me off. I remained at Cawnpore till Tuesday, and put Brother Mūkūrjī into the work as well as I could. He is an earnest, good brother; but his wife, on account of long chronic illness, was ordered to Calcutta, and the work in Cawnpore was not conserved as well as it could have been under more favourable conditions.

Old Sister Phillis, one of our converts there, became very useful, but after a year of service was taken to heaven. Some of them went to the Church of England, and some are still in our Church there. Brother Thoburn came occasionally, and organized the English work; and Dr. J. Condon, one of the Lord's lay-preachers, was appointed civil surgeon at Cawnpore soon after I left, and became a powerful worker in our cause.

A year later Brother Gladwin was appointed there as a missionary, and developed the English work, and also regular native preaching and large schools in the city; and that station became the first self-supporting mission in the Conference, and is also the seat of the "Memorial High School," under Rev. Henry Jackson and Mr. Annett. They have appropriated missionary money there for buildings; but the preacher's salary has been paid by the people from an early period of Brother Gladwin's appointment to Cawnpore.

Tuesday, 24th.—On my return to Lucknow, I found the old Moulvy and his friends on the platform waiting for me; and they called again to see me this evening. Had a family prayer-meeting at Brother Thoburn's to-night, at which we had five Bengālīs—three men and two women. The two latter came out as seekers, and received Jesus. One of them is now the wife of Brother Herbert Moony, and a very useful Christian woman.

It is all arranged for me to go to-morrow to Seetāpore, on my tour through the Mission. Brother Bailey is to go as my interpreter. Every traveller in this country has to "take up his bed and walk," so Brother Mansell gave me an outfit of bedding for my journey.

25th.—We took the road in the "dāk-ghārī" (mail coach), at eight a.m. The old Moulvy and his son came to see me off, and were most anxious to know when I would return. I told the dear old man that I hoped to return in September.

"Oh, that is such a long time: your words give me so much light and comfort. When you come again I will bring our nobles to see you."

Instead of returning in September of that year, as I thought I should, I did not see Lucknow again for three years, and was sorry to learn then that the old Moulvy was dead.

We drove fifty-two miles through a beautiful, but poorly-cultivated country, arriving in Seetāpore at five p.m., and were welcomed by Rev. Brother Knowles, who had a tent pitched for us in the Mission "compound," or yard. ("Seetā" was the wife of "Ram," and *pore* means "city." This is the "city of Ram's wife.") Preached this evening to about sixty natives and half a dozen Europeans.

Thursday, 26th.—White-frost covering the ground this morning. Preaching announced for the chapel at eight a.m., but as the shivering natives had collected in the sunshine on the Mission-house verandah, I preached to them there. Preached in the chapel at eleven a.m. Bailey was master of the situation. Brother Knowles said, "It is a providential thing that you have Bailey as interpreter." We had to-day a general break-down among the natives; and ten women and seven men, including two not yet out of their teens, came forward as seekers, and after a hard struggle, with many tears, professed to receive Christ and peace with God. These were nominal Christians.

We had a dozen Afghān Mohamedan soldiers present, who seemed to be greatly interested. They said to Brother Knowles, "This preaching is all true. It has loosened a knot in our hearts, and we are untying it; but you will have to give us a little time."

In the evening I preached to an English congregation of sixty—about one-half of whom were soldiers. There was a great awakening, and many stood up as seekers; but the soldiers had to leave early for their roll-call, and we had thus an interruption at the opening of the prayer-meeting, before we could instruct them in personal detail. A few civilians professed to find peace.

27th.—Preached, through Bailey, at noon. In our congregation were Captain Risālahdār Ubdoolā Khān, his brother Rashied, and other native officers,—

fine-looking Afghans, belonging to Colonel Robart's cavalry. We explained the constitution of man's body, his mind, and his spiritual functions, with their requirements, and God's supply for all of them; man's fall, and redemption by Jesus Christ; God's basis of faith for man, His prophetic and historic record concerning His Son, and the personal verification of the truth in the experience of believers, exhibited in their lives, and explained and certified by their testimony for Jesus. We gave many illustrations, and the truth went home beautifully.

At the close, the Captain came up and said to Brother Knowles, "We agree with all that has been said. We have received great light. The light has shined into me this day." They followed us to the tent; and the Captain (who is more properly a colonel, having command of 600 cavalry) begged me to come and preach to his men; but as I had to preach again the same evening in the chapel, and leave early next morning, it was impossible for me to do so. It seemed such a pity! Then they said, "We'll meet you in the Colonel's compound in the morning." Brother Knowles was astonished to see these Mohamedans at our meeting, and more to see how they took to it. He says, "The like was never seen here before."

CHAPTER V.

PANAHPORE.

CAPTAIN UBDOOLAH KHAN and his fellow-officers met me early, according to promise, but the colonel ordered them to their lines, so that I could not say much to them.

Saturday, 28th.—Our journey from Seetāpore to Panahpore is about fifty miles. This is my first day's experience in a "dhūlī dāk." The dhūlī is a carriage about seven feet long, three feet wide, and three feet high. In this the bed is spread; so that the occupant can sit, or lie down and sleep, at will. At each side are sliding doors. This, however, is a carriage without wheels or horses. A long, light pole passes through the centre, close under the ceiling of the carriage, extending through each end four or five feet. The whole is carried by four coolies, two at each end. These are relieved by a fresh relay about every six miles. They move regularly in a steady trot, keeping time and stimulating each other by a sort of grunting chorus, oft repeating 'jaldī jā"—that is, *quickly go.*

It is said that some editor in England, in giving his readers an account of a terrible battle in the

Mutiny, made quite a sensational climax by the statement that after the engagement the "dreadful Dhūlies came down upon Her Majesty's wounded soldiers and carried them off." The fact was, they were thus carried off to the hospital to be treated.

A little after dark we arrived in Panahpore (*Panah* means "refuge.") So we were welcomed by Brother and Sister Johnson, and Brother Buck, into the "city of refuge."

This town was founded by the Rev. Dr. Johnson, M.D. He bought nine hundred acres of land, and laid out the town, and opened up little farms, to which persecuted Christians might flee for refuge, and poor Christians gain an honest living by tilling the soil. Bishop Kingsley preached here a year ago in a tent. Now we have a comfortable chapel, and a population of forty families, with 120 souls. Brother Enoch Berge, a native ordained deacon, is the resi dent pastor.

Sabbath, 29th.—Preached at eleven a.m. Good attention; but we did not invite seekers. Again at half-past five p.m. At the prayer-meeting following the preaching, twenty-four men and six women came forward as seekers, and professed to find peace. Some of them are servile, and not very reliable; but I felt a profound sympathy for them, and showed no distrust. Some of them spoke beautifully. One said, "A great light is shining into my heart." Another said, "My soul is filled with joy. It is like a spring bubbling up in my heart."

Monday, 30th.—At twelve o'clock, as the gong

was telling the hour for preaching, there was a sudden cry of fire. Half a mile west the jungle was in flames. Large quantities of long thatch-grass belonging to the "pore" had been cut and bound in sheaves, and much remained ready for the scythe. All this was being consumed. So we all ran to try to subdue the fire. I had had much experience in fighting fire in the mountains of Virginia when a boy; so I went to the front here in the heat of the sun at noon, and wrought with all my might for two hours, till we succeeded in putting it out. Meantime it passed a little beyond the bounds of the Mission farm, into a tract under rent by an old Brāhman. The old man, with three or four of his labourers, came to help. I assisted him in removing beyond danger the only cut grass he had; so that his loss did not exceed a couple of dollars. We had a service on our return; and sixteen women and five men professed to find the forgiveness of their sins. Brother Enoch Berge did not get back in time for the meeting; but later he came in, marching before him seven dhobīs—washermen—and their twenty donkeys. These men had come from Shahjehanpore, five miles distant, to gather fuel, and had carelessly upset one of their big smoking-pipes and set the grass on fire. Firing the jungle here through want of care is an offence punishable to the extent of seven years' imprisonment; incendiary firing, fourteen years. The seat of justice—Likinpore—is forty miles distant. To go so far with witnesses to prosecute the dhobīs, would involve perhaps a heavier loss than the burning of the grass; so the question was, "What shall we do with the dhobīs?" I said, "Send for the old Hindū, that he may see that the Mission people did not let the fire get into his grass, and that he may be a party in trying and punishing the prisoners. Bring them all to the service, and we will preach the Gospel to them." There were plenty of men there who seemed to know all about the law in the case, and who reminded them in advance of what they might expect—seven years in prison, and the loss of their donkeys, to pay for the grass they had burnt. So the poor fellows were weeping bitterly. When the gong sounded, and the congregation assembled, the seven dhobīs were placed in front between me and the body of the congregation. Most of them were large, good-looking natives. I adapted the discourse to Hindūs; but made no allusion to the prisoners, or the fire.

Near the close of the discourse the old Hindū and his counsellor arrived. Seeing them come in, I enlarged, so as to "give them a portion in due season." Brother Bailey and several others then gave their testimony to the saving power of Jesus; and we had several prayers.

When the service was ended, the trial of the men commenced. Our two missionaries, Brothers Johnson and Buck, and the native pastor, were present, and the people all stayed back to see what was to be done.

Some of the men fell down on their faces to implore mercy, but Bailey pulled them up and would not allow it, and told them to "stand up like men, and tell the whole truth about the business." They confessed, and explained how the fire got out, and begged for mercy.

I said to Brother Johnson, "It will cost more than any of you can afford to prosecute them,—and you have no right to impose a fine otherwise; the penalty of the law, moreover, would be too severe for such an accident, so you had better turn it to the best account you can morally, and forgive them.

Enoch Berge was the heaviest loser by the fire. When Brother Johnson repeated to Enoch my advice, he made a telling speech.

He said, "Before I came to the house of God I felt like pursuing these men to the bitter end of justice by the law; but as I sat here, and looked at them listening so attentively to the preaching of the Gospel, I thought of the prayer of our Lord, 'Forgive us our trespasses as we forgive them who trespass against us,' and my heart at once overflowed with love for them, and I forgive them with all my heart."

It was most interesting to see the gathering smiles on the tearful faces of the men, as Enoch proceeded with his discourse. We then appealed to the Brāhman to concur in pardoning them.

He seemed to get into a fearful rage, and screamed out, "I am ruined! My throat is cut! I have lost my religion!"

"Come over to us," said Bailey, "and get the right sort of religion, that will stick to you in the day of trouble."

The Brāhman said, "We must seize the asses, and pay ourselves for the loss occasioned by the fire."

When he saw that we could not be moved, he reluctantly gave in. One of the fellows fell down with his face on the ground between the Brāhman's feet, and so the trial ended. The Brāhman and his friend promised to come to our meeting next day, but did not do it.

Tuesday, 31st.—Preached to believers at noon and night; closing with a fellowship-meeting.

Enoch Berge said, "If I had gained the whole world, I should not be so happy as I am to-night: Jesus has saved my soul from sin."

Soonderlal said, "Jesus removed the heavy burden of my sins. I love everybody as I love myself. I am saved; and if the Lord should call me now, I should go straight to heaven."

Chotey, a large black man, said, "I read Pādrī Taylor's book in 1869. I saw by the papers that he was coming to Lucknow, and I intended going there to see him; but, thank God! he has come hither, and under his preaching I have been led to Jesus and have got all my sins forgiven."

Brother Wāp said, "I am greatly blessed this time. I never was so blessed before."

Brother Paulus said, "A spring of living water is flowing into my mind."

Sister Charlotte said, "I have received the pardon of all my sins, and I am extremely happy."

Brother George said, "For three or four days the grace of God has come upon me."

Daiseis' wife said, "I know that my sins are forgiven; and I am happy. Before I was baptized I was subject to fits. From that time I was free from them till I neglected Christ. Then I had a relapse, and severe fits came upon me. I came back to Jesus; and when His love came into my heart I got quite well."

Chotey's wife said, "I strongly testify that I am cleared from my sins; and I am very happy."

And so on. They nearly all told their experience in great simplicity. Many women came forward as seekers, with their babes in their arms; and to-night I see the same standing up to testify for Jesus, with their babes still in their arms. The dear little things! —I hope they will be brought up spiritually in the house of the Lord.

All their talk, of course, was in Hindūstānī; and hence I have only given the substance of their testimony.

CHAPTER VI.

SHAHJEHANPORE.

SHAH means "king," *jehan*, "the world," *pore*, "city,"—called after Shāhjehān, one of the Great Mogul kings of the country of former days.

On Wednesday, Feb. 1st, we struck our tents in Panahpore, five miles distant, and came to this "pore." We are quartered in Dr. Johnson's mission bungalow; Brother Buck is his colleague.

The great missionary interest of this place is the Boys' Orphanage. Dr. Butler got a few orphans together in Nyne Tāl in 1859, and subsequently opened an orphanage at Bareilly; but it was afterwards removed to this place, secured by Dr. Johnson. The site contains thirty acres of land. The minister's bungalow is sixty feet square, with verandah on all sides, ceiling about thirty feet high,—a fine establishment for an Indian residence. It was built by Captain Sage, at a cost of 9000 rupees; but Brother Johnson got it for 5000.

The Orphanage now contains 147 resident boys and young men, and about twenty day-scholars. These are all instructed in the rudiments of the Hindī, Hindūstānī, and Persian languages; most of the larger boys, also, in the ordinary branches of

English. They all learn a trade, as well, in the industrial department—farming, weaving, shoemaking, printing and press work, cabinet-making, etc.

The school-house and chapel, in one, is sixty-six feet square, with ceiling thirty feet high. There are three recitation-rooms on each side, with chapel in the centre, twenty-four feet broad by sixty-six long: the cost 7000 rupees.

The whole thing, with minister's bungalow, teachers' houses, boys' houses, workshop, and well, cost about 20,000 rupees.

Of this sum our Missionary Society paid 5000 rupees; Indian Government 4250; Col. J. Y. Gowen, 7000; England, principally from Quaker friends, 2000; Dr. Butler, 1000; and smaller miscellaneous sums. For the support of this institution, the Government grants 300 rupees per month for tuition, two-and-a-half rupees each for twenty-four orphans from the famine of 1861, and two rupees per month for ninety-four other boys; and a portion is paid by our Missionary Society.

On this day of our arrival we preached in the Orphanage Chapel at twelve noon and half-past six p.m. All attentive and well behaved.

Friday, Feb. 3rd.—Went out eight miles to Chandapore, to attend a monthly meeting of the Fakīrs and followers of Kabīr. He was born at Benares about four hundred years ago, and to this day a few hundred thousand Hindūs bear his name. His leading dogma was that all who should acknowledge him as their guide would be so united to God as to lose all personal responsibility: that God would do in them whatsoever they were inclined to do, and lay no sin to their charge. They admit all castes into their fraternity, and are in the habit of holding monthly gatherings, I was told, for feasting and religious ceremonies; so we went to one of their feasts, to speak to them in the name of the Lord.

We learned, on arrival at their village, that to-morrow is the great day of their feast. However, they received us kindly, and we got a good assembly of them, including three of their Fakīr priests. We preached to them on "Whosoever will, let him take the water of life freely."

Two of the priests began at once to ask questions and challenge debate.

I said, "If you will kindly hear what I have to say, at the close you can ask questions, and we will answer them so far as we can."

We then got a patient hearing to a sermon over an hour in length, and our testimony to a personal experience of salvation from sin by Jesus Christ, and a closing prayer that God would open their hearts and apply His truth. The people seemed to be deeply impressed, but the priests became greatly excited, seeming to fear that their craft was in danger, or that the people might think that we had spiked their guns, and opened up a warm discussion. Bailey replied with great point and good spirit.

Then the head Fakīr tried to checkmate our testimony by saying, "Oh, I drank of the river of life long ago, and got all that you say you have got. Kabīr was the son of God, and through him all my sins were taken away."

I challenged him to produce Kabīr's credentials. "Where is the proof that he ever set up such a claim for himself? You say that your sins have all been pardoned and taken away: I must have the testimony of your neighbours on that point."

Then I appealed to the people: "Friends, you know this man. He says that his sins have been taken away. Is that true? Does he not cheat you, and oppress you, and tell you lies?"

The people cried out against him, saying, "He is one of the greatest sinners amongst us, and he is telling you lies now."

Then he changed his ground, and said, "We are united to God; we are a part of God. We do nothing of ourselves: God does it all, and never imputes sin to us. We never sinned in our lives."

Bailey replied, "Then if I come and join your clan, and become a worshipper of Kabīr, I may seduce your wife and take her away from you, and do all manner of wickedness, and you would say, 'Mr. Bailey—what a good man he is! True, he has given us a great deal of trouble, but, poor fellow! he is not responsible. It was God who did it all.'"

Many of the people cried out, calling the priest by name, "Shame, shame on you! You know well enough that we are all responsible for our conduct."

Thus we sowed the good seed among the people, silenced the batteries of the priests, and returned.

Preached in the Orphanage Chapel at six p.m. About seventy came forward as seekers, and twenty-five professed to find forgiveness of sins, and publicly testified for Jesus.

Saturday, 4th.—My rest day; but while I was resting—at the earnest request of the leading English residents of the station, it being their only leisure day—I preached to them in our chapel at four p.m. Among them were Judge Henderson, Collector Saunders, and his assistant Mr. Smith—brother of Rev. Jarvis Smith of the British Wesleyan Conference. We had a very interesting service.

We continued special services on Sabbath and Monday. Over seventy, during the series—mostly orphans—professed to obtain peace with God. The greater part of these, as I have heard from year to year, have remained steadfast.

CHAPTER VII.

BAREILLY.

A JOURNEY of fifty miles brought us to this place. Preached to a poor leper on the way while changing horses. His fingers and toes had all dropped off.

I said to him, "Where will your spirit go when it shall leave the body?"

He reflected a moment, and replied, "It will go back where it came from."

We tried to lead him to the cleansing Fountain, that his spirit might be prepared to return to God who gave it.

We found a good and welcome home in the house of Rev. T. J. Scott, the presiding elder of Bareilly district. His residence is a large bungalow built by Dr. Butler, the pioneer of the Mission, but who, some years before, had returned to America.

The next house is the residence of Rev. D. W. Thomas, who, with his earnest, good wife, and Miss Fanny Sparks to assist him, has charge of the Girls' Orphanage—a similar institution to the one for boys in Shāhjehānpore. It contains 140 orphan girls—many of them now young women, well advanced in the rudiments of education, and in handy work to fit them to fill their station in life.

Here we also found Miss C. Swain, M.D., at her post. She is a most successful medical practitioner, and gets access to the best families in the city. She has treated this year 1335 cases, and has in connection with this opened up an interesting zenāna work. (The Hindū harem is called a zenāna.) Ninety-five of these are now open to her and the ladies assisting in this work of teaching the Hindū women the way of life. She cured recently the wife of an influential Hindū, who had been given up by her regular physicians as a hopeless case. The Hindū had been an uncompromising opposer of our Mission before, but from this time became a friend. Thus God, through the agency of Sister Swain, is breaking down the barriers of caste, and removing mountains of prejudice. His Highness the Nawāb of Rāmpore visited her medical school, and was so pleased that he first gave for its support 1000 rupees, and felt so well disposed afterwards, that he made over by deed a palace and forty-two acres of land, located near to our Mission premises, for the purpose of a hospital for native women, a medical school, and a home for the medical missionary. The property is worth about 35,000 rupees.

Bareilly is a large native city, and military station. On the evening of my arrival, at the request of our missionaries, I went with them to a temperance tea-meeting for her Majesty's 25th Regt., and heard some good temperance talk, and preached a little to the soldiers.

Wednesday, 8th.—I visited a native Christian village under the pastoral care of the chaplain and a native pastor. The chaplain and our own missionaries united in a request that I should try and do something to reform the so-called Christians who live in it, and who scandalize the name of Christ by their gross immorality. I found that they were engaged in a lawsuit with the chaplain about the title to their village lands; and while I was there they severely beat their native pastor; so I could not see my way open, in the midst of such confusion, to do them any good.

Preached in the Orphanage Chapel at noon to the 140 orphans—all old enough to sin, and hence old enough to be saved from sin—and to a few visitors; Bailey interpreted.

Preached in the bungalow used for regular native services at six p.m.; Brother Scott interpreted, and did it well. Brother Bailey heard to-day that Justice Walker, whom he knew in Lucknow during the Mutiny, was residing in Bareilly, and was a justice of the peace and treasurer of the city.

"I will take Brother Taylor to see Walker," said Bailey; "and we will get him converted to God."

The missionaries laughed at Bailey's new-born zeal, and said, "You can do nothing with Walker. His wife is a Musulmānī, and he has a lot of her Mohamedan kindred in his house: he never comes to preaching."

"Oh, I am sure we can get him saved," replied Bailey; and left abruptly, and went to call on his old friend. After reviewing their memories of the Mutiny, he said, "Mr. Walker, I want to introduce Mr. Taylor to you."

"No, Mr. Bailey; if you please, don't bring Mr. Taylor here. He'll be pitching into me about something or other; and I don't want to see him."

"Nay, nay, Mr. Walker; Mr. Taylor is a world-wide traveller, and a kind gentleman. He will interest you on many subjects, and not pitch into you at all."

So Mr. Walker consented, and Bailey came in haste for me to go and get his friend saved.

We went to his office, and after a long talk on various topics, as I was about to leave, I said, "Mr. Walker, as I am stopping at Mr. Scott's, near by, and have but a few days to spend in your city, if agreeable to you I shall be glad to come some morning and conduct family worship for you."

"Thank you, Mr. Taylor; but I am a man of business, and have to go early to office daily, and cannot possibly command the time."

"How about Sabbath morning?"

"Well, I have no particular engagement Sabbath morning."

"Suppose, then, you invite a few of your friends, and allow me to come to your house, and we will have family worship together?"

"Very well, Mr. Taylor; come next Sabbath, at eight a.m."

Thursday, 9th.—Preached in the Orphanage Chapel at noon, from Luke vii. 50. Illustrated the narrative by my map, nine feet by twelve. Great seriousness.

A Mohamedan giant who lives with Mr. Walker, whom we called "Goliath of Gath," was present at our meeting in the bungalow. Bailey recognized him as an old friend whom he knew in the Mutiny. He seemed much pleased to see Bailey, and said to him, "You have found God. I wish I could find Him too!" We had about 100 hearers, and good attention.

Friday, 10th.—At the Orphanage Chapel Bailey interpreted well, as usual. The missionaries in different places often expressed surprise at his clear, terse translation of my Scripture quotations,—so original and so forcible. Before his conversion to God he had never read but two chapters in the Bible in his life. His wife was ill, and some one told him that if he would read to her out of the Bible she would get better; so he read two chapters to her, and she got better; and he read no more till our meeting at Lucknow.

A grand meeting to-day among the orphans. Sixty-seven of the elder girls came up as seekers, and twenty-six professed; sixteen of them had been professors before, but now got a clearer experience.

At seven p.m., in the bungalow, twenty-five men and fifteen women, native nominal Christians, came out as seekers, and professed to find Jesus. "Goliath" seems under deep concern.

Saturday, 11th.—Witnessed the distribution of prizes in our native mission school in the city (of 100 Mohamedan and Hindū boys). I gave them an address; Brother Scott interpreted.

In the evening we had a meeting in Brother Scott's house for his native helpers; and I gave them a talk on personal holiness.

Sabbath, 12th.—Had a service at Mr. Walker's at eight a.m. Eighteen persons present, including his family. At the close, seeing that a good impression was made, I said, "Now, Mr. Walker, if you like I will come again to-morrow morning at seven o'clock, and conduct your family worship. We can have a family service from seven to eight, and then you can have from eight to nine for breakfast, and get to office in due time—at ten a.m."

"All right, Mr. Taylor; we shall be glad to see you again to-morrow morning."

At the Orphanage Chapel at noon we had about seventy seekers, and nineteen professed to find Jesus. The following are a few specimens of their testimony as given in Hindūstānī before the congregation:—

A young woman said, "I have received the forgiveness of my sins. No one has told me in my ear, but I feel the testimony of it in my mind, and I will always be true to Jesus."

Another said, "I submitted myself to Jesus. The burden of sin is removed from my heart. It was a crushing load, but I don't feel any of it now. I know my sins are pardoned."

Another said, "When I heard from Miss Sparks last night that I could receive the pardon of my sins, I tried to find it, but did not. This morning I have received Jesus, and now I feel that He has taken away my sins."

Another said, "I was very miserable last night, and did not know what to do; but to-day I submitted myself unreservedly to Jesus, and God has acquitted me."

Another said, "I am a very great sinner. I wonder why I have been so wicked, and that I never could do any good; but now my sins are pardoned, and I feel very happy."

Another said, "Last night I was praying, and reading about the Ten Virgins, and said to myself, Shall I be like one of those foolish women to whom Jesus said, 'I know you not'? I was very unhappy; but to-day I have received Jesus, and He has comforted me."

Another said, "I was very much troubled last night, and did not feel like praying. I thought Satan was after me; then I prayed, and found Jesus. He acquitted me, and pardoned all my sins, and now I am happy."

Another said, "Jesus is mine; I will never leave Him. I will be in His bosom when I die."

Many of these witnesses for Jesus had been picked up in the huts of dead and dying Hindūs during the great famine of 1861. Preached in the bungalow at half-past six p.m. A dozen seekers, and five professed to find peace.

Monday, 13th.—Preached in Orphanage Chapel on the "babes and sucklings"; and the truth took hold on the smaller orphans. Some of them came forward; but more of the larger ones: thirty-eight professed to find forgiveness of sins. At six p.m. I preached in the City Schoolhouse to the English-speaking Hindūs, Mohamedans, and Brāhmos. About 100 present, crowding the room. I discoursed to them an hour. The Spirit of God was manifestly present to apply the truth. At the close Judge Bakhtāwar

Singh, a Hindū judge receiving a Government salary of 800 rupees per month, arose and tendered his thanks, and the thanks of the hearers, for what they had heard.

If I had time to "dispute daily" with these people, and pursue fully St. Paul's methods—having the same Gospel, the same Jesus, and the same Holy Spirit—I am sure we should see corresponding results. But I have promised to make as fair a division of my time as possible among the whole of our missions before the hot weather shall set in; and my appointments are announced. Such seems to be the best for the whole work,—to help to develop and adjust the working agencies of the Mission at large, rather than a long siege in any one place among the heathen. Indeed, we cannot expect very great results among the natives, in the presence of a nominal, ineffective Church. If there were no such Church, we might hope for more immediate results among them; but now our only hope is to make the Church effective. Some weeks after this sermon to the educated natives, a Hindū merchant told Sister Swain that for many nights afterwards he could not sleep, but lay awake and wept on account of his sins. Four years afterwards, Mr. Drummond, the Commissioner there at that time, told me that a high Hindū official in the Government said to him, "If Taylor sāhib had remained in Bareilly I should have become a Christian." Thus my regret that I could not stay and follow up that work has often been revived. We have good and earnest missionaries, in most respects better qualified for this work than myself; but their engagements cover large districts of country, and embrace a vast variety of work, especially school-work.

Tuesday, 14th.—Preached at Walker's at seven a.m. About thirty present, and deep awakening. At the close Mr. Walker said: "Mr. Taylor, I hope you will come to-morrow morning, and every morning while you remain in the city."

"Thank you, Mr. Walker; I shall (D.V.) do so with much pleasure."

Preached at the Orphanage Chapel at twelve noon. Fifty seekers, and twenty-seven professed to find Jesus. Many of them, this time, were little girls. The large ones were saved first, and now the little children are coming to Jesus.

Brother Thoburn writes that the work in Lucknow is progressing well: three or four saved each week.

Wednesday, 15th.—At Justice Walker's again at seven a.m. Great awakening. All of them—about twenty souls—went down on their knees as avowed seekers of salvation.

Good service at twelve o'clock in the Orphanage Chapel. During preaching in the evening in the bungalow, a cry of fire broke up our meeting for half an hour. In the next lot to our bungalow was Brother Thomas' "kārkāna" or workshop, an institution he got up at the close of the famine in 1861, to give employment to starving mechanics and a refuge for poor Christian natives. In the centre of this workshop compound stood a tent with thatch walls, which he was using temporarily as his office, while his office proper was undergoing repairs. The tent was in a blaze. As I came out I saw his desk, containing valuable books and papers, turned end-over-end in the midst of the flames by a young native, who seemed to be fire-proof. The desk flew open in one of its somersaults, and out came the books and papers: by means of a general grab-game everything of value was rescued, but somewhat blackened and scorched. We soon returned to the bungalow, and about a dozen of the Walker family came out as seekers, and professed to receive Jesus.

Thursday, 16th.—At Justice Walker's at seven a.m. I preached, through Brother Scott, on the two baptisms,—but one, in fact,—the water-baptism being but the seal of the soul's indenture to the service of God, and sacrament of initiation into His visible Church, and sign of the inward baptism "by the one Spirit into the body of Christ."

Mrs. Walker, the Musulmānī, came forward for Christian baptism. Brother Scott read the baptismal service in Hindūstānī, and we prayed for her and for Mr. Walker till they were filled with the Holy Spirit; and then I baptized her with water.

I then read our "General Rules," and gave them an address on church organization, and organized "a church in the house" of Brother Walker; and appointed him to conduct a public service in his own house every Sabbath morning, assisted by the missionaries when they could command time.

At the noon meeting that day, in the Orphanage Chapel, Mrs. Walker publicly related her experience in her own language: she could not speak English.

At the close of the meeting, Brother Scott said, "She has great command of the Hindūstānī language, and is most clear and emphatic in her testimony to the saving power of Christ." I may simply add that Justice Walker kept up the meetings at his own house, and sometimes took meetings at the bungalow. Mrs. Walker was a large, fine-looking woman, apparently in the vigour of life and health; but a few months after her conversion to God she took ill and died. Brother Scott wrote me that she remained true to Jesus, and died in the Lord.

After a year or two Brother Walker also died in the Lord, and the family has moved away I know not whither. The giant passed through all this, deeply awakened, and came to spend the evening with me at Brother Scott's the night of my departure: admitted everything; anxious to be saved, but hesitated. I know not what has become of him.

Four years after I spent one night in Bareilly, and in the afternoon visited the Orphanage. Many of the grown-up girls had married and gone away; and many younger ones had come in: but the majority of them knew me, and jumped for joy when they saw their old friend who helped to lead them to Jesus four years before. A very large proportion of them remained steadfast in Jesus,—so said Sister Sparks, who had been with them all the time.

CHAPTER VIII.

MISCELLANEOUS.

LEAVING the pleasant home of Brother Scott about nine p.m., we travelled that night by dhulī dāk forty miles, to a camp-meeting on the Budāon circuit,—Rev. R. Hoskins missionary.

We arrived at the camp just as the cheering rays of the morning sun began to stream through the mango groves. Brother and Sister Hoskins gave us a welcome home in their tent.

[My limited space will preclude the diary details of daily toil for the next eight months, except occasional illustrative specimen facts and incidents.]

At this camp-meeting over thirty nominal Christian natives professed to find the pardon of their sins; and one Mohamedan was baptized by Brother Scott, who spent a few days at the camp.

The singing, led by a native fiddle and the tumtum (a kind of drum), was charming to my ears and heart. I have heard nothing to equal it in this country. Brother Hoskins is an earnest and successful missionary. His work is principally among a low class of farmers, but the most of them after their baptism remain at home and support themselves; and this work gives greater promise of an indigenous permanent growth than any that I have yet seen in India. He also has flourishing schools,—supplies the people with good books from our press in Lucknow; and his farmers are becoming a reading people, and will, I believe, become an intelligent, thrifty, Christian people. This was my last appointment in the Bareilly district; and my regret was, that I could not stay longer and accomplish more for God and His dear servants whom I love so much.

From the camp-meeting we passed into the Morādabād district,—Rev. E. W. Parker presiding elder. Our first station was Chandousī. It was late at night when we arrived, and very dark, but after much difficulty we found the Dāk bungalow, where two very earnest missionary workers were waiting for us —Brothers Mansell and Wheeler. We made an itinerating tour of hard fighting and varied success at Chandousī, Bābūkherā, Joā, Sambhal, Bāshtā Amrohā, and Morādabād. Brother Parker, a grand educator and presiding elder, and his wife, a true helper, were with us during most of the campaign—which occupied a space of six weeks.

He refers to our visit in those towns in his annual report as an event for its good fruits long to be remembered.

Brother Wheeler, in his report of the work in Morādabād, says: "Brother Taylor's tour through my part of the field was a most important event. The helpers were both quickened in their experience and instructed for their work. Some eighteen or twenty English-speaking people were converted in

Morādabād under his ministration,—one of whom has passed peacefully and triumphantly home."

A few natives at each place professed to find the Saviour, but most of them were nominal Christians before; indeed, in so hasty a visit in each place, and a working agency not up to the point of effectiveness, it was impossible to make a fair test of the saving power of the Gospel among the heathen, as we did in Africa and in Ceylon. A vast amount of valuable preparatory work has been done in India, especially in education, and in the translation of the Scriptures into nearly all the languages of this great empire; but the spiritual development and adjustment of agency are entirely behind that of any other mission-field in which I have laboured—while the combinations of the opposing forces here in India probably exceed those of any other part of the globe. My brethren here, having read of my labours and successes in Africa, got an idea that I would at once attack the masses in the streets, and mow them down like grass in a hay-field; but instead of that I began, where I always begin, with the members of the church. In other fields we found them in such an advanced state of preparation, that with but little loss of time we were ready with a powerful force of holy men and women to march at once to the front and rescue captive souls from the enemy; but here my limited time was nearly all taken up in barracks, hospitals, and parade-grounds—where, to be sure, much good was done of its kind.

In these remarks I bring no charges against any, and do not wish to cast any reflections indirectly upon any, but simply to explain the situation.

When I closed my services in Morādabād, Brother Bailey was most anxious to take me to the native state of Bhopāl, in Central India, where he has kindred in high official position, and strike for the establishment of a new mission where none existed. He was as confident of success as he was of getting Justice Walker converted to God; but I was simply on an evangelistic tour, as I had been for so many years, labouring to help stir up existing organizations, and was expecting to go home, according to previous arrangement, the next year; so I could not see my way to Bhopāl. But early in April we went to Meerut, a large native city and military station. We had a letter from Brother Parker to an old Church missionary in Meerut, which we presented, thinking he might invite us to give him a helping hand in some special services in his native work; but he did not invite us.

But Rev. Mr. McKay, Church chaplain, and Rev. Mr. Gillan, Scotch Kirk chaplain, gave me a most cordial and earnest invitation to work for them in English work. So Brother Bailey returned and took work under Brother Parker, where he has been working earnestly ever since. He now (in 1875) has charge of Sambhal Circuit, and has become a powerful preacher of the Gospel in Hindūstānī and Hindī.

I preached daily in the Kirk in Meerut for three weeks. I did not for a fortnight invite a seeker to come out avowedly on the Lord's side. The chaplains were both in attendance on all occasions, and often spoke publicly of the great good they had received at the meetings. I was most hospitably entertained at their houses; and no brethren could be more kind to me than they were. I dearly love them as brethren in Christ, and hoped gradually to get them to see with me the necessity of having awakened sinners to come out from among the wicked, renounce their rebellion, and avow their allegiance to God. Finally I invited them to come to the front, and seven came promptly forward; and we had a deeper awakening among many who did not yield, so that I hoped for a great harvest of souls; but it struck the dear ministers as a novelty, because they had never seen the like before. They did not object publicly, but afterwards expressed their feelings so that I did not consider it safe to repeat the call for seekers to come out avowedly; for as I was working under their auspices, I could not see it my duty to lead the people in a way that their pastors would not approve. That would tend to schism; so I had to choose the less of two evils. Hence, with many under awakening, I did not certainly believe that a single one was saved. Hoping that some good might be conserved, I secured the concurrence of both ministers in the organization of a general fellowship band, composed of the awakened sinners and quickened members of the two congregations. I appointed two leaders for the band—one a young lieutenant, of the English Church, and the other a quartermaster in the army, and member of the Kirk: both fine men. The ministers both wrote to me at different times, saying that about forty persons attended the fellowship band every Wednesday night, and that a truly spiritual work was progressing among them. I was very glad, and hoped that they would keep it up. After a few weeks, however, the lieutenant was transferred by an army order to some other station; and a few weeks later the quartermaster went to the Sanitarium in the hills; so that the band was left to scatter abroad, and was never again collected together. I cannot say that no good was accomplished, but I heard that the rumour abroad was that our revival in Meerut was a failure; and I believe it was.

I went from Meerut to DELHI, and laboured three weeks with my old friend Rev. James Smith, the Baptist missionary whom I met in Australia eight years before. The weather now was so very hot that we did not attempt to hold special services in his chapel, beyond the regular Sabbath appointments—at which a few soldiers professed to find Jesus; but we had preaching every week-evening in native verandahs and open courts, and prepared the soil, and sowed the good seed; and in the following cool season Brother Smith, as his report states, gathered a considerable harvest. He is trying hard, and with a good degree of success, to place his mission on a purely self-supporting basis.

One night, when we were preaching in an open court surrounded by flat-roofed native houses, to about 100 attentive Hindūs, there was a sudden commotion in the crowd, and some of the men ran up on the roofs of the houses. My first impression was that a fire had broken out; and I enquired, "What is it all about?"

"Here is a man who has been hit on the breast with a brickbat," replied one—holding up the brick in his hand. Bang came another brick, hitting a man on the foot; then brick after brick fell among the people, and were picked up, and brought and laid down at my feet. While Brother Smith went on the housetop, to see where they came from, I told the people to sing, and while they sang, smash went an earthen water-pot close to my right; but we stood quietly and sang, till the shower of bricks ceased; then I resumed and finished my discourse.

Friday, May 12th.—Visited the Great Mosque of the Mogul emperors of Delhi. It is really a magnificent structure. From the top of a minaret about 300 feet high I got a full view of the city and a wide radius of the surrounding country. The buildings are greatly superior to any I saw in Cawnpore or Lucknow.

As I was driven from time to time to all parts of the city, many places of interest, and incidents belonging to them, were brought to my attention: such as, "The forlorn hope was led through this gate. Twenty-three men were told off, each one to carry a bag of powder and lay it down at the gate, and fire a fuze to set it off. Seventeen of them were killed and mortally wounded. These gates were thus blown open, and the English soldiers marched into the city. Then it took seven days of hard fighting to take it; for inside were 60,000 Sepoys, who had been trained in the British army by all the military skill of their commanders,—and no end to the guns and ammunition at their command. Besides this great force of mutineers inside, they had 10,000 men posted outside. These were conquered by 6000 English and 25,000 native troops.

"That is the gate where the chaplain was slain. His daughter and another young lady were dragged down those steps and killed in that little alley.

"That great cross marks the spot where some hundreds of Europeans and East Indians, slain by the rebels, were buried in a mass together.

"Under that tree, the rebels took 120 English and East Indian women and children, and murdered them.

"That English church was built by the vow of a wounded colonel, on the result of his living to see the rebellion crushed." Etc., etc.

Brother Smith told me the following story of a martyr in the Mutiny,—Walāyat Ali :—

"He belonged to a respectable, and once a wealthy family, in Agra. He possessed all the fiery enthusiasm of the Mohamedan sects; and hence, after his conversion to God, his boldness in defence of the truth was striking. His faith in the Gospel, combined with his child-like sincerity, rendered him impregnable to bribes or flattery; and his thorough knowledge of the theory and practice of Mohamedanism made him a formidable opponent. He was brought to God through the agency of Colonel Wheeler in 1848, and baptized in 1857. He taught his wife Fatīmā to read; and although she had been all her lifetime secluded in the zenāna, she came out boldly with Elizabeth, her eldest daughter, and they were baptized."

Brother Smith introduced me to Fatīmā and her children. She told me the following about her husband :—

"On Monday, the 11th of May 1857, about nine a.m., my husband was going out to preach, when he was told that the Mohamedans of the city were killing all the Christians. He was urged to flee, or he would be killed. He replied, 'No, no, my brother; the Lord's work cannot be stopped. This is no time to flee—except to God in prayer.' We then had our family prayers, after which he kissed us all, and said, 'See that, whatever comes, you do not deny Christ.' Then I began to weep bitterly; and he said, 'My dear wife, I thought your faith was stronger in the Saviour than mine. Why are you so troubled? Remember God's Word, and be comforted. Know that if you die, you will go to Jesus, and if you shall be spared, Christ is your Keeper. I feel confident that if any missionaries live, you will be cared for; and should they all perish, yet Christ liveth for ever. If your children are killed before your eyes, oh, then take care that you do not deny HIM who died for us! This is my last charge; and God help you!'

"Then came a crowd of Mohamedans, and seized my husband, and dragged him along on the ground, beating him on his head and in his face with their shoes, with taunting shouts,—'Now preach Christ to us!' 'Now where is your Christ, in whom you boast?'

"Then they commanded him to recant, and forsake Christ.

"'No,' he said; 'I never will. My Saviour took

up His cross, and went to God. I will bear my cross, and lay down my life, and follow Him to heaven.'

"'I suppose you want some water?' said one of his murderers.

"'When my Saviour died He got vinegar mingled with gall. I do not need your water, and your swords have no terror for me. Let them fall on me, and I fall a martyr for Christ.'

"Then a trooper rode up, and asked, 'What is all this?'

"'We have here a devil of a Christian, who will not recant: so do you kill him.'

"My dear husband exclaimed, 'O Jesus, receive my soul!'—when a stroke of the trooper's sword nearly cut off his head.'"

While detailing these facts the good woman would wipe off her tears, and say, "Well, why should I sorrow? He gave his life to Christ who died for him, and he is now with Jesus." She continued:—

"I was close by under a tree, and saw them kill my poor husband, and could not help but shriek out. I then went back to the chapel compound, and saw my house in a blaze. I took my children, and went to the house of Mirzā Hādjī, where I remained three days; when an order was issued that if any were found harbouring Christians they should be put to death. Mirzā Hādjī told me about the order, and said, 'You must at once leave my house, or become a Mohamedan.'

"Then he and another man urged me to forsake Christ—saying that 'every Christian in India was killed, and for me to hold out was madness and folly.'

They offered me a house, and protection, and thirty rupees per month for the support of my children.

"God helped me to resist the temptation; and I said 'No, I cannot forsake Christ. I will work to support my children, and if I must be killed, God's will be done!' So I left, with my seven children. Some Sepoys at the police-station attempted to kill us; but one man, knowing who I was, told them that I was under the protection of the king, and not to kill us. I tried in vain to get a place to live in; for no one would take us in, lest they should be murdered for harbouring us. So we wandered about, having no place to rest, and but little to eat.

"On the thirteenth day of our tribulation a large body of Sepoys went out of the city, and we managed to mix with the crowd, and thus got out to a place called Tulwāree, and got a room for eight annas per month. All the money I had was taken from me except six rupees. I afterwards went to Soonput, forty miles from Delhi, and remained three months, employed in grinding corn, at an anna (three-halfpence) for eighteen pounds in weight. I often had to work night and day; yet the Lord was good to us, and we did not starve. After the English re-took Delhi, I returned to Tulwāree; and there we all took fever, and I was in great distress. My youngest child died, and I had not a pie to pay any one to help to bury him. The Mohamedans tantalized me, and said they would bury him if I would turn Mohamedan. I wrapped the little corpse in a cloth, and took it outside the village, and was digging a grave with my own hands, when two men came and asked me why I was crying; so I told them, and then they kindly helped me dig the grave, and left. I then took up the little corpse, and looking up to heaven, I said, 'O Lord, Thou hast been pleased to call to Thyself this little child, and I have been able to bring his little body to be buried. But, O Lord, if Thou shouldst call one of the big ones, how can I bring it? Have mercy on me, O Lord, and permit me to meet with some of Thy dear people again: and if not, O Father, take to Thyself the mother and the children.'"

Fatīmā is a Christian worker in Delhi now; of whom Mr. Smith, in one of his reports, says: "Fatīmā has great courage and fluency of speech. She is of high respectability, and is therefore received by very many Mohamedans willingly; and many who once hated the name of Jesus now allow her to speak freely of His love."

From Delhi I went to AMBALA, and preached two Sabbaths for Rev. Wm. Morrison, to Her Majesty's 72nd Regt.; and in the week intervening we opened an English work in Sudder Bazār—which continues, I learn, to the present, with the prospect of becoming a nucleus of a church there. I was most hospitably entertained at the house of Rev. Dr. Morrison.

I went thence to BIJNOUR, and wrought a few days for Rev. Henry Jackson, and had some souls saved; thence by dhūlī dāk on a very wet night forty miles to MORĀDABĀD; thence about forty more, to the base of the mountain, *en route* for NYNE TĀL; and thence fifteen miles up the Himalāya Mountains, on Rev. Dr. J. L. Humphrey's pony.

The Doctor is not only an indefatigable missionary, but a successful medical practitioner. From April to November of this year he treated 1830 patients. He is also the founder of a medical school in Nyne Tāl. Colonel Ramsey, commissioner of Ghurwāl and Kamāon, has been his ever-ready patron, and a firm support to all our mission work in the Himalāya Mountains.

A large number of mountaineers—native Christian men and women—have graduated from Dr. Humphrey's humble college at Nyne Tāl, and are very useful as doctors and as Christian workers. Besides all this, in day-schools and Hindūstānī preaching Dr. Humphrey is very successful. Referring to my visit in his annual report, he says: "He preached and held daily meetings for several weeks, which resulted in the forming of a class of about thirty members. We hope the fruits of his highly acceptable labours may remain, and be seen among us for years to come." It was during this visit that Sister Humphrey and I compiled "Hymns New and Old," which have been so valuable to our rising Indian churches.

Spent a week preaching for Rev. J. Budden, of the London Mission, at ELMORA. He is an earnest Christian gentleman, and a grand interpreter in Hindī. He is doing a great educational work in the mountains.

Spent a Sabbath at RANI KHET, and went on, a week's journey through the mountains, to PĀORĪ: Rev. Henry Mansell presiding elder, and Rev. P. T. Wilson preacher in charge. This was my last work that year in our Mission Conference. All the missionaries and their wives, and our female missionaries, have my fullest confidence and sympathy. A few hundreds of nominal native Christians professed to find peace at our meetings, and also a small number of Hindūs and Mohamedans; and God gave a fresh Divine impulse to the work, which thrills on with increasing power year by year. My work closed in Pāorī about the last of August. It was not considered safe to return to the plains earlier than October; so I set apart the month of September for a pilgrimage with the natives, to study them, and learn what they did and suffered to get rest for their souls. Captain Garstin, sub-commissioner of Ghurwāl, lent me a tent and a chaprāsī—a native to provide by the way—and Brother Wilson a native cook; so in company with the Hindū pilgrims, without an interpreter, I visited the most celebrated shrines of the north—Badrīṇāth and Kidernāth—away on the borders of eternal snow, in the Himalāya Mountains. I can't stop for details. They would fill a volume.

We reached Mussourī on the 5th of October. Spent a few days preaching for Rev. Mr. Woodside, American Presbyterian, in Dheradoon; and went thence and spent a few days with Rev. Dr. Forman, and the Newtons, of the same Mission in Lahore: and at the call of the missionaries of the American Board of Foreign Missions to attend their annual meeting at Ahmednugger, I started for Bombay, about 1500 miles distant, on Wednesday, the 19th of October, 1871.

CHAPTER IX.

BOMBAY.

THIS city was built on several small islands, which have been gradually united to each other by levelling down the hills and filling up the separating valleys. Thus the whole became one island, and that has been united to the mainland, and firmly anchored to it by railway lines.

When Charles II. was married to the daughter of the king of Portugal, he received the island and dependencies of Bombay as part of her dower.

"A grand expedition was despatched to India by the Crown, under the Earl of Marlborough, to receive possession of the settlements; but after having held it for six years, the ministers of the Crown found that it cost more than it yielded, and ceded it to the East India Company—under whose fostering care the population grew from 10,000 to more than 800,000, and the trade from 100,000 to more than 300,000,000 rupees.

"The year in which Bombay was ceded to the Company was the year in which the first order for the purchase of tea was sent out by them to the East."

Tea was spoken of, then, as a "regalia in high treatments and entertainments, and presents to princes and grandees," and was sold as high as a hundred shillings per pound. "In 1657, Thomas Garraway, the founder of Garraway's coffee-house, which still exists in London, was the first to sell it 'in drink made according to the directions of the most knowing merchants and travellers in the Eastern countries; and many noblemen, merchants, and physicians resorted to his house in 'Change Alley, to drink the drink thereof.' He sold it at a rate varyng from fifteen to fifty shillings the pound. But it was not till ten years after, that the Company issued an order for 'one hundred pounds' weight of the best tey they could gett, to be sent home by their ships.'"

PARSEES are not a very numerous, though a very influential class of the population of Bombay. The whole Parsee nation in India numbers less than 100,000: of these about 50,000 reside in Bombay. They are Persians in nationality, Zoroastrians in religion. They fled from Persia 1200 years ago, under the pressure of the "great Mohamedan conquest," when their nation had to choose to accept the Koran or the sword. They settled in the Surat country, a couple of hundred miles north of Bombay —where a large portion of them still remain. They were allowed a peaceable settlement by the king of the country, under certain treaty conditions—one of which was, that they should not eat beef; and thus they *politically* adopted some customs of the Hindū religion. The Parsees believe in one God, in heaven and hell; are not idolaters, but, instead, assume to worship God through the medium of the elements, especially fire, and are hence called fire-worshippers; but they have many religious ceremonies as ridiculous as any among the heathen. I cannot here attempt a description of them. In commerce and trade they are very enterprising, and have been very prosperous. In the reaction following the great cotton speculative mania occasioned by the civil war in America, many of them, in common with the mass of English and Hindū speculators in shares, collapsed, but a large number of them are now wealthy merchants, and some of them liberal.

Sir Jamsetjee Jejeebhoy founded and endowed a hospital in Bombay bearing his name, which has no rival in the city, and is a refuge for thousands of sufferers of all nationalities annually. As a class the Parsees are well educated; and a large proportion of those in Bombay speak English. They do not patronize mission schools, but have schools of their own; and many are educated in the Government schools. Rev. Dr. Wilson, a pioneer veteran missionary of the Free Church of Scotland, had many fine Parsee lads in his school in Bombay thirty-five years ago; but when he baptized a couple of them, leading to a lawsuit for their recovery, which was decided in the Doctor's favour, and stirred up all the bad blood of the Parsee nation, they took their children from Christian schools, and have never sent them back. With all their progress in education and social elevation, they are probably the most uncompromising haters of Christianity in the country—not so vindictive as some of the Mohamedans, but fewer of them become Christians. Indeed, up to the time of my going to Bombay, history, so far as we can learn, only records eight cases of Parsees becoming Christians. The Parsees do not bury their dead, as do the Mohamedans, Christians, Būdhists, and others—nor burn their dead, as do the Hindūs—but turn them over to the vultures to be devoured. They have on a high hill near the city what is called the "Tower of Silence." It is an enclosure of several acres of ground in its wild jungle state, except scattered stately palm trees, and a few towers of solid masonry, flat on the top—covered, I am told, with gratings of iron bars, on which the bodies of the dead are exposed to be devoured by birds of prey. This enclosure is surrounded by a high wall, and no one is admitted "except on business"; and none but Parsees have any business there. I went one day and climbed upon the wall, and got an outside view of the premises. I saw huge vultures in countless numbers perched on the palm trees, waiting for a dead Parsee. I fancied they sharply eyed every living one, and said to themselves, "You are our man : we'll clean your bones for you one of these days." The funeral obsequies at the house of the dead are, I am told, quite elaborate; and on each side of the street leading to it long lines of venerable Parsee gentlemen are seated in honour of the dead. Many of the Parsees, though entirely opposed to Christianity, are rather apt learners of European entertainments and drinking customs. They have as many as four theatres within a stone's-throw of each other, in Bombay. We shall have many of them converted to God yet, and they will become powerful evangelizers among the nations of India.

HINDŪS of every variety of caste constitute the great majority of the population of Bombay.

Many of them are well educated, and speak the English language, and are successful merchants and operative producers in every possible department of industry. Every caste has its own profession or trade; indeed, the business to a great extent established the separating walls of caste; so that the descendants of any particular caste are bound to pursue the business or occupation of their ancestors. Their temples are not massive buildings, as I formerly supposed, but generally very small, tower-like constructions, with pyramidal spires studded on all sides with small statues of their antiquated gods. The few they worship are in the interior, exposed to view below. The worshippers, singly or in small clusters, stand outside, while a few priests inside ring bells, beat drums, swing incense-lamps, sprinkle "holy water," and go daily through a vast routine of ceremony. The worshippers bring flowers for the gods, and presents of money and food for the priests. Their great assemblies, mostly in the open air—often swelling to tens of thousands—are their regular festivals, partly social and partly religious: indeed, they are so intensely religious that everything they do is combined with some religious ceremony.

The Hindūs are transmigrationists in common with the Būdhists. The system of the latter is more clearly defined as to the ultimate state of the soul. The Būdhists' heaven is not annihilation, but the rest of utter unconsciousness. This rest is reached through a series of innumerable births, miserable existences, and deaths. The soul having thus expiated all its misdeeds by suffering, is subjected to no more births, and loses all consciousness of joy or sorrow. The Hindū heaven does not appear to be even so clearly defined as that. A large number of the Hindūs are pantheists—that is, as God is everywhere and in everything, therefore all space and every form of matter are component parts of God; hence an idol is a tangible part of God selected by them as a medium through which they hope to get access to the more vital, intelligent heart of God. Speak to a Hindū about worshipping an idol, and he will give you the same answer that a Roman Catholic will, when accused of idolatry in bowing down to pictures. There is a large and wealthy caste in Bombay called *Jains*, representing a compound system of religion made up of Hindūism and Būdhism. They have much larger temples than the Hindūs.

The MOHAMEDANS, next to the Hindūs, are the most numerous race in Bombay; and they represent there every Mohamedan country on the earth, and carry on a large traffic with Arabia, Persia, and all countries east of Constantinople. They do not like the Europeans, nor their institutions; and hence they do not avail themselves half so largely of the educational institutions of India as do the Hindūs. They however have some good schools of their own. They are traditionally opposed to idolatry, but in the popular forms of idolatrous worship—in feasts, processions, and pilgrimages—and in their reverence for dead men's bones, and in amulets and charms, they largely imitate the Hindūs, and mix with them in some of their ceremonies.

The EUROPEANS and EAST INDIANS of Bombay constitute a population of about 7000, sparsely scattered through the great mass. Many of the latter class are a cross between the old Portuguese settlers and the natives, and are Roman Catholics, and have several churches in Bombay. They have a large high school in Byculla, and are building a college on the Esplanade. Among the Europeans, and the higher class of Protestant East Indians, the English Establishment has half a dozen churches and a few schools.

The Scotch Kirk has a church and a large educational institution for natives; the Free Church of Scotland the same, with the addition of a female orphanage and native church. The American Board of Foreign Missions has a native church; and the Baptists have recently built a chapel for English preaching.

Bombay is the great commercial rival of Calcutta. The latter commands most of the trade in the great valleys of the Ganges and its tributaries, and the navigation of those rivers, besides her system of railroads—the Eastern Bengal and the East Indian Railways. The latter extends to Delhi, 955 miles direct, besides various branches, and there connects with the Scinde, Punjāb, and Delhi division, 556 miles further to Mooltān; and connects also with the Oudh and Rohilcund railway, and by its Jubbulpore extension connects with the Great Indian Peninsular, with its many branches: but Bombay, on the direct line of travel to European countries, commands the advantage of a share of the trade, and a large proportion of the travellers to and from India and the West. The Bombay and Baroda line of rail, north about 400 miles, and south to Madras, about 800 miles, and commerce by sea with the Indus and the Persian Gulf, afford great advantages to Bombay.

CHAPTER X.

THE MĀRĀTTĪ MISSION.

TRAVELLED from Lahore to Bombay in the third class—first, because my funds were low; and secondly, because I wanted to study native language and character. All were exceedingly kind and agreeable, except one old Hindū, who in all his waking hours was repeating his "Ram," "Ram," "Ram," and passing his beads along the string to keep the tally of his "Ave Marias." He seemed to be the most religious man, and certainly the greatest grumbler, of the whole crowd. Arrived in Bombay at eleven a.m. on Saturday the 22nd of October, put up again in the Byculla Hotel, and spent a quiet Sabbath. On Monday, at eleven a.m., took a third-class ticket for Dhond, about 180 miles S.E. The guards offered me a second class, but I declined. The carriages were crowded; but by a new system—new in India—of squeezing and packing, there was room for a few more. I looked, and learned. There sits an old Brāhman in the corner, behind a pile of his luggage, to preclude the possibility of touch by any ordinary mortal; he raises his hands, and screams at an intruder, and then draws himself up into the corner again in a great state of trepidation; his caste may be broken, and his soul lost. Now in comes an Irish guard—a regular packer; and stuffing the Brāhman's things under the bench, makes the Brāhman the base of a layer of coolies. He smashes down the separating barriers which have stood the storms of ages, and indiscriminately packs away high castes and low castes together, like herrings in a barrel. Now full up, we touch at another station. Here comes another old Brāhman: he looks into one carriage after another, and sees the packed-in coolies and low castes. He is in a great state; the bell is ringing the signal to start, and he stands hesitating at the door. Along comes the guard; and with the stentorian order, "Chuck him in there," we suddenly see the Brāhman tumbling into the midst of the common herd.

These railroads are a wonderful institution for India, and are as certainly crushing caste barriers as that they are climbing and tunnelling these mountains: and these railway guards are missionaries in their way,—not directly engaged in building the ark, but preparing the highways for bringing in the timber for its construction. Noah's shipbuilders and roadmakers were very useful men in their day. They got their wages, no doubt; but it was a great pity they did not go into the ark and secure a free salvation.

I reached Dhond at ten p.m. As I stepped on to the platform a thick-set Scotchman introduced himself to me as a Baptist missionary from Bengal—

the Rev. Mr. Ellis, also on his way to the annual meeting at Ahmednugger. "Here is a tonga waiting for us," said Brother Ellis; "and I have just received a letter from Rev. Mr. Bissell, saying that we can both come on in the same conveyance; but if you like I will get another, and you can have this one to yourself."

"No, Brother Ellis; we will go together."

A "tonga" is a small two-horse cart, with two seats across—one facing toward the horses, on which the driver sits, with room for one passenger beside him, and the other for two passengers facing in the opposite direction, sitting back to back with the two in front. When I got in, Brother Ellis, seeing that I covered so much of the seat, seemed to hesitate, and said, "I hope I shan't put you out" (meaning that he did not wish to inconvenience me).

"No, Brother; if you try that you will get put out yourself." He laughed, and at once became as familiar as if he had known me always. I found him a very genial, earnest Christian gentleman and missionary, and we passed the time very pleasantly and profitably together; but the wind blowing on our backs through that long, chilly night, we both took a severe cold. We arrived in Ahmednugger, the principal centre of the Mārāttī Mission, at the dawn of day. This Mission was established many years ago by the American Board of Foreign Missions. Its missionaries in Mārāttī land are not numerous, but very influential and successful, compared with other Missions. We were welcomed to the home of Rev. L. Bissell, D.D., and greatly enjoyed our sojourn in his charming family—consisting of his wife and five children.

This is an annual meeting of great interest—consisting of the eight or ten of their own missionaries, a few visiting ministers, and their own native Christians, helpers, and pastors: making up an aggregate assembly of about five hundred. On this occasion we had as visitors—besides myself and Brother Ellis—Rev. Dr. Wm. Scudder, of the Arcott Mission, and Rev. W. Chandler, of the Madura Mission, in the south,—a sister to the Mārāttī Mission, established and sustained by the same Board.

My first preaching service was on Thursday the 26th. My interpreter is a converted Brāhman, an able minister of the Gospel, and pastor of the Ahmednugger church—Ram Krishnā Punt. The missionaries work as evangelists and general superintendents, and as far as possible secure native pastors for their churches. Brother Ram Krishnā Punt is a fluent interpreter.

On Friday evening we preached again, and also on Saturday at eight a.m. There is a manifest awakening. Preached on the Sabbath at nine a.m.; when seven seekers came out avowedly, and two professed to find the Saviour. In the evening Dr. Scudder preached on "The past and present of the Christian Church,"—a very interesting historical sermon.

Then I preached daily during the ensuing week. We had ten seekers on Monday, twelve on Tuesday, fourteen on Wednesday, eighteen on Thursday, and the same number on Friday. The attention of the people was much divided: those from a distance had the business of the meeting in its variety requiring their time; the residents were much occupied with their company; but God was with us, and good was done. A good number—mostly nominal Christians, with two or three Hindūs—professed quietly to find the pardon of their sins. Many of the same seekers came up again and again; but the whole number of them for the week was about twenty-five. Contrary to my plan—always subject to modification as the Lord is pleased to give new intimations—I arranged to remain here in this work till Wednesday of next week.

On Saturday evening, November 4th, we had a concert of native Christian music in the chapel, which attracted a crowd of Hindūs. The narrative of the Prodigal Son in poetic measure was detailed in short chapters, and then sung by a choir of native singers, accompanied with several instruments. Some of the missionaries said at the close, "We hope to see the day when we shall have as many Hindūs to come and hear the Gospel preached as have come to-night to hear the singing." To their surprise we had a similar crowd of Hindūs on Sunday, Monday, Tuesday, and Wednesday evenings of the ensuing week; and about a hundred of them became regular hearers henceforth, as I have learned since,—some few of whom have been saved. The missionaries expressed themselves as greatly pleased with the results of our meetings; but I was not. I am no croaker; but I have been accustomed to see results in other countries which did honour to an Almighty Saviour.

I arrived again in Bombay on Friday, the 10th of November, 1871. Rev. C. Harding, of the American Board of Foreign Missions, met me at the station, and drove me to his house in Byculla. Commenced a series of Mārāttī services in Brother Harding's chapel on the following Sabbath, the 12th. Rev. Vishnu Punt is the pastor of his native church, but Brother Ram Krishnā Punt came from Ahmednugger to interpret for me in Bombay. Preached at nine a.m. to a congregation of thirty persons. At four p.m. we had about a hundred. "By whom shall Jacob arise? for he is small,"—very small indeed in this great Pagan city!

Monday, 13th.—At seven a.m., twenty-seven hearers; at half-past six p.m., about fifty.

Tuesday, seven a.m.—About forty persons. I gave an account of the zeal of the Singhalese Christians in Moratū Mulwā, Ceylon—who, in anticipation of my visit, went into the jungle and got out the timber, and in two days built a temporary chapel thirty-five by fifty-five feet, and thatched it so well that fourteen inches of rain which fell in forty-eight hours did not penetrate it; and there in one week we had 130 Singhalese converted to God, and not an Englishman concerned in the transaction.

At half-past six p.m. about seventy hearers. Five native ministers are in attendance now, taking note of my way of doing the work of the Lord.

Wednesday, 15th.—At seven a.m. fifty-six hearers. Gave them a detailed account of our great work of God in the Church Mission in Badagam, Ceylon; where 100 Singhalese professed to receive Jesus in ten days.

At half-past six p.m. about 100 hearers. God is with us; but I apprehend His workers in this city are but few and feeble.

One good man met me at the door as I came out, and exclaimed, "Except the Lord build the house, they labour in vain that build it."

"True; but He needs builders, nevertheless. He has never yet built a house among men without the labour of human builders."

Then he quoted "Thy people shall be willing in the day of Thy power."

"Exactly so; and if we can only secure the fulfilment of that prediction—the willingness of God's people to witness and work for Him—then we shall see His saving power manifested in this city; but while they stand shivering on the brink, and merely talk about it, they will but obstruct the progress of God's great work."

There is no Methodist organization within less than 800 miles of Bombay. The Christianity here is of the Calvinian type. Among Methodists, the world over, I can at once introduce incisive, effective methods of work; but among the older organizations I must preach very cautiously for a week or two, to allay prejudice and secure their concurrence and intelligent co-operation. (Thank God! they are all coming to the front now, in all Christian countries.)

It remains to be seen what God can do here with such agency as we have at command. The ministers are most earnest in their efforts to promote God's work; but as for lay workers—I have yet to see them.

Thursday, 16th.—Seven a.m., sixty-four out. We

had with us Rev. Mr. Small, of the Scotch Free Church Mission, Rev. Mr. Weatherhead, of the Church Mission—both of this city; and Rev. Mr. Welland, of Calcutta. I repeated the testimony for Christ of many of the Singhalese who were saved in Badagam, Ceylon; which seemed to interest the people much, and to show them the saving power of God among the Budhists.

At three p.m. preached to the schools of the Free Church of Scotland: about 120 present.

At half-past six, again in the American Chapel, to about 130, including a few Hindūs and Mohamedans, who have not been coming before. There was deep seriousness; and I believe the Spirit of God is applying the truth.

Friday, 17th.—Rained this morning, but we had thirty-seven hearers. I discoursed on prayer, and four or five led in that exercise. After we dismissed, they all sat still for some time, when the pastor got up and made a confession of hindrances in himself, and proposed that we should remain longer, and pray for the removal of obstructions to the work of God. Three native pastors also confessed their want of zeal and soul-saving skill. It was a good season of heart-searching, humiliation, and confession. The work is beginning in the right place.

Half-past six p.m.—After preaching, we invited believers to come forward and unite in praying for power to do the work God wants us to do. About thirty came; after which three or four spoke with great feeling. A native editor prayed, weeping all the time, and said many striking things to God,—

among which were the following: "As hot iron thrust into the water is hardened, so our hearts, heated by Thy Word and Spirit, thrust into the chilling waters of worldliness, have been hardened. The many prayers we have said are such poor things that we do not know whether to call them prayers or not: I think we should change the '*heading.*'"

Sabbath, 19th.—Preached at eight a.m. to an English congregation in the native chapel of the Free Church of Scotland. I hope to see a good work in this Mission. The ministers, Rev. Messrs. Small, Stephen, and Dhanjībhāī, seem greatly interested. Rev. John Wilson, D.D., the pioneer head of it, is absent in Scotland.

At four p.m. preached again in the American Chapel. The largest crowd we have had; good attention, but nothing decisive that I can perceive. It may be my own fault in not demanding earlier an avowed surrender to God. I have been trying to prepare the Church for it, and waiting to see manifest proofs of awakening. Lord, help me to see Thy way clearly, and to walk in it! I fear our workers are too few and feeble for a great advance; but, through the mighty Spirit of God, something must be done this week.

Monday, 20th.—At seven a.m. a quiet, but interesting meeting.

At half-past six p.m. a good audience. At the close of sermon called for seekers, and eleven came —nine men and two women. Two professed to find peace, but did not witness publicly. "With the heart man believeth unto righteousness, and with the mouth confession is made unto salvation." When a sick patient submits to treatment, all the friends are anxious to know how it succeeds, and rejoice to hear that the patient has been relieved and cured; so when poor sick sinners submit to the great Physician, and get healed, God intends, for the honour of the Healer and for the encouragement of the dying masses without, that the healed shall be witnesses of His power to save.

21st.—At seven a.m. forty hearers; good meeting.

At half-past six p.m. deep awakening; thirteen seekers, four or five of whom were new cases. This old Gospel method of having awakened sinners to speak out, enquiring, "Sirs, what shall we do to be saved?"—to come out on the Lord's side, and to consent at once to renounce their rebellion and avow their allegiance to God—seems entirely new in Bombay. We signally lack power, and facility to use what we have. But the people seem willing to learn, and by the help of God we shall get the agency adjusted to His purpose before long. Two or three profess to find peace, but they appear to be still-born souls.

22nd.—At seven a.m. forty-four out. Ram Krishnā Punt interpreted for me this morning for the last time, and returns to-day to Ahmednugger. We shall miss him greatly,—a kind-spirited, good man, and a superior interpreter, with a very quick ear and most fluent utterance; though some less fluent will make sharper points than he.

At half-past six p.m. good congregation; twelve seekers—three or four new ones. The ministers are quite willing, but have never before worked in this way, and require time to get their heads and hearts into it,—not into any particular outward form, but the direct hand-to-hand fight with the powers of darkness for the rescue of souls, to be led at once to Jesus. The lay workers are not visible in any public effort to save souls yet: whether or not they work at home, I cannot say. We are in a pitiable condition. As said a prophet of old, "We have come to the birth, and there is not strength to bring forth." O God! we look to Thee for deliverance. Save, or we die! Help Thy people here to receive Christ, and thus lay hold on Thy strength.

23rd.—Morning meeting as usual. Evening congregation much disturbed by the blowing, fizzing, and bursting of rockets close by the chapel—indeed, all over the city. It was a great marriage celebration, in which millions of Hindūs throughout the country participate. It is the annual marriage of a small plant to one of their gods—a most ridiculous farce, yet arousing the profound religious sensibilities of millions of devout Hindūs, and affording great entertainment for millions more. We had five or six new seekers—one a Mohamedan. A good show of missionaries: besides five resident in Bombay, we had with us Rev. Messrs. Haeberlin, of the German Mission among the Kohlds, beyond Calcutta; Swartz, of the Church Mission; and Angus, of the Free Church of Scotland, Poona.

Brother Haeberlin called at our house, and Brother Harding asked him if he had any sudden conversions among the Kohlds.

"No," he replied; "they are not Hindūs, nor Mohamedans. They are all like children,—easily led, and never manifest any sudden change."

I ventured to remark that, in my experience with children, "their penitential grief and tears, and the manifest joy of their newborn souls, were as distinctly marked as the same experience in old sinners."

They have baptized 14,000 Kohlds; but he says, "Their experience and the outward fruits of it are not satisfactory."

As I walked this afternoon, I saw a good-looking Hindū in the street—shoes off, hands up in supplication, and bowing in acts of worship. I looked, and saw a little temple opposite, and little gods of stone mounted on the front battlement, to which he was giving the adoration of his heart, which is due to God alone. Such things are of constant recurrence in these streets.

Friday, 24th.—At seven a.m. Perfect loyalty to God, and perfect confidence in Him, was the subject we pressed upon the attention of the people. Our officers are taking drill pretty well, but the rank and file is just what we lack. Officers, but no army.

At half-past six p.m. large congregation,—I mean, for this place. At the close of the prayer-meeting five witnesses stood up and stated to the congregation that they had obtained the pardon of their sins—three of them to-night, and the others two nights since. A few more have confessed privately that they have found salvation in Jesus.

Sabbath, 26th.—At eight a.m. preached again in the Scotch Native Church to an English congregation of about 150. Good attention, and great seriousness.

At four p.m., in the Mārātti work, we had ten seekers—one a Hindū, one an African, one a Scotch sailor.

27th.—Morning meeting as usual. At half-past six p.m. Rev. Apājee, of the Church Mission, interpreted. Thirteen seekers, among whom were four Hindūs and one Mussulman. Deep awakening, apparently, but scarcely any workers. When myself, Rev. C. Harding, and Rev. George Bowen are engaged in speaking to penitents, the general worship of singing and praying seems to collapse. Brother Harding is most earnest, and is daily acquiring facility in personal-detail work. I am most anxious that his church shall become a living, working power in Bombay. A number of them are getting into a clear experience of salvation. Captain Jacobs, of Poona, interpreted my words to the seekers to-day. He is an earnest Christian man, an inspector of Government Mārātti schools. Made a number of calls to-day in East Indian families, and prayed in two or three.

29th.—At the evening service one man professed conversion.

Thursday, 30th.—Morning meeting as usual. Large audience in the evening, with six or seven seekers: three professed. One of them was an old member, and I fear is not very clear after all; one a young Englishman—a medical student; and one the said Mohamedan. Visited an old woman in the hospital to-day; sang and prayed with her. She wept, and seemed very penitent. She afterwards became an earnest Christian.

Friday, Dec. 1st.—Two services, as usual. In the evening a woman whom I had visited when sick was at the meeting, and came forward as a seeker. She was weeping bitterly, and saying, "I do submit myself to God. Why can't I get relief?"

"Because you are trusting to your submission, or something else, and do not receive Christ." It was some time before I could get her to say, "I receive Christ."

Then she began to say, "I receive Christ: I do receive Him"; and while saying the words with her lips, she did in her heart receive Him; and began to say, "Oh, I feel a little better!"

"Never mind about the feeling: keep looking to Jesus." Soon she got into clear light, and praised God for His saving mercy.

This evening closes a series of eighteen days. Fifteen persons who came forward as seekers have testified publicly and clearly. I have heard of a number of members of different churches who profess to have found pardon under the preaching by quietly receiving Jesus in their pews. The wife of a native minister has professed to get pardon at these meetings, though a nominal Christian for fourteen years. It has been a hard fight, with some victories on our side.

I have arranged for a series of English services in the Institution Hall, in connexion with the school of the Free Church of Scotland; with morning services in the Scotch Orphanage for native girls.

CHAPTER XI.

ENGLISH WORK IN THE INSTITUTION HALL.

PREACHED at eight a.m. on Sabbath, December 3rd, in the Scotch Native Chapel, to an attentive English audience; and again in the evening in the Institution Hall, to about 140 English-speaking people, including a good sprinkling of Hindūs. A hard field, and but few helpers.

Monday, 4th.—Preached to the Orphans at seven a.m. Brother Dhanjībhāī interpreted in Hindūstānī. At half-past seven p.m. in Institution Hall. About 150 persons present, and good attention.

5th.—A good service with the Orphans. Went to-day to stop awhile with Brother Dhanjībhāī—native pastor for Dr. Wilson. He was a Parsee lad, a student in Dr. Wilson's school over thirty years ago, and was by him led to Jesus and baptized. He was four years under training in Edinburgh, and was ordained there twenty-five years ago. He is now fifty years old—an earnest, liberal Christian minister; but has never succeeded in getting Parsees converted to God. They are very hard to catch. Brother Dhanjībhāī is now residing in a mansion adjoining a Hindu temple, near the Byculla railway station. This mansion was built by a young Hindū merchant—at a cost, I learn, of 250,000 rupees. His father built the temple adjoining. Gas tubes, with hundreds of burners, are laid all along the verandahs of the mansion (first and second storeys)—to be lighted on the festive days of the temple; so this great mansion is designed as an appendage to that idolatrous concern. The young merchant, however, did not long enjoy it. Like too many merchants besides Hindūs, he went into some grand speculation, and failed in business. A money-lender under a mortgage-deed got the mansion; and I fear his master got the Hindū, for the poor fellow died with a crushed spirit of disappointment. The property is now in the market, and no purchaser. Its gas burners have gone out. Brother Dhanjībhāī has it at a nominal rent, to keep it in order, and I occupy one of its large wings; and God is worshipped here.

Tuesday evening.—Good assembly in the Hall; but not so many as last night. Not much sign of awakening yet.

Wednesday, 6th.—Good service with the Orphans. I think we shall get many of them saved soon.

In the evening had a good time preaching on holiness; and what may seem strange, the Hindūs present seemed much more interested in that subject than any I had brought under their notice. Their eyes sparkled, and frequently they gave manifest expressions of approval,—which they are apt to do when pleased.

Thursday, 7th.—Had an extraordinary meeting

with the Orphans this morning. Sixteen of the young women came forward, and with great penitential weeping received Christ, and found pardon. Each one afterwards stood up and gave a clear, plain statement of the facts in her experience. They could understand English, but only one of them spoke in it.

I made many visits during the day, and prayed with families for seven hours.

In the evening we had a large increase in the congregation. We have a prayer-meeting for half an hour before preaching, in a back room. To-night, for the first time in the Hall, I requested believers and awakened persons to stop for an after-meeting. They all stopped; and we tried to hold a prayer-meeting, but there were few prepared to pray before so large a congregation. We however had a little quickening in some hearts. God will yet do a great work in Bombay.

Friday, 8th.—At the Orphans' meeting Brother Dhanjībhāī interpreted. Thirteen girls came forward, and told the simple story of their awakening and salvation. I did not, however, see the same degree of interest expressed by the heads of the Institution as was manifest yesterday. For a dozen to be saved yesterday seems as much as their faith can stand; and they rather objected to these being allowed to testify at once—saying that "it would be better to wait awhile and appoint a day to examine them, before they should be allowed to make any public profession."

I afterwards talked to them. They confessed that they "had not the least ground to doubt any one of the girls who had professed to find peace, but thought it possible, among so many, that some of them might be mistaken." I replied, "It is possible that some of them are mistaken: I don't pretend to know the heart of any one of them; but to show suspicion and doubt in our conduct towards them, is to give help to Satan in his first assault. The very first thing the devil will say to all who are truly saved, will be, 'Take care that you don't say anything about this, for you may be mistaken; and to make a false profession will bring you into the shame and disgrace of a hypocrite. Indeed you are mistaken. It is all excitement, and will soon pass away.' If Satan can have backers so good and influential as you are, he is sure to carry his point, and will rob these lambs of the confidence and comfort which God has given them to keep. God's plan is to 'put a candle on a candlestick as soon as it is lighted, that it may give light to all that are in the house'; your plan, it appears, is to 'put it under a bushel,' to see whether it will burn without oxygen. God's plan, when a babe is born, is to put it to the breast of a healthy, hopeful mother, to get nourishment; your plan is to put it out into the jungle, among the jackals, to see how it will get on in the world."

They all received my talk, as it was meant, in great kindness, and theoretically gave in; but they cannot at once get rid of the dark shadow of their education on this point. They must find out the certainty of a *secret* eternal decree of God, selecting some of these girls to be heirs of eternal life, and dooming the rest of them to perdition, before it will be entirely safe to risk a public profession of their experience of the love of Christ in their hearts. These are dear good people, and I love them; they are unwittingly victims of their creed. Having sound teaching on most essential points, and having received Jesus, they are good in spite of the wretched, distorting dogma of fate which they hold. Twenty-nine of the Orphans professed to find Jesus; and Rev. S—— said the testimony of every one was simple, natural, and clear. Dr. Wilson baptized a number of them subsequently, and so far as I could learn, they all did well.

Friday evening, in the Hall, we had a large crowd. After preaching, Brothers Harding, Bowen, and two others, testified that the Lord Jesus was alive, and that they knew Him as a personal Saviour. No break here yet; but it dawns upon my mind that God will lead me to organize many fellowship bands in the houses of the people who will be saved at my meetings. We cannot have an organized, witnessing, working church without them. I am satisfied that this is the only thing that can grapple successfully with the tremendous combinations of Satan in this country, and bring deliverance to these millions of Hindūs, Mohamedans, and Parsees. But whether, in Central and Southern India, God intends a regular distinct Methodist organization alongside of existing churches, or whether He may not leaven all these with the true leaven of the Gospel, and amalgamate the whole, or draw out from the whole, a "Desi Kalīsiyā"—an indigenous Church of Christ, without

8

formal connexion with any foreign church, or support from any—I cannot tell. I have no plan, and don't intend to have any, except to discern and follow, at any hazard, the Lord's plan, as He may be pleased to reveal it. At any rate, I must organize the fellowship bands to nourish the babes God is giving us. Some English-speaking persons were saved at our Mārūttī meetings. Brother Harding advised them to go and join the Church Mission; but I don't know what help they may get there. I only know that they will not allow me to preach in their church, because my ordination parchments were not signed at the same office as their own; so that their pastoral care may not suit for the development of my spiritual children.

Saturday, 9th.—By invitation of Mrs. Major Raitt, I took tea and spent the evening at the house of her mother, the Widow Miles,—a Christian Jewess. I was introduced to her large and interesting family, all except a daughter and her husband in London, and another married to Rev. Mr. Cassidy, a Baptist missionary,—both having died and gone to heaven. We had with us her sons-in-law—Major Raitt, James Morris, C.E., William Ashdown, C.E., and their wives; George Miles, assistant secretary to Government—her only son; her single daughters—Dorathea, Emily, and Alice; and four orphan daughters of the Cassidys—Mary, Julia, Sarah, and Matilda; also her sister-in-law, Miss Matilda Miles.

Brother Bowen was with us, and we had some good singing. What a grand thing to get such a family truly converted to God! I had once before spoken to Mr. George Miles. Rev. H——, at the Mārāttī meeting one night, said to me, "Go and speak to that gentleman"—pointing him out; "he is Mr. George Miles, a very good Christian man, but he seems to be in some distress"; so I went and talked to him, and tried to administer Gospel consolation to him as a believer in some difficulties. I had no time then to find out his state. To-night we had a talk in the back verandah alone. In the course of our conversation he said, "Since you spoke to me that night in the American Chapel, I have not played a single game at billiards, nor taken a glass of brandy." So I began to find out the true state and standing of that "very good Christian"; and, thank God! he is finding out his own condition,—and I believe we shall get him saved soon. We had a good season in family worship, and I believe the Spirit of God is working in their hearts. I think the old mother is saved.

Sabbath, 10th.—Preached at eight a.m. in the Scotch native chapel. Went with Brother Bowen at three p.m., and preached to twenty-five vagrants in the House of Correction. Major Raitt is the superintendent of this institution. The House of Correction proper contains about 300 prisoners, with an outside apartment for these vagrants, who are not there under any sentence, but from poverty and want of employment. Major Raitt came to my service for his paupers.

At six p.m. I preached in the Free Church of Scotland, on the Esplanade. Dr. Wilson has just returned, and was present at the meeting, though not the minister of that church. I suppose we had 300 or 400 hearers. I preached on "What think ye of Christ?" and hoped to do great good, and not raise a point of disagreement,—that I might be so made a means of blessing to that Church, and perhaps be invited to hold some special services there.

Monday, 11th.—Had a small service at seven a.m. in Balassas Junction Road: fifteen present.

At the Hall in the evening. Large audience. Called for seekers for the first time; and none came.

Tuesday, seven a.m.—Thirty hearers, and some interest. As soon as I awoke this morning, I felt a gush of fresh vigour in prayer and faith for the salvation of sinners in Bombay. It is an awfully hard tug: some days I feel great heaviness, but not at all despondent. God will give us victory. Many think we have had a great success in Bombay; but I know that it is only preliminary to what God is most anxious to do for this people. I hope He will be able to secure a suitable adjustment of agency for His purpose of mercy. If so, there is no reason why we may not have hundreds of sinners saved in Bombay this season. I am convinced, from all I can learn of the state of the churches here, that they have no strength to nurse and build up any more converts than we have already had; but we shall organize them into bands, and set them to helping each other.

At half-past seven p.m., in the Hall, two came forward as seekers. One was an American sailor. Both professed to find peace. They are but birds of passage, yet I am glad they passed this way, for the good they got and did.

13th.—At seven a.m. twenty-two hearers, and one a seeker.

At the Hall we had about 150 hearers and five seekers, but nothing noteworthy besides.

14th.—Nothing special at the morning service, except that one seeker professes to have found Jesus. To-day the steamship "Nemesis" arrived, bringing missionaries for our India Mission Conference: viz., Brother Judd and wife, who have returned from a furlough of a couple of years; Brother Gill and wife, Brother Cunningham and wife, and Brother Gladwin, who are fresh recruits; also from our Female Missionary Society, Sisters Tinley and McMillan, and Sister Ashley of the American Board of Foreign Missions. Miss Ashley is bound for Ahmednugger; the rest for Lucknow.

At four p.m. preached at the Pensioners' Home to about thirty persons. At half-past seven in the Hall again. Large congregation; four new seekers, and one man professed to find peace. All our newly-arrived missionaries, except Sister Judd, were present; and some of them gave us help in the prayer-meeting. It was a great surprise, on their first night in India, to drop straight into soul-saving work.

15th.—Meetings morning and evening, as usual; but no advance to report.

Sabbath, 17th.—Preached at nine a.m. at Berkeley Place, in a small private house. Brothers Gill, Cunningham, and Gladwin were present, and spoke. Preached at three p.m. to the twenty-five vagrants again. Addressed a little Sunday School at the Baptist place of worship, and preached there at six p.m. Brothers Bowen, Judd, Gill, and Gladwin gave distinct witness for Jesus; and a deep impression was made, I believe, on many hearts. I am looking out daily for the development of God's plans. We must see a work in this city worthy of God and His Gospel. All the glory shall be His.

18th.—Missionaries all left at ten a.m. I wanted them to leave Brother Gladwin to help me, but they did not. Went to the gate of the Great Indian Peninsular Railway Works this afternoon, to try an out-door service as the men were leaving their work. I sang "The Eden above," to collect them; but they took other paths round the corners, and only one man had the courage to come and stand to hear: the only blank failure in all my thirty years of out-door preaching experience.

Then I had a service at Berkeley Place at five p.m.; and twenty came. At half-past seven p.m., in the Hall, we had nine seekers—Major Raitt among them. None of them saved. The seekers seemed long in coming; and now that they had come, we had but little power to lead them. The outside pressure is tremendous; while the internal force of the Church is but the opposite of strength,—entire weakness, and not taking hold on God.

Tuesday, 19th.—Preaching service at Mrs. Miles', at half-past seven a.m. Major Raitt was present, and asked me to visit him. I breakfasted at Mrs. Miles', and then called on the Major. He took me into a back room, and told me how utterly wretched and helpless he was, as a poor sinner. I instructed him, and prayed for him. He remained on his knees, and prayed audibly and very sensibly, but in great simplicity, for himself. He cried out, "O Jesus! accept me now."

"That is just what He wants you to do—to accept Him. 'As many as received Him, to them gave He power to become the sons of God.'" I think he will soon come into liberty. I do not expect physical miracles; they are not necessary: but I do expect the Spirit of God to produce awakening so deep, and conversions so powerful, with the outward manifestations and proofs of His work so demonstrably clear, accompanied by an explaining testimony for Christ, that they will serve better than physical miracles to convince this people that the Bible is true, and that Jesus Christ is alive, and the only Saviour of sinners. God is anxious to do all this, and we must have it. We shall, blessed Jesus, we shall!

Preaching service at five p.m. at Berkeley Place; nineteen present.

At the Hall in the evening we had ten or eleven avowed seekers.

Near the close of the meeting Mr. George Miles stood up before the congregation, and said, "I found the Lord at home last night, and He has pardoned all my sins." He is the "good Christian" I spoke to in the American Chapel four weeks ago, and again in his mother's house last week. Thank God!

Wednesday, 20th.—Good meeting at Mrs. Miles'. Took breakfast with Major Raitt. Prayed with him again. He is in great distress, but seems near to the kingdom of heaven. He drove me into the city. Called for the first time at the "secretariat," to see Brother George Miles. Found him, his brother-in-law James Morris and his wife, and Captain Winckler and wife, all living in the same establishment. Brother Miles' wife and nine children are in England. Found Mrs. Morris under deep awakening. She and her husband were seekers last night. At her request I gave her advice and prayed for her. Captain Winckler has been an avowed seeker for a fortnight; but, though in great agony of soul, seems to be hard aground.

Service again at Berkeley Place at five p.m. Twenty-three out, but no advance visible.

At half-past seven in the Hall again. Large congregation; ten seekers. Captain Winckler told the congregation that last night he had received Christ, and got the pardon of all his sins. He told us what had barred him out of the kingdom for a fortnight. He had an enemy against whom he had vowed vengeance. All the time he had been praying so fervently for pardon, it was his purpose to "punch the head" of his enemy on the first opportunity. "When Brother B—— told his experience last night, I saw that this was my hindrance," said the Captain, "and that I could not be forgiven unless I would forgive. So I began at once to pray for my enemy, and very soon God gave me power to forgive him; and at once I received Christ and got forgiveness."

Thank God! He has been a puzzle to me for a fortnight; for he was so thoroughly broken up, wept and prayed so earnestly, and sought on all occasions public and private, saying, "I do submit, I do receive Christ, but I can get no relief." Now it is all explained.

He is nephew of Mrs. Miles,—his mother also a Christian Jewess.

Thursday, 21st.—Good meeting this morning at Mrs. Miles'. Her daughter, Mrs. Morris, with whom I prayed yesterday, received the Saviour at this meeting. Thank God! She will make a good worker for Jesus.

Meeting at Berkeley Place; interesting, but no special result. Good meeting at the Hall this evening; several ministers were present. Four new witnesses publicly testified for Jesus: viz., Sister Morris, William Ashdown, Mr. Thomas Marsden, and another; all saved to-day and to-night. Glory to God!—we are gaining ground.

Friday, 22nd.—Good service at Mrs. Miles'. William Boyd told the audience that he had received Christ, and got forgiveness of sins, at the meeting in the Hall last night. Visited Major Raitt again to-day: he is in very great distress, but hard aground on the shoals of unbelief. He is a fine specimen of a Scotchman; and if he shall get a clear experience, he will be a very useful man.

Mr. James Morris, before named, called to see me this afternoon. I spent an hour in explaining the way, and praying for him.

He said, "I can't attend to my business now, nor do anything." He is not far from "the kingdom of God."

Very small meeting at Berkeley Place, at five p.m. In the evening we had a large crowd at the Hall. Including Brother Boyd, who spoke this morning at Mrs. Miles', we had seven new witnesses to-night.

Mr. Morris told about his visit to our house to-day, and how I had instructed and prayed for him; and, said he, "I had only gone about a hundred yards, near to the railway bridge, when I accepted Christ, and He took away my load of sin."

Mrs. Major Raitt said, "I received Jesus at home to-day, and now I have peace with God. I have long been trying to be a Christian, but never knew the way before. To-day I gave up my own trying, and received Christ, and He has given me rest."

Mrs. Ashdown received Christ to-night, and testified for Him. Also, Mary and Julia Cassidy. Their father was an educator of youth, and a Baptist minister in Poona; but both he and his wife died, within a few months of each other, a few years ago.

To-night closed our series at the Hall. Including natives, over sixty persons have, up to this date, professed to receive Jesus at our meetings in Bombay. Thank God!—"the morning cometh."

Saturday, 23rd.—Brother Dhanjibhāī drove me to Malabar Hill this morning, and we called on Rev. J. Wilson, D.D., on Captain and Mrs. Oldham, and on Mr. and Mrs. Johnson.

Sabbath, 24th.—Preached at Berkeley Place at nine a.m. Captain Taylor, son of an old Indian missionary, long since gone to heaven, gave a warm exhortation. Preached to twenty-five vagrants at three p.m. Poor Major Raitt is down with fever. The Lord bless him! Preached at four p.m. in the American Chapel.

Christmas Day.—At seven a.m. had a meeting in the private house of a native Christian. After meeting he served us with good coffee. Met one of our Hindū seekers there, who has found the Lord. Also our Mohamedan seeker, who had professed clearly to have found peace with God through our Lord Jesus Christ. The native pastor says, however, that he is not clear now. I am afraid, from what I heard, that he was not properly looked after. If sympathizing, loving Christians had been as zealous to help, as his Mohamedan friends to hinder him, I have no doubt that he would be happy in the Lord to-day.

Preached in the American Chapel at seven p.m. Good congregation; a number of Hindūs, and one Parsee among them. Four or five persons witnessed for Christ—among whom was Brother Morris. Hope to see, this week, a further advance among Brother Harding's natives; but their workers live in such proximity to the icebergs of heathenism, that they soon get chilled unless their blood is kept in quick circulation by constant action,—to which they seem disinclined.

26th.—Morning meeting in a native private house; eighteen present. Preaching again in the evening in the American Chapel; one young native professed to find peace.

27th.—Morning meeting at the house of another native; forty persons present. At the chapel in the evening, three seekers.

28th.—Morning and evening services as usual; three or four seekers.

29th.—Half-past six p.m. Having many English hearers, I preached in English alone; and Brother Harding followed with a powerful exhortation in Mārāttī. Eight seekers came and kneeled down at the front seats. Four of them were Hindūs; and down alongside of these was poor Major Raitt, who was now recovering from his attack of fever, and was earnestly struggling for deliverance in company of the natives he so looked down upon in the days of his pomp and pride. Two of the Hindūs professed to find Jesus.

Took breakfast this morning with Captain Oldham. He is a military officer, but now Government inspector of railroads. He was in India for many years; and although a nominal member of the Church of England, became a sceptic. He returned to England, and through the death of a friend was awakened by the Spirit of God. Groping in the dark in great distress, he one day, in Scotland, found his way into a small Baptist chapel. The text was the key that opened to his soul the kingdom of God: "He ever liveth to make intercession for us." The fact came home to him as a vital verity—"Oh! my Jesus is alive, and I accept Him, and trust Him as my Saviour"; and that moment he experienced salvation. He is anxious to co-operate with me to advance the work of God in India. His wife, too, seems a person of rare excellence. God bless them!

Saturday, 30th.—This evening, in the house of Mrs. Miles, I organized the first fellowship band, or "class," ever organized in this city. There has, of course, always been the spirit of fellowship in the hearts of God's children here, and often manifested in their casual meetings with each other; but this is undoubtedly the first organic, regular arrangement for it. I appointed Brother Bowen leader. At this our first meeting for fellowship, twenty-eight persons told their Christian experience—most of them young converts. In circumstantial detail, variety, simplicity, and point, I never before heard better testimony for Christ. Some of these will join our second band, to be organized next Monday night at the house of Brother George Miles.

Sabbath, 31st.—Preached at three p.m. to the vagrants again, and laboured till six p.m. with one who bowed down as a seeker, till he obtained deliverance. At half-past six p.m. preached in the Baptist preaching-house a second time. Great crowd, and good feeling; but I was not at liberty to call for seekers, having no arrangement with the minister on the subject. He has been ill, but is now recovering.

New Year's Day, 1872.—Had an interesting service in Balassas Junction Road at seven a.m. A young man in great distress came home with me to Brother Harding's. He said, "For five years I have been a professing Christian, and have been engaged in Christian work as a teacher in the Sunday School, —often praying in public. Others regard me as a good Christian, and I hoped that I was indeed one; but, alas! I am continually relapsing into sin." He went on to say that, attending some of my meetings, he was awakened somewhat; then he read my book

"Reconciliation, or, How to be Saved," and was clearly convinced that he never had been saved; and is now in great distress. He is earnestly seeking in secret, but will have to consent, publicly, to confess his sins and his Saviour.

At half-past seven p.m. I went to the house of Brother George Miles, to organize Band No. 2. The young man who went home with me this morning met me at the gate rejoicing, saying that at four p.m. he had obtained mercy. I learned that he was at the head of the correspondence department of the Bombay Bank,—his name, C. W. Christian. We had a blessed fellowship-meeting. Sixteen spoke in charming simplicity. Not a technical, commonplace remark, and not a single old fogy to teach them any.

Brother Christian said, "Brother Morris came into the Bank, and told me that Jesus had saved him from sin, and was preserving him from sinning daily. It brought forcibly to my mind two facts: first, I have never had an experience of that sort; second, if Mr. Morris has got it, why cannot I get it? That was my starting-point." He described the struggle of last night, which precluded sleep, and the visit to me in the morning, and the final struggle this afternoon. He was called to dinner, but could not cease his pleading with God for pardon.

He proceeded to say, "I said, 'What is the matter? I can't believe.'

"The Spirit said to my heart, 'What is it that you can't believe? Do you not believe that God is able, and willing, and ready now to save you, if you will but receive Christ?

"I said, 'Yes; I believe all that.'

"'Well, then: why not receive Him?'

"I said, 'I will, I do receive Him.'

"I did receive Him, glory be to God!—and He saved me, and I went at once and told the joyful news to my dear parents and sister, as they sat at the dinner-table."

Captain W—— and his wife had both yielded to temper, and brought darkness into their souls. We all immediately kneeled down and prayed for them, and they both received a renewed application of the pardoning blood of Jesus, verifying what is written —"Confess your faults one to another, and pray for one another, that ye may be healed." They were both healed and happy before we arose from our knees.

CHAPTER XII.

MAZAGON MEETINGS.

PREACHED at Mr. Thomas Graham's, in Mazagon Road, Jan. 2nd, at half-past seven a.m. House well filled, and good attention.

At half-past seven p.m. preached in the Library room of the Peninsular and Oriental Co.'s dockyard. About 130 hearers.

Wednesday, 3rd.—At the close of Graham's meeting, Mr. Walter Abraham, superintendent of Government printing, came and asked me to pray for him. I laboured with him a long time, when "Abraham believed God, and it was counted to him for righteousness." I went home with him, and prayed for his family. His wife is dead, but he has with him three daughters and two sons. Brother Abraham drove me in his carriage to visit families in Mazagon. Among others, called to see a family in bereavement,—Mr. and Mrs. Williamson, who teach a school in their own house. They had a married son who went out swimming a few days ago, and was drowned. His wife was looking at him when he went down, but no help could be afforded him till he had gone. They have hope in his death, as he was a devoted Christian. I prayed with the family.

At seven p.m. we met in the Library room half an hour before preaching, to practise singing from our new book—"Hymns New and Old." This became from this time a regular part of each evening's service, and thus our people became rich in the acquisition of choice hymns and tunes. About 150 present: deep attention; and several brethren gave a good testimony for Jesus.

Thursday, 4th.—Good meeting at Graham's; fifteen seekers, and fourteen of them professed to find the Saviour. Many of these were young people. This is said to be a very cold day here—62° Fahrenheit this morning, and 74° at three p.m. It was very hot till a day or two before Christmas, but has been cool since.

Large meeting at seven p.m. After preaching, Brothers Bowen and Morris exhorted. No seekers.

Friday, 5th.—Good work at Graham's. At seven p.m. our meeting was in the Peninsular and Oriental Co.'s Theatre, instead of the Library room, being larger and better suited to our purpose—which they kindly lighted with gas, and gave us the free use of the whole. Five men this evening stood up as seekers, and we stayed back with them till nearly ten p.m.; but they did not find relief.

Saturday, 6th.—Prayed an hour with Major Raitt. He has a hard tug to get rid of self. Good fellowship-meeting this evening at Mrs. Miles'. Several more joined the band. It is not a church organization, but a general band regardless of church relations.

Sabbath, 7th.—Preached at a private house at seven a.m., and to eighteen vagrants at three p.m.

Twenty were shipped for England last week, including the one who received Jesus last Sabbath. At seven p.m. we had a great crowd in the Theatre: eight seekers; and two lads professed.

Monday, 8th.—Four seekers this morning at Graham's. Glorious fellowship-meeting to-night at Brother Miles'. Mrs. Harry Wilcox received Christ at it, and was filled with joy. Seven months afterwards she died, sweetly resting in Jesus.

Tuesday, 9th.—Good meeting at Graham's. A man was deeply awakened, and wept much.

"Will you not submit?" said I to him.

"Yes, but not to-day; I want to wait and bring my wife with me."

He was so convinced of sin that he went and sought reconciliation with several men with whom he had long been at enmity, and spoke freely of me and my meetings as the means of his awakening. Poor fellow!—instead of receiving Christ, and getting on his armour, he thus exposed himself, and the arrows of the archers hit him, and within a few days he was one of my bitter opposers, and never came to my meetings again.

At seven p.m. eight seekers, and one man professed to find the Lord.

Wednesday, 10th.—Good meeting at Graham's. At the Theatre, about 200 hearers: eight seekers, and four professed to find the Saviour. It is a hard pull all the time: God is slowly but surely developing an infant, witnessing, working church from the foundation. The old ecclesiastical "bottles" of this city have neither strength nor capacity for such a work; and hence we shall require "new bottles,"—new here, but indeed the same that the Lord Jesus put into the market 1800 years ago, and that are now extensively used, especially among "the people called Methodists," throughout the world.

Thursday, 11th.—Four professed at Graham's, and six or seven at the Theatre.

Friday, 12th.—No conversions at Graham's this morning. A dozen seekers, and four saved, at the Theatre. Major Raitt bore a distinct testimony to the saving power of Jesus in his heart.

Captain Christian and others applied for the use of a church in the Fort, but did not succeed. The tide of opposition is rising, and the papers are beginning to open fire upon us. Our people are evidently gathering strength proportionate to the increasing pressure from without.

Saturday evening organized Fellowship Band No. 3 at Mr. Graham's, and appointed Brother Harding leader. Sixteen joined at this our first meeting.

Sabbath, 14th.—Preached at Berkeley Place at half-past nine a.m. Four seekers. Arranged to organize a fellowship band there next Sabbath at half-past eight a.m. A fine class of our converted men and women live near, and will join it. At three p.m. organized Fellowship Band No. 4 in Mazagon; and eleven joined. We are establishing the custom of weekly fellowship thank-offerings: though we have no use for the money, we need to develop the habit of giving among our people. When God shall establish this self-supporting church, these sluices will be open, and the funds already flowing in to supply all the purposes the Lord may approve.

Preached at the Theatre at seven p.m. Large crowd: a growing spirit of work among the young converts. Six persons professed to obtain remission of their sins to-night.

Monday, 15th.—Twenty at the fellowship band at George Miles' at seven a.m. Marvellous simplicity and candour in the mutual confession of their "faults one to another," and sympathy and prayer for each other.

The progress of the members in the knowledge and love of God is very manifest. Their testimony is full of variety and incident. For example, Captain Winckler said: "I met an old acquaintance the other day, and he shouted out,—

"'How are you, Captain Winckler? how are you? I have not seen you for an age.'

"'Very well, thank God!'

"'What has come over George Miles? I understand that he has become a Bible distributor of the Tract Society, or something of that sort.'

"'He has become a Christian,' I replied.

"'What! was he not always a Christian?'

"'He was a nominal Christian; but now he has received Christ and got his sins forgiven, and has thus become a real Christian.'

"'Ah, indeed! Well, Captain, how are you?'

"'Oh, thank God! I have received Christ, and become a Christian too.'

"'Good day, Winckler; good day,'—and he was off in a moment."

Six new cases of conversion to-night in the Theatre.

Tuesday, 16th.—At seven a.m. preached in Balassas Junction Road. Again at the atre at seven p.m. None found the Lord to-night that we know of. Timid seekers quail before the rising floods of opposition. Two daily papers have opened their batteries against us, and several ministers are preaching against the possibility of sudden conversions.

Sifting will do us good. God is leading, and we will follow.

Wednesday, 17th.—Thirty hearers at Junction Road at seven a.m., and a good prospect. Major Raitt tells me that he has succeeded in his application to the Government Committee of the House of Correction, to allow me to preach to all the European prisoners who may desire it. (Many of the prisoners, hearing of my services for the vagrants, requested the Major to arrange for me to preach to them also.)

The chaplain will go into fits. He had one the other day, when he saw my name on the visitors' book—which I signed, by request, when I went to preach to the vagrants. When the chaplain opened the book to sign his own name, on his next visit after I had committed the grievous offence of preaching to the vagrants, to whom he did not preach, he saw my signature, and shouted out, "What! has that man Taylor been in here?"

"Yes," said the deputy; "he has been preaching to the vagrants." He got into a dreadful rage, and stormed as but few even high ritualists could do.

This chaplain has some good points, but is a victim to his own hot temper. After raging about in the office for a time, he said, "Take this book away from here. I'll never sign a book that has Taylor's name in it!" So now, when he learns that I have Government authority to come into his department to preach to the prisoners, a fit extraordinary will take hold on him. Poor man!—I wish he knew my meek and lowly Saviour.

Nothing noteworthy at the Theatre to-night.

Thursday, 18th.—Fair meeting at Junction Road, but no breaking down of sinners. Preached at four p.m. to over fifty prisoners, and taught them to sing a hymn. Many of the poor fellows wept as they sang—

> "What a Friend we have in Jesus,
> All our sins and griefs to bear!
> What a privilege, to carry
> Everything to God, in prayer!
> O what peace we often forfeit,
> O what needless pain we bear,—
> All because we do not carry
> Everything to God in prayer!"

"How true that is, my friends! If you had in your youth accepted this Friend, and all through your toilsome journey of life taken everything to God in prayer, where and what would you be today? Think of the happy homes you might have been in possession of now, the wife and children, and sunshine which would have made your homes little heavens of earthly blessing. What a pity! How did you get into this miserable place? 'All because you did not carry everything to God in prayer.' Now sing it again" ;—and the poor fellows sang and cried by turns, till they learned the first verse.

"Now we will go on with the hymn—

"'Have we trials and temptations?
Is there trouble anywhere?—
We should never be discouraged:
Take it to the Lord in prayer.
Can we find a friend so faithful,
Who will all our sorrows share?
Jesus knows our every weakness:
Take it to the Lord in prayer.

'Are we weak and heavy-laden,
Cumbered with a load of care?—
Jesus still will be our refuge:
Take it to the Lord in prayer.
Do thy friends despise, forsake thee?
Take it to the Lord in prayer;
In His arms He'll take and shield thee,—
Thou shalt find a solace there.'

"Dear friends, you are indeed weak and heavy-laden, burdened with sin and sorrow,—hard toil and no pay. This Friend from heaven speaks to you. He says, 'Come unto me all ye that labour and are heavy-laden, and I will give you rest.' He will not interfere with your disjointed relations to society, and the legal penalties of British law; but if you will take His yoke and receive Him as your Saviour, He will plead your cause before the throne of His Father, and the penalty of eternal death entered in the books of Divine Justice against you will be cancelled. You will stand acquitted before

God, and be restored to heirship in His glorious kingdom—a grand rise for poor prisoners, to gain a standing in the Royal Family of heaven! It is written, 'As many as received Him, to them gave He power to become the sons of God.' It will be so with every one of you to-day, if you will submit to God and receive Jesus."

This is but a specimen of the way we proclaimed liberty to those captives.

At seven p.m. we had a large gathering at the Theatre, and more of them than usual remained for the after-meeting; yet but few came out as seekers.

Friday, 19th.—Several seekers at Junction Road at seven a.m. In the evening a great crowd at the Theatre. Among the seekers were Mrs. Captain O——, and Colonel A——'s daughter.

Saturday, 20th.—Visited Mrs. Captain O——. She has found the Saviour. The Colonel's daughter was there in great distress. Just as I was commencing, in family worship, to show her the way to Jesus, Miss P—— came in, saying, "I have come for you, Miss A——. Here are two letters from your Pa. He is coming in the train, and wants you to meet him at the railway station." She talked like a governess, but I did not yield the floor, and she sat down; then I proceeded with my instructions to the penitent young lady, and sang softly,—

"'The Master is come, and calleth for thee,—
He stands at the door of thy heart;
No friend so forgiving, so gentle as He:
Oh, say wilt thou let Him depart?

Refrain,—
Patiently waiting, earnestly pleading,
Jesus, thy Saviour, knocks at thy heart.

'The Master has come with blessings for thee:
Arise, and His message receive;
Thy ransom is purchased, thy pardon is free,
If thou wilt repent and believe.

'The Master is come, and calleth thee now:
This moment what joy may be thine!
How tender the smile that illumines His brow!—
A pledge of His favour Divine.

'He waits for thee still; then haste with delight,—
Oh, fly to the arms of His love;
Press on to that beautiful mansion of light
Prepared in His kingdom above.'

"The great Teacher here uses the simplest occurrence of every-day life to illustrate the sublimest fact in all history—a knock at the door—a call: 'Behold!'

"'Who's there?'

"It is Jesus! The Redeemer of guilty sinners, the crucified, but risen Saviour, has come. Your father is coming by the train. Jesus has already come. He is knocking now at the door of your heart. He has often knocked before, but you have shut the door against Him, and bolted it from top to bottom. Pride—what a bar, right across the door! Fear of man, and shame, and love of the world, and every other habit of sin indulged, bars the door. The Spirit of God has already come into your heart, to show you the situation, and to give you the power to drive back or break these bolts and bars, and admit the Heavenly Guest. Will you do it? You don't see Jesus, any more than you see the air you breathe; but He is as really present as the atmosphere that surrounds you. Oh, receive Him now!"

We kneeled down and had a season of silent prayer; and there upon her knees Miss A—— gave her heart to God, and received the Saviour; Miss P—— also broke down in penitential tears, and soon after, at her own home, professed to find forgiveness of sins.

Sabbath, 21st.—Organized a fellowship band at Berkeley Place at nine a.m. Fifteen joined. It was in the house of a Plymouth Brother, who seemed cheerfully to consent to the organization of the band; and I meant to appoint him the leader, as he appeared to be an earnest Christian of several years' standing, but he declined to join the band. Those who joined seemed very promising cases, but recently converted in the Theatre. At eleven a.m. opened a little Sunday School in the Theatre. Led Fellowship Band No. 4 at three p.m., organized a new band at the Theatre at half-past four p.m., and preached there at seven p.m. to a crowd, and had a few saved. Thank God!

Monday, 22nd.—Glorious fellowship-meeting at Brother Miles', at seven a.m. The members are growing beautifully. At the Theatre at seven p.m. Just as I announced the text, "Prepare to meet thy God," all were startled by the cry "Fire! fire! fire!"—the light of the flames already flaring through our windows. Then followed the announcement, "The north-east wing of the Company's buildings is on fire." I requested all who could be of any use to put out the fire to go, and the rest to remain quiet; and then I proceeded with my discourse, to show how needful to heed the admonition of the text, "Prepare to meet thy God."

Presently an order came from the dock-master for all the families in the Company's buildings to leave instantly, as the fire was nearing a barrel of powder. So we adjourned, to meet all who were not required to fight the fire, at the house of Mr. Thomas Graham. We had there a good prayer-meeting. Many of the converts prayed. I called on Brother George Miles. We don't usually call on brethren or sisters to pray —preferring spontaneity as moved by the Spirit, or their own convictions of duty or propriety; but not having heard Brother Miles pray, I called on him this evening for the first time. After a little delay, when I was waiting to hear him open his mouth in earnest prayer, like the rest, he said, "Brother Taylor, I have a physical disability, and cannot pray in public."

CHAPTER XIII.

NEW OUTPOSTS.

TUESDAY, 23rd.—Opened morning and evening services at a private house in Falkland Road. I closed special services at the Theatre, and told the people to go home and rest a week; in the meantime I made this quiet arrangement for a work in a neighbourhood in which we had not done much. We had twenty-four persons in the morning, and thirty-four at night,—mostly new cases. My people were resting; and not many knew that I was opening a new place.

At three p.m. preached again to "the spirits in prison," and had sixty-five hearers. Major Raitt witnessed for Jesus, and exhorted the men earnestly: "Submit to God, and receive Christ as I have done, and you will, like me, obtain the pardon of all your sins," etc.

An application for the use of the Town Hall for my meetings has been before the council for some time; but through the opposition of two ministers, as I learn on good authority, the matter was staved off, and finally referred to the Governor, and refused,—though freely accorded to Keshub Chunder Sen, the

Brāhmo. Of course I know that I am in a great Pagan city, and that the authorities, naturally enough, try to conciliate the natives as far as possible; and I have nothing of which to complain.

Newspaper war waging fiercely. George Bowen is responding to their guns splendidly, both in the *Guardian* and in the *Times*. Most of the editors seem disposed to deal fairly; but correspondents say what they like, and many of them have no regard for the truth.

Wednesday, 24th.—Increasing number and deepening interest at Falkland Road, both morning and evening.

Thursday, 25th.—Preached at Falkland Road at seven a.m., and at three p.m. to seventy hearers in the prison. A military prisoner was found to be under awakening, and Brother Harding and I took him into a room assigned us by Major Raitt, and prayed with him till he professed to receive Christ. He is in simply for some military irregularity, and the Major speaks well of him. In the evening Rev. W—— was at our meeting at Falkland Road, and professed to be in sympathy with our work. He is a good man, but under the authority of a High-Church Bishop.

Friday, 26th.—Three letters in the *Times* to-day—two against "the revival," and one on our side. I have not read any of them; I seldom ever read what the papers say about me, but I hear of these things from others.

Visited two of the Peninsular and Oriental Co.'s sick men to-day. Mr. Macey is near his end, but says he is resting in Jesus. Smails is recovering. He is one of the Company's divers, and has recently returned sick from Galle, where he had for some time been engaged in raising the passengers' luggage and the mails of the steamship "Rangoon." He says, "She lies on a beautiful plain of very white sand, 100 feet below the surface of the waters. The pressure of the water at that depth is so great that all the divers got sick; indeed, it nearly killed them. Two men had to do most of the work. We raised 430 mail-bags. I never saw so many fish in any one place, in all my diving experience, as I saw there;—fields of them in every direction, shining and flashing in the most brilliant beauty. I saw many sharks, but they were always near the surface. I saw a most beautiful serpent of many colours, about nine feet long. I saw also a vast variety of small animals, such as are never caught, because they abide in such depths that none but divers could catch them,—and they are otherwise employed."

To-night, at Falkland Road, we had about sixty hearers, crowding the room; and four professed to obtain pardon. Had a slight interruption by a man who wanted to debate; but we politely invited him to sit down, and he did so.

Sabbath, 28th.—Fellowship band at Berkeley Place. Our host stopped out in the verandah till the meeting closed, and then, in the presence of most of the members, he came in and gave me an awful blowing-up, and smashed up the band. I saw then that he hoped to get them all to join his "sect"; but seeing that they were all falling into line with me, he allowed his feelings and prejudices to get the mastery of him, and let off steam so terrifically that the converts took fright and forsook us both,—though I did not reply to him, except quietly to say that he was entirely mistaken. He came afterwards and confessed, and apologized, and I freely forgave him; but the little flock had gone, and but few of them ever came back to my meetings. I saw in that the utter weakness of a heterogeneous fellowship band, outside of proper church organization. So I got a valuable practical lesson from that bit of unpleasant experience.

Led the two bands in Mazagon this afternoon, and preached in the Theatre in the evening. A great crowd, and good meeting for believers; but no conversions.

Monday, 29th.—Blessed fellowship band at Brother Miles' this morning. We enquired into Brother Miles' "physical disability." He said, "It is a nervous affection,—which, however, never troubles me except when I attempt to speak, or to pray, in public."

"Oh, Brother," said I, "that is the same kind of disability that troubled me in my early ministry, and I have not quite recovered from it yet; but you have not got it so badly as my old friend J. H. Lynn. His superintendent thought he was called to preach, and told him to go and fill a certain preaching appointment for him. The news got out, and a crowd of people assembled to hear him. Lynn accordingly came up to time, and walked into the pulpit. After sitting there awhile, he got up and looked out through a window in the rear for a few moments, then suddenly turned towards the congregation and said, 'Friends, the heavens are covered with blackness; a dreadful storm will soon be down upon us, and I think we had better get home as soon as we can.' He bolted straightway, and was the first man out of the house and off for home. The storm was all in his own mind—the result of his 'physical disability.'"

I then prescribed that Brother Morris should ask Brother Miles to take the family worship alternately with himself; and it worked like a charm.

Had this evening a pleasant social gathering at Mrs. Miles'. Good singing, social cheer, and religious edification.

Tuesday, 30th.—Preached in the prison at three p.m., and one prisoner in the seekers' room professed to find Jesus.

At Falkland Road this evening three professed. We had with us my old friend Barker, from Sydney, New South Wales. He gave us a good account of the progress of the work of God in Australia. He is on his way to England.

Wednesday, 31st.—Service at seven a.m. at Junction Road. At Falkland Road, at seven p.m., we had six seekers, and three saved.

Feb. 1st, 1872.—Good meeting at Junction Road. Colonel Styleman was with us, and went visiting with me. Prayed with a poor old woman in great distress. She had lost three daughters, but had hope in their death; but her son, forty years old, got drunk, and by mistake walked out of an upper window instead of the door, and was picked up dead. Poor old broken-hearted widow!—we tried hard to lead her to Jesus. She felt much better before we left her; but I could not tell whether or not she had really received the "Comforter."

One man saved in the prison this afternoon. Preached this evening at Morley Hall, in Colāba—a remote part of the city of Bombay; while Brother Harding continues the services at Falkland Road.

Feb. 2nd.—Discoursed this morning at Junction Road on Christian fellowship—showing the ground, the Scriptural authority, and true bonds of fellowship,—and gave notice that I would (D.V.) organize a band there next Sunday morning, at seven o'clock.

Preached at Falkland Road at half-past seven p.m. Had several hopeful cases of conversion to God and gave notice that I would (D.V.) organize, a fellowship band there next Sabbath at nine a.m.

A very curious thing occurred one night there, after one of our preaching services. A number had just been saved, and I gave them an opportunity to bear witness for Jesus. After half a dozen new converts had spoken just to the point in their newborn simplicity, a very red-faced burly-looking man, whom I had never seen before, stood up and gave a long detail of twenty years' experience of miraculous deliverances which God had wrought for him; stating that he loved the Lord with all his heart: finally Rev. George Bowen rose to his feet, and the man sat down. Bowen knew him well, as a man who had just lost a good appointment under the harbour-master, on account of his habit of getting drunk. He was well-read in the Scriptures, professing high attainments in religious experience, and most pious when drunk. Here he was in our meeting, vitiating the testimony of true witnesses. Bowen was horrified, and prayed that God, without injury to him, would shut his mouth ; and from that time the man could not speak a word for some weeks. I saw him in the hospital a few days after, and he wrote on paper what he wanted to say. He seemed in good health; but his tongue had borne false witness in the Lord's house, and God thus rebuked him. He recovered his speech, but did not give up his sins and hypocrisy.

Saturday, 3rd.—Glorious fellowship-meeting to-night at Mrs. Miles'.

Sabbath, 4th.—At seven a.m. we organized Band No. 6, at Junction Road. Ten joined it; and I appointed Brother William Ashdown the leader.

At Falkland Road, nine a.m., twenty-one joined; and I appointed Major Raitt the leader. I shall of course continue to lead all the bands ; but I appoint leaders to help to bear the responsibility of caring for so many newborn souls, and thus train the leaders to be efficient sub-pastors.

Preached in the evening in the Theatre on "Christian perfection." Brother Barker, from Australia, was at several of our fellowship bands to-day, and witnessed a good confession to-night. Brothers Bowen and Raitt also spoke right to the point.

God is leading, and we are succeeding.

Monday, 5th.—Removed to-day from the house of

my good Brother Harding to Brother Miles', as I was preparing to work in that part of the city. Brother Bowen has rented Frāmjī Cawāsjī Hall, belonging to the Parsees, for our services. The lower storey is used for a public library, the second is a fine hall to seat over 1000 persons ; but we cannot command so many hearers, for Bombay is about seven miles long, and the English-speaking population is sparse and widely scattered; hence we have to take them in detail, by special services in each of the most important English-speaking centres. We are not yet ready to advance directly upon the native lines; we must first collect and drill an army. We heard that the Parsees would not rent the hall for any religious purpose; but they are in want of funds, and consented to let us have it for about forty rupees per night. Some friend of Brother Bowen furnished the funds.

We opened there on Tuesday the 6th, at half-past seven p.m. About 250 persons in attendance, including a good sprinkling of Hindūs, Parsees, and Mohamedans.

At the Wednesday, Thursday, and Friday evening meetings there, we had about the same number, and a growing interest.

Sister Morris first, and a number of others at different times, asked me what I would do to provide for the pastoral care of all these converts. I advised them to pray to God, but say nothing about it till we should see more clearly the Lord's leading in that matter. I have laboured as an evangelist for sixteen years, but always in conjunction with organized churches—to which I entrusted the care of the converts saved at my meetings. The only pulpits to which I have been admitted in this city, with the exception of one night in the Free Church on the Esplanade, are the two native mission chapels to which I have so often referred. To be sure, within a few days past, a sort of invitation has been given, but encumbered with conditions which we cannot accept. Rev. W—— told me he would be glad to have me preach in his church: "not consecrated, and hence no legal bar; but—but—the Bishop," etc.

He afterwards said to one of my converts, "Mr. Taylor is doing a great work. He will get the people to be good, and then they will all join my church." We have been advising the converts to continue to go to the churches they had been most inclined to attend. But pastors who will not allow me to preach in their churches—some of whom preach against my work—are not the men to nourish and lead to usefulness those who have been saved at my meetings. It has long been manifest that I must in some way provide for them; but I have not been clear as to whether or not it is the will of God that I should take the responsibility of organizing a church. I had myself been saved in the Methodist Episcopal Church, of which I have been an ordained minister for more than a quarter of a century; yet I have for years been so free from the fear of man and from sectional prejudice, that if I had anywhere in my world-wide evangelistic tours found a church holding purer doctrines, employing methods more incisive and effective, and manifesting a loving spirit of soul-saving work more in harmony with the mind of Christ and the example of the apostles, I should have left the Methodist Church at once, and joined it; but I have found no such church on the earth, and hence expect to live and die in the Church of my early choice. But to establish a church here is to found a mission in a great heathen city. It is over four years since I saw my dear wife and boys, and my plan was to return home this year; so I have waited for the clear light of the pillar of fire, and now I see it unmistakably leading the way. To organize a witnessing, aggressive Church of Christ in India, in organic union with existing churches here, we have found to be entirely impracticable; to try to run on a purely independent line, outside of existing organizations, is to fail, or to found a new sect—and we have too many of them already. The Methodist Episcopal Church of America has as good a right, as God may indicate her line of advance in her world-wide mission, to organize in Bombay, or anywhere else, as any other branch of the Church of Christ.

CHAPTER XIV.

METHODIST CHURCH ORGANIZED IN BOMBAY.

ON Thursday, the 8th of February 1872, Brother George Miles drew up the following letter :—

"To the Rev. WILLIAM TAYLOR.

"DEAR BROTHER,—We the undersigned, who have by God's mercy been awakened through your preaching to a sense of our sins, and who have found the Lord Jesus to be our Deliverer, are desirous for the establishment of a Methodist Episcopal Church in this city.

"We are satisfied, from all that we have yet learnt, of the Scriptural authority for the methods practised by the Church to which you belong; and we therefore unitedly invite you to take the necessary steps for the accomplishment of our wishes, and to act yourself as our pastor and evangelist until such time as you can make arrangements with the Home Board for sending out the necessary agency to this city."

Brother James Morris the same day showed it to a number of the converts, and thirty of them signed it; so in the evening, when he came home and showed me the list of signatures, I said, "Now before you go any further with this business, I must read our

'General Rules' in the bands, that they all may know what we shall expect of them, and act intelligently. So by Monday morning, the 12th of February, I had read the Rules in the seven bands we had up to that time organized. Brother Morris, meantime, had increased his list of signers to eighty-three; and on Wednesday the 14th I formally accepted their call by the following letter, which was published in the *Bombay Guardian*:—

[REPLY.]

"DEAR BRETHREN AND SISTERS IN THE LORD,—

"In response to your letter allow me to state a few facts.

"Though an ordained minister, and for many years a pastor, in the Methodist Episcopal Church of America, I have, with the concurrence of my Church, for many years past wrought as a missionary evangelist in foreign countries, among all denominations of Christians. I came to Bombay Presidency by invitation of the American missionaries of 'the Mārāttī Mission.' I enjoyed the pleasure of working with them at Ahmednugger and in this city, and in return have had their hearty sympathy and co-operation—the same also, in a good degree, of other ministers—in all my work for God in this city. Our gracious God will reward them. I had also the pleasure of giving a little help to the Mission of the Free Church of Scotland.

"I expected by invitation of ministers here, as in other places, to assist many churches in Bombay in seeking the soul-saving power of God, and in the development of a more effective working agency in their respective organizations.

"As you all know, we have been Providentially brought, 'by a way that we knew not,' to a somewhat different result.

"A number of you will bear me witness, that when at different times you spoke to me on the necessity of organizing a Methodist Church in Bombay, to conserve and extend the fruits of this work of God, I advised you not to think about that, but to go on in the soul-saving work in which the Holy Spirit was using you, and that God would in due time manifest clearly the course you ought to pursue. I could not anticipate what it might be, but was fully resigned to follow wherever He might lead.

"Under later unmistakable indications, I now see with you the guiding hand of God by which you have been led to your present conclusion, and I am bound by my loyalty to Christ to concur with you in this movement. After I received your letter, I read to the 'fellowship bands' the 'General Rules of our Societies,' that all might know from the start the self-denying, cross-bearing life necessary to constitute a true Methodist,—that is, to find out God's Gospel *Methods*, and pursue them with a martyr spirit of fidelity to Him and to mankind. So our organization has now become matter of history. Let it be distinctly understood that we do not wish to hinder, but to help the spiritual progress of all pre-existing Churches in this great country.

"We attach no importance to the nominal relation of an unconverted man or woman to any Church. When, therefore, God by our agency leads such to receive Christ and salvation in Him, they naturally look to us for spiritual guidance, and we are bound to extend to them hands and hearts of fraternal sympathy, and receive them into our church-fellowship; unless they conscientiously believe they can get and do more good in some other branch of the Church of Christ. But persons who have a vital spiritual union with any Church, and a field of usefulness therein, we sincerely advise to remain in their own Church. We are not at liberty to refuse any persons who have a 'desire to flee from the wrath to come, and be saved from their sins'; but we do not wish any truly saved man to leave his Church to come to us. On the other hand, persons who are influenced by worldly motives would make a very great mistake in trying to ally themselves with us. All who join the Methodists should make up their minds to 'endure hardness as good soldiers of Jesus Christ,' and prove the truth of the Saviour's saying, 'Blessed are ye when men shall revile you, and shall persecute you, and shall say all manner of evil against you falsely for my sake.' Dr. Chalmers said, 'Methodism is Christianity in earnest.' That is a thing directly antagonistic to the carnal spirit and life of the world; and hence the emphatic statement of St. Paul, 'All that will live godly in Christ Jesus shall suffer persecution.'

"It does not follow that such are a long-faced, gloomy people, but rather, a people who 'rejoice evermore, pray without ceasing, and in everything give thanks unto God.' They daily cheer their heavenward journey with songs and shouts of victory over sin and Satan, speaking to each other in 'psalms and hymns and spiritual songs, singing and making melody in their hearts to the Lord.' All of us further agree, that ours is to be an Evangelistic, self-supporting Church. We know no distinction of language, caste, or colour, as it regards our relation to God and to each other as His children.

"Every member is expected to be a witness for Christ, and help to herald the fact that every human being on the face of the earth, or that may be born, to the end of time, has, and shall have, chartered rights under God's 'eternal purpose' to a full restoration of his filial relation to God, and a present salvation from 'all sin,' on the one simple condition of receiving Christ. 'As many as received Him, to them gave He power to become the sons of God.'

"Every such one becomes our real brother or sister, and fellow-heir to an eternal inheritance in Heaven. All such, who remain 'faithful unto death,' are enabled in that last mortal struggle to exclaim, 'O death, where is thy sting? O grave, where is thy victory? . . . Thanks be to God which giveth us the victory through our Lord Jesus Christ.' To give one illustrative case: Dr. Sewall, an old Methodist of Washington City, when dying, shouted aloud the praises of God. His friends said, 'Dr. Sewall, don't exert yourself. Whisper, Doctor; whisper.' 'Let angels whisper,' said he; 'let angels whisper: but a soul "cleansed from all sin," by "the blood of Christ,"—a soul redeemed from death and hell, just on the threshold of eternal glory,—Oh, if I had a voice that would reach from pole to pole, I would proclaim it to all the world! Victory! victory through the blood of the Lamb!'

"I will make application at once for missionary pastors to be sent to assist you in your great work. I will meantime (D.V.) serve you to the best of my ability till they shall arrive; but must be allowed, as heretofore, to decline to receive any fee or reward for my services.

"Your brother in Jesus,

"WILLIAM TAYLOR.

"*Bombay*, 14*th February* 1872."

It was from the start distinctly stated and unanimously concurred in by all our members, that ours should be purely a Missionary Church, for the conversion of the native nations of India as fast and as far as the Lord should lead us: that while it should be true to the discipline and administrative authority of the Methodist Episcopal Church, it should neither ask nor accept any funds from the Missionary Society, beyond the passage of missionaries to India; nor hence come under the control of any Missionary Society, but be led directly by the Holy Spirit of God, and supported by Him from Indian resources. For the sake of establishing, as nearly as possible, an indigenous Indian Church, regardless of colour or nationality, our ministers will forego their rights as regards salary, and also the ministerial social standing—equal to that of an officer in the army—which in India has been considered essential to success in their high calling, and live on subsistence allowance as near the level of the natives as health and efficiency will allow.

We shall thus preclude a "pādrī-log" caste—white preacher caste, which causes such an impassable gulf between foreign and native ministers. Whether Jew or Greek, Parsee or Afghan, Hindū or American, Scythian or English,—all our saved ones are indeed one body in Christ, and ministers are their servants for Christ's sake. Of course we have no control over the social distinctions of society. God's Gospel arrangement for fellowship, without ignoring social distinctions, provides within His Church a sphere and time for all needful social and spiritual fraternity as one great brotherhood, in which even its Divine Founder stands as a Brother. He says, "Whosoever doeth the will of my Father which is in heaven, the same is my brother, my sister, my mother"; and it is written, "He is not ashamed to call them brethren." It is our earnest wish to help all other Christian organizations in their soul-saving work, so far as God may give us ability; and to hinder none.

We are not opposed to Missionary Societies, nor the appropriation of missionary funds to any and all Missions which may require them. Our ground on that point is simply this: There are resources in India—men and money sufficient to run at least one great Mission. If they can be rescued from worldly waste, and utilized for the soul-saving work of God, why not do it? All admit that self-support is, or should be, the earnest aim of every Mission. If a work in India—the same as in England or in America—can start on this healthy, sound principle, is it not better than a long, sickly, dependent pupilage, which in too many instances amounts to pauperism? I am not speaking of missionaries, but of Mission churches. We simply wish to stand on the same platform, exactly, as our churches in America—which began poor, and worked their way up by their own industry and liberality, without funds from the Missionary Society. When such need help in some great enterprise, of building a church edifice or literary institution, it is considered no infringement of their self-support and self-respect to get help from churches or friends beyond their bounds; nor to accept help from the Missionary Society for the beginning of work in their bounds too poor to start of itself. So our self-supporting principle in India applies particularly to the support of ministers of the Gospel, and as far as possible to all our church buildings and institutions, but would not preclude foreign help for the latter from liberal Christian friends who might feel it a privilege to help us ; nor would it preclude help from the Missionary Society for extending Mission work, just as is done in all our self-supporting conferences at home, if need be. But it is a sound principle in political economy to develop the resources in hand, before you begin to subsidize them. Appropriations in advance will hinder, if not preclude, a healthy development. We hope for such an adequate development of Indian resources as to render it entirely unnecessary ever to draw on any Missionary Society for any purpose. The opening pioneer Mission work in any country may require, and in most cases has required, and does require, some independent resources which the pioneer missionary brings to his new work, before he can develop it, or make it self-supporting. Thus St. Paul depended on his skill as a tent-maker; I depend on mine as a book-maker; and missionaries ordinarily have to depend on Mission funds. Ten times the amount of all the money now raised for Mission purposes would not be adequate to send one missionary for each hundred thousand of heathens now accessible. God has within our day opened the gates of all the heathen nations of the earth to His Gospel messengers ; and now He wants the men to go, and the money to send them, and give them such help as they may require in sowing, till they can reap, and make their fields self-supporting and reproductive.

The old existing Missions of India have accomplished, especially in education and translation of the Scriptures, a vast preparatory work, which we thankfully accept as part of the available resources we propose to utilize. All honour to the patient, good men who have spent their lives in this preparative dispensation! But we see the disadvantages of what is known as the "compound system." It is not likely that any missionary ever planned such a system as a theory, but it gradually grew upon them as a fact; and thus the theory has been adduced, and facts which should have been set down as incidental and exceptional, have attained the status of an unavoidable necessity; so that with many good missionaries it is accepted, as a foregone conclusion, that it is impossible for persons converted from Hindūism, or Mohamedanism, or Parseeism, to remain at home with their own people; they must be at once protected and provided for. Hence the "compound," with houses for native converts under the eye and protection of the missionary. All missionaries deplore this necessity,—many are trying to abate it; and among low-castes many converts now are taught with success to remain in "whatsoever calling" or relation they may be when called by the Spirit of God. Still so many native teachers have been nurtured in the compound, who teach others by their own experience, that it is very difficult to measure the motives of the candidates they bring to the missionary for baptism,—especially when they know that a large amount of foreign funds are annually distributed from the missionary treasurer's office. So we escape a danger that many, unacquainted with the native Indian character, cannot appreciate, in being able to say, —"We get no appropriations of money from any foreign source. We have no rupees to give you, and no compounds in which to shelter you. If you receive Christ among us, we will baptize you, and say to each one, 'Go home to thy friends, and tell them how great things the Lord hath done for thee.' They will persecute you, of course; but God has given you a guarantee that you shall never be tempted or tried 'above that ye are able, but He will, with the temptation, also make a way of escape, that ye may be able to bear it.' If they kill you, accept the first good chance you get to have your head cut off, and seize a martyr's crown. Don't provoke opposition, nor court danger; but don't fear or shun either, in the plain way of your duty to God."

On this principle we may not for awhile get so many native converts; but they will make up in quality any lack of numbers. To ensure sound instruction on this subject, we seek no native agency from other Missions; and, as far as practicable, discourage all native Christians from joining our Mission.

We state our principles to the Hindūs, Mohamedans, and Parsees; and they approve of them. They are all familiar with the newspaper reports of lawsuits,—and many of them have footed the bills involved by them to recover their sons from the compound of the missionary; and from their standpoint they can but regard the man of God as a kidnapper.

We say to them on all suitable occasions, "We claim for your wives, children, or servants, as for yourselves, liberty of conscience. The laws of the British Constitution and the laws of God support this claim; but, on the other hand, we recognize your rights of property to the persons of your wives, children, and servants, and we pledge our word and honour that we will not infringe your rights. If we can get your wives, children, or servants, to receive Christ and salvation, we will baptize them, and send them home to you. You must not suspect that we will hide them: we will not; we will send them back to their friends and kindred; and we will require of you that you treat them properly, and not interfere with their conscience. Give them a fair trial, and you will see that they will fulfil all their duties better than they ever did before. If you persecute them they will bear it patiently; but we will put you upon your honour to do justly, and trust that you will show yourselves worthy of our confidence,—for we love you, and will place confidence in you, if you will not destroy in yourselves a ground of confidence."

I have often made such statements to hundreds of heathens, and never without profoundly enlisting their attention; and by their eyes, actions, and words, they have on every such occasion expressed their approval. Our platform has not a single new plank in it, and we don't want any new thing. We simply claim the privilege of carrying on a Mission, for the salvation of as many of these millions as God shall give us, on the very principles so fully exemplified in the Acts of the Apostles, and repeated in the great revival of apostolic methods by Whitefield, the Wesleys, and their coadjutors—first in England, and then in America.

In regard to our Mission in the North, commenced in 1857, I have always taken the ground that, as it was planted in the new provinces of Oudh and Rohilcund, it was quite proper for us as a Church to found educational institutions, orphanages, printing establishment, etc., and do from the foundations what older Missions have done for nearly all other parts of India. I have always, from my arrival in India, done what I could to advance their work. I knew that in planting a Mission on these plain, old-fashioned principles, I should be misunderstood and misrepresented by many; and have not been disappointed, nor for a moment discouraged. I am sure we are on the right platform for India,—God Himself, without our seeking or planning, put us on it,—and we intend, by the power of His Spirit, to stay on it.

Our first Circuit Plan (of which we give the reader a specimen over-leaf), will help to convey an idea of our organic proportions at this early stage of our existence.

That we might conduct our Mission without any possible complications with our India Mission Conference, or our Missionary Society, I thought if the General Conference would grant a provisional charter for a Bombay Conference, to be left to the judgment

PLAN OF BOMBAY CIRCUIT—

MARCH

Meeting-Places.	2	3	4	Four days for Special Services.	9	10	11	Four days for Special Services.
FRAMJEE COWASJEE HALL. Preaching each Lord's Day, at 11 A.M. and 6 P.M.		11 A.M. No. 1. 6 P.M. No. 1.				11 A.M. 1. 6 P.M. 1.		
MAZAGON. P. & O. Co's Hall		S. 15 F. 10	P. 1			S. 15 F. 1	P. 3	
Tinckom's		F 9				F. 1		
COLABA. Preaching each Lord's Day, at 9 A.M.	p. 11	P. 1	F 4		p. 6	P. 3	F. 4	
GRAHAM'S.	F. 3				F. 3			
BYCULLA. Mrs. Miles'	F. 2		P. 4		F. 2		P. 1	
Almeida's	F. 8		p. 14		F. 8		p. 13	
Grey's		F. 6	p. 7			F. 6	p. 10	
Berkley Place	F. 1				F. 12			
THE FORT. George Miles'			F. 7 p. 5				F. 7 p. 8	

The Sacrament of the Lord's Supper to be administered first Sabbath evening of each month. Quarterly tickets will admit *members* to the Quarterly meeting of the Bands, and to the Sacrament; *others* should have notes of admission from the Pastor.

"F." For Fellowship Band, or "Class Meeting," which is for the saved, and the seekers, only.

"P." For the public Preaching of the Gospel.

METHODIST EPISCOPAL CHURCH.

1872.

16	17	18		23	24	25		30	31	Ap. 1.
	11 A.M. 3. 6 P.M. 1.		Four days for Special Services.		11 A.M. 1. 6 P.M. 1.		Four days for Special Services.		11 A.M. 2. 6 P.M. 1.	
	S. 15 F. 10	P. 1			S. 15 F. 13	P. 2			S. 15 F. 10	P. 4
	F. 9				F. 1				F. 9	
p. 7	P. 1	F. 4		p. 11	P. 2	F. 4		p. 4	P. 1	F. 1
F. 3				F. 3				F. 3		
F. 2		P. 5		F. 2		P. 1		F. 2		P. 3
F. 8		p. 10		F. 8		p. 11		F. 8		p. 6
	F. 6	p. 11			F. 6	p. 5		F. 6		P. 13
F. 12				F. 1				F. 12		
		F. 7 p. 2				F. 7 p. 10				F. 7 p. 14

Ministers.

Wm. Taylor 1
George Bowen .. 2
Charles Harding 3

Prayer-Leaders.

James Shaw 4
C. W. Christian.. 5
Major Raitt 6
James Morris.... 7
Wm. Ashdown .. 8
Walter Abraham 9
George Miles 10
Capt. J. Winckler 11
George J. Pointer 12
Edwin Blackburn 13
Wm. Boyd 14
Joseph Head ... 15

"p." For public Prayer Meetings.
"S." For Sunday School.
1st Quarterly Conference, 7 A.M. 30th March.
1st Quarterly Meeting of the Bands, or "Love-feast,' 9 A.M. 31st March.

of the bishops having charge of our work, it would be well. The following are copies of my letter to Bishop Janes, and to the General Conference, on the subject :—

"BOMBAY, INDIA, *March* 4, 1872.

"DEAR BROTHER,—The enclosed printed letters will indicate to you the leading of God which has resulted in the organization of a Methodist Episcopal Church in Bombay. We have now nine classes, in which over 130 converts meet weekly; and newly-saved souls are being 'added daily.'

"We hereby ask you, and our Missionary Committee, to send us men as we may require them, but not money. If you wish to pay their passage to Bombay, and can, by the liberality of a few friends or otherwise, do it, without placing this Mission on the list of *dependent* Missions, all right. One appropriation of funds from any Missionary Society would set upon us the brand-mark of existing Indian Missions, and tend to bring us down to their dead level.

"We do not underrate the valuable preparatory work accomplished on these vast plains of heathenism by faithful missionaries, living and dead—especially in the translation of the Scriptures into most of the languages of these nations; but we believe the time has fully come when God wishes to demonstrate the soundness and practical utility of His own Gospel methods of aggression—one principle of which is self-sustentation. Our Mission Conference in the North—planted, as it is, in a new heathen field—cannot live on the principle on which God intends to run this work in the South; where we especially desire that the Holy Spirit be allowed to test His simple Pauline methods.

"We believe that He will thus lead us through this great Indian Empire.

"After we learn to walk without crutches,—then if, in any emergency, our American brothers wish to help us, all right; and our Indian Methodists, according to their ability, will also make a collection for the 'poor saints in Judæa,' or in New York. We now ask the Committee, through you, to send *two* young men—single men—if engaged, well; if not, better. We want men of good practical common sense: if liberally educated, well; but sound in body, wholly devoted to God, ready to do or die for Jesus in India, and who will trust God and His Indian Methodists for food and raiment. We can't promise high salaries; but no faithful minister here need incur debt for food or raiment, nor suffer want of either.

"It is considered unsafe, on the score of health, for new recruits to land here in the summer. So the said missionaries for Bombay need not arrive till November of this year. I will (D.V.) be here to receive them, and initiate them into their work.

"Your Brother in Jesus,

"WILLIAM TAYLOR.

"Rev. Bishop Janes, D.D."

The following is a copy of my petition to the General Conference which held its session in Brooklyn, New York, commencing May 1st, 1872:—

"To the General Conference of the Methodist Episcopal Church.

"DEAR FATHERS AND BRETHREN,—The God of our fathers has planted Methodism in Bombay. You may see by enclosed printed letters that our cause here is but in its infancy.

"I have been but three-and-a-half months in this city, and the first month was devoted to the Mārāttī natives through interpreters; but you may see from enclosed Circuit Plan an indication of our growth. This is a city containing a population of nearly a million of souls; Morādābād, the seat of our recent session of the India Mission Conference, is about 1400 miles distant; hence this Mission cannot in reason be appended to that Conference. Moreover, we believe that God intends to run this soul-saving concern on His old Pauline track, which must pay its own running expenses, and help 'the poor saints in Judæa' as well; and therefore we cannot be tacked on to a remote dependency.

"We have asked our Missionary Committee, through Bishop Janes, to send us two young men, to arrive in November of this year; but it is already manifest to us that God will raise up ministers here from the recruits He is now levying. One young man had over thirty seals to his ministry before he was two months old. We have nine classes, in which more than 130 new converts meet weekly; and others are being 'added daily.' Nearly all these speak the different native languages spoken in this city; and God will lead us down upon the native masses as soon as we are sufficiently developed and equipped for such an advance. We shall want the facilities for initiating and organizing into a regular Methodist ministry the men whom God may call in Bombay for this work.

"We therefore respectfully ask the General Conference at its present session to grant us a charter for the organization of a Bombay Conference,—not a Mission Conference. If we stand alone on our own legs, by the power of God, and draw no Mission funds, why call it a

Mission Conference? We have a number of spacious places of worship in our Circuit, named in the accompanying Circuit Plan; but we are also raising funds for the erection of a Methodist Episcopal Church. For further information I refer you to Rev. R. S. M'Clay, D.D., and Rev. Henry Mansell. As it regards myself, I am subject to the Master's orders, to stand at this post till He shall release me, and order me to some other.

"Your Brother in Christ, on behalf of the Methodist Episcopal Church in Bombay,

"WILLIAM TAYLOR.

"BOMBAY, *March 4th*, 1872."

You naturally enquire, What was the result of the petition? Well, the Committee on Foreign Missions were about to consign it to the waste-basket without even reading it, when Brother M——, who had recently passed through Bombay, and was a member of that Committee, called for the reading of the petition. It was read and laid on the table—not to be taken up again. The idea of a man laying the foundations of a Conference in a heathen country in the short space of three months!

CHAPTER XV.

FRĀMJĪ CAWĀSJĪ HALL.

FEBRUARY 13th.—Good audience; two or three seekers. Rev. Henry Mansell, of the India Mission Conference, was with us, and gave a powerful exhortation.

Feb. 16th.—Rev. R. S. M'Clay, D.D., missionary from China, preached a beautiful sermon here this evening.

A few saved here last week, and more this.

Since we organized, our young members have been put to a severe persecuting test; but most of them stand undaunted. Many of the pulpits, and the press, are denouncing us; but God is with us, and we will not fear what man may say or do.

Saturday, 17th.—Organized a soldiers' band to-night at Captain Christian's in Colaba. Brother James Shaw the leader.

After special services for three weeks in Frāmjī Cawāsjī Hall, the details of which I have not given, we engaged the Hall for Sabbath services, morning and night, for thirty-five rupees per week.

On Sabbath, March 3rd, we held our first sacramental service; and had sixty-five communicants.

Brother Harding said that it was much the largest communion in the city; and yet, owing to the great distance of our extreme wings from this centre, not more than half of our people could be present.

Held a successful series of services of over a fortnight in Morley Hall, in Colāba. Krishnā Chowey, a young Hindū, was awakened there. On my first interview with him, he said, "I am fully convinced of the truth of your preaching, and have a great desire to become a true Christian; but there are great difficulties in my way. My uncle spent thirty years in Bombay, and made a great deal of money, and has good estates on the Malabar coast, where he resides. He has no children, and has adopted me as his heir, and given me his name. (My proper name is Canāren.) If I become a Christian, I shall forfeit my inheritance. The girl to whom I was betrothed when a child is in his power, and I shall have no end of trouble. I shall lose my situation in the Customs; and shall fail in an examination to come off in July on custom-house laws."

I said, "If you cannot give up all these things for Christ, you cannot enter the kingdom of God. What you have to do, is to consent to part with all idolatry and sin, and make over and entrust to God all these temporal interests—to have and to hold, or to lose, as He shall see best." I prayed with him; but he did not fully make up his mind.

Mirza Ismael, a Persian Mohamedan, was a regular hearer at the Parsee Hall meetings; and in Morley Hall, on March 7th, he came out as a seeker. In his penitential struggle, while I was talking to him and praying for him, he had a sort of vision. He saw before him a beautiful garden. He wanted to go through a gate into that lovely place, but could not advance. In every attempt he went either to one side or the other, and could not reach the gate. In his fruitless struggle a charming-looking man appeared at the gate, and beckoned to him to come, and he believed that he could; and in the effort he recovered proper consciousness, and heard me saying to him, "Receive Christ; He has come to save you."

"I did in that moment receive Him," he added, "as my Saviour; and I was filled with light and happiness."

As a Mohamedan he may have needed some such tangible stimulus to his faith; and the Holy Spirit in that simple way helped him. It is written, "Your old men shall dream dreams, and your young men shall see visions." These are means of light and leading to those who have not sufficient light through the written Word of God. We had no facilities for baptism at the Hall; so he came home with us to Brother George Miles',—and there, in presence of that large threefold family, I baptized him. He is thirty-one years of age; and is a teacher of the Persian language in one of the schools of the city. He took our advice to go home to his place among his Mohamedan friends, and proceed with his school duties as before.

"Why baptize him so quickly?"

Because I have learned in heathen lands, as I never did before, the importance of following strictly the apostolic precedent, in this as in everything else.

The last night I laboured in Caltura, Ceylon, we had fourteen Budhists forward as seekers; and most of them professed by very intelligent statements that they had received Christ and the forgiveness of their sins. I never thought of baptizing them at once. One of these was a young man who had come nine miles to the meeting. Many weeks afterwards I learned that the father of the said young man kept constant watch to prevent him from returning to the Mission chapel to be baptized. Baptism is the sacrament of initiation into the visible Church of Christ, and the outward act which cuts the relation of the subject to heathenism. When converts are thus properly enrolled and mustered into the army of Jesus, their position is clearly defined and known; and fully committed to their work—the bridge behind them cut away—they have nothing to do but abide in Christ and march along. Of course, the first thing is to accept the Lord Jesus, and be "baptized by the Spirit into the body of Christ." Thus the 3000 who believed on the great Pentecostal day in Jerusalem were not allowed to fall back into their home associations for a single hour, till they were all baptized. So when the Philippian jailer believed, Paul did not wait till morning, but there and then baptized him and his household.

Our dear Ismael had been under instruction for weeks, had seen many souls brought to God, and had publicly come out himself, and received the baptism of the Spirit: then why any distrust or delay?

March 11th.—Organized Fellowship Band No. 10, in Middle Colāba, appointing Brother James Shaw the leader; and appointed Captain Winckler leader of Shaw's soldier band at Captain Christian's.

"Why note so many details of this sort?"

All my facts and details belong to the early history of a Mission that is to span this empire, and has been the subject of rejoicings in the presence of the angels of God; yet I can only in my limited space insert illustrative examples of large classes of such facts. I am so familiar with them that I feel the danger of undervaluing them, and of leaving out many that should be written.

Sabbath, 17th.—Preached to the soldiers in Colāba at nine a.m. At Frāmjī Cawāsjī Hall, at eleven a.m., Brother Harding preached a good sermon about the penitent thief on the cross. I preached there at seven p.m. to the best congregation we have had. Contributions in the boxes at the door, sixty-three rupees: a little gush of one of the streams on which to float our self-supporting Mission.

Monday, 18th.—Had a glorious fellowship band at Brother Miles' to-night. Brother Mirza Ismael was present. He is very happy, and gave a rupee as a "fellowship thank-offering." He gave a full account in the band of his penitential struggle, and the vision that had helped him to receive Jesus.

Tuesday, 19th.—Regular visiting-day with Brother George Ainsworth. He gives me one day in the week for a certain round of about eighteen families. He is in the Customs department, and was saved at one of our meetings at Falkland Road.

In our singing-practice I was in the habit of repeating the first verse of a hymn, till the congregation could catch the tune, and then proceed. Mr. Ainsworth, with his wife, came that night for the first time to hear me preach. They entered and got seated while we were engaged in singing-practice—for which we took half an hour before the time appointed for preaching. We had just taken up the first verse of one of Charles Wesley's grand hymns (the 109th in our "Hymns New and Old"):—

> "And can it be that I should gain
> An interest in the Saviour's blood?
> Died He for me, who caused His pain,—
> For me, who Him to death pursued?
> Amazing love! how can it be,
> That Thou, my God, shouldst die for me?"

A book was handed to Mr. and Mrs. Ainsworth, and the hymn indicated; but to their surprise the same verse was sung again.—"A mistake, perhaps." Then we sang it over again.—"What does this mean?"

It was sung again and again; and Ainsworth said to himself, as he told us subsequently, "And this is the great preacher I have heard about! I came to hear him preach; and he seems to know nothing but one verse of a hymn. When he gets to the end of it, he begins, and goes over the same verse again. What nonsense!"

On we went, singing the same verse; and the rest of the congregation, who knew the value of repeating in order quickly to master the tune, were getting on beautifully; but Ainsworth, there for the first time, and knowing nothing of the design of this method, was first surprised, then disgusted, and then got angry, and was tempted to get up abruptly and leave the house; but the small room was greatly crowded, and he had difficulty to get a seat; and being a man of good breeding, he made up his mind to stand it patiently, and see the end. On went the repetition —and now the whole crowd had got the tune; and George began to reflect, "What wonderful words are these, that must be sung thirty times over before we go on to the second verse?—

"'And can it be that I should gain
An interest in the Saviour's blood?'

"'That *I* can gain,'—I, George Ainsworth: can I gain an interest in the Saviour's blood? Oh, would not that be a gain worth more to me than to gain the world? To gain the world, and lose my soul: dreadful!—

"'And can it be that I should gain
An interest in the Saviour's blood?'

Why not? I hear of many who have gained this, at these very meetings. What's to hinder me from finding this 'pearl of great price'? 'He tasted death for every man'—hence for me."

Repeated again by the congregation, it came ringing into his ears,—

"Died He for me, who caused His pain,—
For me, who Him to death pursued?"

"Yes, He died for me—for George Ainsworth; and I have, in the murderous spirit of carnal enmity to God that pursued Him to the death of the cross, been rejecting Him all my life, and am a rebel against Him now, with the brand-mark of His murderers upon my soul."

(I have merely given the substance of what he said passed in his mind.) We then went on with the hymn, and came to the verse,—

"Long my imprisoned spirit lay,
Fast bound in sin and nature's night;"——

"True," said George to himself; "and I am a poor condemned prisoner to-night."

"Thine eye diffused a quickening ray;
I woke: the dungeon flamed with light:
My chains fell off, my heart was free,—
I rose, went forth, and followed Thee."

"Oh that I could feel that quickening ray to-night!" was the throb of a new life that the Holy Spirit was beginning to inspire in his dead soul. It grew and increased, and when seekers were invited at the close of the sermon, George Ainsworth was one among the first to respond; and in the agony produced by a sudden, deep awakening of the Spirit of God, he surrendered, and received Christ; his wife also: then they could indeed sing with that little host of Jesus' witnesses,—

"Long my imprisoned spirit lay,
Fast bound in sin and nature's night;
Thine eye diffused a quickening ray;
I woke: the dungeon flamed with light:
My chains fell off, my heart was free,—
I rose, went forth, and followed Thee.

"No condemnation now I dread :
Jesus, with all in Him, is mine ;
Alive in Him, my living Head,
And clothed in righteousness Divine,
Bold I approach the eternal throne,
And claim the crown, through Christ, my own."

Brother Ainsworth afterwards showed me a beautifully written statement of the leading facts of his experience of salvation in his Bible—closing with two verses of another grand hymn (No. 279 of "Hymns New and Old"):—

"'Tis done ! the great transaction's done !
I am my Lord's, and He is mine ;
He drew me, and I followed on,
Charmed to confess the voice Divine.

"Now rest, my long-divided heart,
Fixed on this blissful centre, rest ;
Nor ever from my Lord depart,
With Him of every good possessed."

19th.—Had a grand preaching service in the prison. Among the poor fellows who have come to Jesus is a Roman Catholic.

We are now in the midst of the "Maharram," a great annual festival of nearly a week, kept by the Mohamedans. It is often the occasion for avenging any old score with the Hindūs, Parsees, or Christians: grand street processions, night illuminations, the clatter of cymbals, and confusion of sounds. Then woe betide a Hindū procession that may meet the "Maharram" in the streets! So it was rumoured this afternoon that the Mohamedans were killing the people, and that the military had been called out to restore order. My friends said, "You should not attempt to go through the city this evening."

I said, "I am not responsible for Mohamedan riots, but I am responsible for my appointment in Colāba to-night." On my way I learned that since the soldiers had marched to the front, the threatening aspect of affairs had been modified; but the streets were still crowded with excited people, and no one could tell what the next hour might bring forth.

Sabbath, 24th.—Commissioner Drummond, from Rohilcund, was present at Frāmjī Cawāsjī Hall this morning. He afterwards told me that he came early to the Hall; and the first one who came after him was a Hindū, with whom he had the following conversation:—

"Salām, bābū!"

"Salām, sāhib!"

"What is your religion?"

"I am a Hindū."

"What have you come here for?"

"To hear Pādrī Taylor, sahib."

"He's not a Hindū: why do you come to hear him?"

"Well, sahib; there is a very mysterious work going on here in connexion with his meetings. Many men, whom I knew to be drunkards, swearers, and dishonest men,—tyrannical men, too, who were before always abusing the natives in their employ,—have been entirely changed at these meetings. They are now all teetotalers; they are honest and true in their dealings, and speak nothing but words of kindness to everybody; and instead of hating and abusing their servants, they show real love and sympathy for them, and are all the time trying to do them good. I have looked into these things closely, and know that what I tell you, sahib, is true; and this kind of work is going on all the time at Pādrī Taylor sahib's meetings. I don't understand it, but I feel so anxious to know more about it that I can't keep away."

Six p.m.—The largest crowd we have had. Sydenham Smith, and three others, came out as seekers.

We now organized our workers into three divisions, to carry on special services for a few weeks in three different parts of this wide-spread city.

Sabbath, 31st.—Good meetings at Frāmjī Cawāsjī Hall morning and evening; several saved.

Monday, April 1st.—Held this afternoon our first Quarterly Conference, at Major Raitt's, and at six p.m. our first love-feast, at Mrs. Miles' bungalow. Over 100 sisters and brothers partook of the sacrament; and the speaking was most interesting. We did not introduce the custom of taking a little bread and water at the love-feast. No law of the Church is violated by its omission. My people had never seen nor heard of such a thing. I always appealed to the Bible as my authority for everything I said or did, and challenged them to "search the Scriptures daily," like the noble Bereans, "and see if these things were so." I could not claim Scriptural authority for introducing a *ceremony* so closely resembling the sacred feast ordained by the Master; so I administered the sacrament of the Lord's Supper at the love-feast instead. The time may come when we may bring food to our fellowship-meetings, to supply the need of the multitude of poor persecuted saints, and revive the real "agapē," or ancient love-feast, instead of a commemorative ceremony of it. In old countries, where it is established and understood, I should observe it, and say nothing about it; but in these days of ritualistic ceremonies, and in this country of heathenish feasts, having the opportunity of breaking entirely new ground, we just quietly leave this ceremony out.

We also, without altering any of our doctrines—which are the simple doctrines of the Apostles—prune off all ecclesiastical cant phrases, and correct and sharpen much of the terminology of the pulpit. For example, we never ask a poor sinner to look to the *cross*, or to come to the *cross*, but to look to Jesus, and to obey His words, "Come unto me all ye that labour and are heavy-laden, and I will give you rest." When Paul was preaching to the heathen in Athens, he did not tell them to "behold the cross," but to "feel after God, if haply you may find Him, for He is nigh unto every one of you." We have to do with a risen, invisible, but living, personal, present Jesus. The historical facts of the sacrificial offering of Christ belong to the basis of faith, and should be stated plainly, and vividly reproduced to the minds of our hearers; but we don't take them to seek the living among the dead: we assure every poor awakened sinner that the living, loving Saviour is nigh—even now knocking at the "door of his heart"—and beseech the seeker at once to open and receive Him.

We don't ask anybody to seek *religion.* Everybody in this country has religion of some sort; and it requires too many words to define the kind you wish him to seek. We urge people to seek *salvation*—to seek redemption through the blood of Jesus, even the forgiveness of sins. They thus obtain "pure and undefiled religion." We do not ignore the word; but it is an abstract term, not so well suited to represent the object of a poor sinner's search as the terms the Apostles used in that connexion. Our awakened sinners seek Jesus; and when they find Him they don't say, "We have got religion," but with Philip say, "We have found Him of whom Moses in the law, and the prophets did write—Jesus of Nazareth"; or with Paul, "Being justified by faith, we have peace with God through our Lord Jesus Christ."

None of our people are "*instruments*": they are all intelligent, responsible *agents.* God never, by word or by implication, calls a man an instrument —a mere tool. Men may be sovereigns, subjects, slaves, ambassadors, witnesses, workers, "kings and priests unto God," children of God, and heirs of eternal glory,—but not instruments. We use the word in its proper connexion according to the Scriptures, "Yield not your members instruments of unrighteousness, but yield your members instruments of righteousness." Our members—hands, feet, etc.—are instruments; but it is quite a mistake to call a man an instrument. I would not stand a debate about it; but, teaching my people from the foundation, I choose to give them correct, clear, and unambiguous terms. I explain these things to our newly-arrived missionaries, and they see it at once, and cheerfully follow in that line.

Friday, April 5th.—Special services this week in three different centres; but I am preaching at George Ainsworth's. To-night James Bapty, the miller, came forward as a seeker.

Saturday, 6th.—Visited Brother Ismael this afternoon. He told me a great deal about his old religion —Mohamedanism. He is getting on well as a young follower of Jesus. Brother Boyd brought Mr. Bapty to see me. He is a Yorkshireman, about six feet four inches in height, and large every way in symmetrical proportion. He is in great distress of body and soul. He says he has never been a drunkard, but has been an habitual drinker for thirty-five years. He keeps an open sideboard, at which he and his visitors put away a bottle of brandy daily. I doubt not, from what he tells me, that he takes enough to kill two or three ordinary men. Last night, at our meeting, upon his knees he bade adieu to the brandy and all intoxicating drinks. To-day he is suffering from an awful head-ache, and is tempted to think that "it will hazard his health to stop so suddenly, and that he had better taper off."

"If you attempt to 'taper off,'" said I, "you will just taper on again. If you were down in delirium tremens, then, under suitable medical restrictions, a little might be necessary; but you are a strong man, with a vigorous constitution, and you should stand to it, like old Christopher Fry, a blacksmith of my early acquaintance.

"Fry had been a great drunkard, but went to a

camp-meeting, and was converted to God, and of course gave up the grog. Some time after that he became dangerously ill, and was brought down apparently to the gates of death.

"The doctor said, 'Fry, you must take some brandy, or you will die.'

"'Doctor, there is no bar between me and death. I have never resolved that I will not die; but I have resolved, by the strength of God, that I never will drink intoxicating liquor. If I had not been so addicted to it, then as a medicine it might do me some good; but as it is, it would do my body no good, and might destroy my soul. I am ready to die, thank God!—but I won't take the brandy.'

"The doctor gave him up as an incorrigible teetotaler, and a hopeless case.

"Fry lingered long—till he got the effects of alcohol worked out of his system—a mere skeleton; then his flesh came upon him gradually like the flesh of a little child; and he got up a new man, lived to a great age, honoured God to the last, and then went to heaven."

So Bapty said, "I'll stand it, by the help of God."

Sabbath, 7th.—I preached at Colāba at nine a.m. As I came out I met Krishnā Chowey. I had not seen him for about three weeks.

"Krishnā," said I, "where have you been?—I have not seen you for weeks."

He then gave me an account of himself. He was so awakened one night when I was preaching in Colāba, that he spoke out spontaneously, "I am determined to be a Christian"; but did not come forward as a seeker. A native pādrī, hearing his exclamation, went out with him at the close of the service, and said, "Oh, Krishnā, I was so glad to hear you declare for Christ!—now come home with me, and we'll talk about it." He took him to his missionary, and they tried to persuade him to be baptized. The native pādrī removed his family to a house just opposite where Krishnā and his two brothers lived, and thus hoped to bring the three brothers into their church. Krishnā was told that I was not a properly ordained minister. The pādrī, too, said, "I know something about Mr. Taylor." Thus Krishnā was kept away from my meetings, and was often asking the pādrī what it was that he knew about Mr. Taylor,—who finally answered, "Oh, nothing; Mr. Taylor is a very good man": so Krishnā saw through it, and the spell was broken.

I said, "You know, Krishnā, I have not said a word to you about being baptized, and joining my church. Those good men would baptize you in your sins—a thing I never will knowingly do. My first business is to get people saved from their sins; and even then I don't persuade any to join my church. I instruct them clearly from the Word of God, and leave them to the decision of their own judgment and conscience in regard to their church relations." He came with me to Frāmjī Cawāsjī Hall, and heard Brother Bowen preach at eleven a.m.

I preached there in the evening; and two men came forward and found Jesus—one of whom was my tall friend, James Bapty.

Tuesday, 9th.—Went this evening to Railway

George Ainsworth's—(not the "preventive service" George Ainsworth). The wife of Railway George, a large, dark, East Indian woman, was one of the first converts at our meetings in the American Chapel. I remember I called attention to her hard struggle, and to her testimony, and remarked, "She says now that she has received Jesus, and has got all her sins forgiven; and I have no reason to doubt her testimony."

She added, "Yes; it is all true: I wouldn't tell a lie about it."

She lives in an obscure neighbourhood beyond the Byculla railway bridge; I had not seen much of her, and felt concerned to know how she was getting on, —but to my joy find that she is doing well, and has opened her house for meetings. As I was busy in other parts of the city, Brother Harding had been holding meetings there, and had a number converted to God; but having no English church, he wished to turn this band of young believers over to me; so this evening I went with him, and found over a score of people assembled in Ainsworth's second-storey verandah,—a long, narrow, well lighted, and of course well ventilated place. I preached to them; and a number of witnesses spoke for Jesus,—among whom was Brother Jurain, a dark East Indian from Madras, who was saved about the same time as Mrs. Ainsworth last November.

He told us of his great wickedness, and said, "I got to be such a rebel against God, and such an enemy of man, and so utterly wretched, that a year and a quarter ago I determined to put an end to my miserable life by shooting myself. It was an old flint-lock gun that I had. I put in a heavy charge, that the business might be done quickly. I put the muzzle under my chin, and pulled the trigger with my toe; but as the pan opened by the stroke of the flint, the powder fell out. I then primed it again, and lay down on my back; and as I was fixing the gun so that the powder could not run out and miss fire again, a woman called aloud,—

"'Henry, where are you? Come here: the man who bargained for your gun has come with the money to get it.'

"I was at the door of hell. God held me back, and has saved me, and is daily preserving me from sinning."

12th.—Prayed with Brother Bapty to-day in the balcony of his mill. He is up to his chin in financial difficulties with his Parsee partner in business.

Bapty had made and lost a fortune in India. He again made some money, and went to England and bought machinery for a flour mill, and took his brother in as a partner. But his brother died; and on the way back Bapty got acquainted with a rich Parsee, a fellow-passenger, who agreed to furnish half the funds necessary, and become half-owner of the concern; but Bapty, for a consideration agreed upon, was to build the mill and run it. They signed the articles he had drawn up for his brother (not very carefully worded). He built a splendid mill, and was making about 500 rupees per day. But the Parsee, seeing it was such a grand thing, determined to get it all into his own hands; and taking advantage of some defect in the articles, he brought a suit in chancery against Bapty, and closed up the mill. All that Bapty had in the world was now locked up in this chancery suit—that might last for years, or quite long enough to starve him out. They each had an interest in it of about 20,000 rupees. The Parsee was willing to take 30,000, or give Bapty 13,000. He could not give the former, and was not willing to take the latter. He was in a sad dilemma; so we went up into the balcony and laid the matter before the Lord. The outlook was very dark; but God gave comfort to our souls, and we thought we saw a fringe of light round the edges of the heavy financial cloud that overshadowed the mill, Dear Bapty is cleaving to Jesus, and casting his care upon Him. He says he never had anything to break down his spirit till this trouble came upon him. A blessing in disguise, from Him who maketh "the wrath of man to praise Him"! But for this trouble, he thinks he never would have been brought down to the feet of Jesus. [God did in a marvellous way lead His child, Brother Bapty, out of all his troubles. He is now sole owner of his mill,—all paid for; and from the fortune he is making he intends to build a house for the Lord.]

19th.—Read from the *New York Christian Advocate* to-day the report of a presiding elder in the Virginia Conference, in which he says: "Father Taylor is well, and in fine spirits. This Father Taylor is father to California William. An excellent meeting was recently held at his house." Good as a letter from home. Thank God for the health and vigour of my dear parents!

CHAPTER XVI.

OPERATIONS AMONG THE HEATHEN.

ON Friday, the 10th of April, I said to a number of our young workers: "Sisters and brothers,—I have for months been absorbed in our English-speaking work; the margin of the available stuff of that sort is very narrow, and we seem to have cut through it; but we have got out of it a good working force. It is now upon my soul specially to seek power from God to lead this band of workers through the heathen lines. As a church we are young and feeble, and may not be able to accomplish much at first; but we must begin in good earnest, and go on and acquire skill in the work. We must read and study with special reference to this thing, maintain entire consecration to God, receive and trust Christ for everything we may require to save ourselves and the heathen about us. God will gradually lead us down into this dark empire of heathenism, and enable us to bring them to the Light. I don't know how it is to be done; but He does. I see no opening at all. Its walls have stood unscathed for thousands of generations, and seem to be impregnable; but God will show us the way through them. This is my confession of faith, based on God's adequate, available provisions in Christ, under the immediate administration of the Holy Spirit. 'Why not long ago?' He lacked suitable agency. His ancient soldiers died and went to heaven; their successors were corrupted by a compromise with heathenism. The Reformers of the sixteenth century broke the fetters of the unholy alliance, ignored their traditions, and got back an open Bible for the world—but, unfortunately, added their own speculative dogmas; and, owing to the alliance of State and Church, the struggle led to great political revolutions, so that the movement became more political than religious. The Reformers of the eighteenth century, under more favourable conditions, got hold of the right adjustment of Gospel doctrines and methods of work, and the spirit of Christ-like, loving aggression for the salvation of the world. The organic outgrowth of that great revival manifested such uniform and incisive methods of work, that its agents were stigmatized by the name of Methodists. One important part of their providential mission, from the first and all through, has been to diffuse their doctrines and infuse their spirit into the old Calvinian bodies, and to provoke them to love and good works. The Bible and Tract Societies, and nearly all the Missionary Societies of all the churches, have, within the last 135 years, grown out of this great revival of apostolic religion. The organic development of it called Methodism has just made its first entrance into Bombay, and in connexion with our Mission Conference in the North, has begun its grand work of evangelizing India. The old organizations have done a great work; but they need help, and God has sent us to help them."

We all prayed that God would pity us, and use us in His own way to save the heathen. It was a solemn meeting, and we got an increase of faith and power.

Sabbath, 12th.—Organized a fellowship band in Umercarry at eight a.m. Brother W. J. Coen opened a work here in a private house, and got about fourteen persons converted to God; and now they have joined us in church fellowship. Brother Coen is an earnest and successful worker.

Monday, 13th.—Heard Brother C. W. Christian preach this evening at Mrs. Miles'. He has had many children saved at his meetings, and now leads two juvenile fellowship bands. Though only converted to God last New Year's Day, he is an earnest preacher, whom God has called. The fear is, that with his heavy duties in the Bank, his zeal in soul-saving work may break down his health. God will teach him wisdom to use and not abuse his powers. [He has since become a regular minister of the Gospel.]

Tuesday, 14th.—At half-past seven p.m. commenced a series of special services in the Old Strangers' Home building, in Middle Colāba. Brother Bowen has been preaching here four evenings per week for three weeks, and has had some very interesting cases of conversion,—among whom were W. Curties and George Gilder, jun., young men in the Government Marine Telegraph Office. [Both of these young men have been received into the India Conference, and are earnest preachers in our Mission.] This evening we had about eighty hearers, and several saved.

Krishnā Chowey came out as a seeker this evening, and, after a weeping struggle, surrendered and received Christ. He has been under awakening for months, but never came out on the Lord's side till to-night.

Wednesday, 15th.—Brother Shaw and I visited Brother Krishnā and his two brothers, Trimbuck and Anā, and prayed with them. Krishnā told me to-day that when I was leading him to Jesus last night, the things that other missionaries had told him about me kept ringing in his ears, and were a great trouble to him; but finally he got the victory, and accepted Christ, and is now resting in Him. Glory be to God!

16th.—Good service as usual in the prison at three p.m. We have it twice a-week regularly.

The chaplain is in great difficulties. He opened his mind freely to Major Raitt, and said, "Taylor is a dreadful man: he has driven me out of the prison, and also out of Mazagon and Parell."

The Major tried to show him that he was quite mistaken: "Taylor has got some people saved in all these places, but that has not affected you in the least. I know that, so far as the prison is concerned, he has greatly increased your congregation. Before he came here, this prison was a bedlam. It was almost impossible to get on with them—they were so profane, so quarrelsome and insubordinate; but now I have no trouble with them, and from morning till night they are singing Taylor's hymns; and I believe that more than a score of them are truly converted to God."

"They ought not to be allowed to sing in prison," rejoined the chaplain.

Paul and Silas were allowed to sing in a Roman prison.

In visiting the hospital, the chaplain said to one of our converted Romanists, "What made you leave your mother-church, and go and hear this foreigner?"

The convert pointed him to his Bible, and said, "You will find my reasons in this book."

The chaplain administered the sacrament to our prison converts—they being members of his church. We led them to Christ, but did not interfere with their church relations. He never could have got them to the sacrament before, and did not attempt it. He thus unwittingly endorsed our work among them; but afterwards saw that he had committed himself, and tried to get out of it by telling them that, having been baptized and confirmed, they had always been Christians. Prisoners, convicted by the judges of all the crimes known to the law, locked up here in the interest of society,—a rare lot of Christians!

Friday, 17th.—Three men came out as seekers to-night; one of them was Trimbuck Canāren, Krishnā's brother. After meeting, I walked with Trimbuck on the beach in the light of the moon. As he was fresh from the ranks of Hindūism, I asked him what he thought of missionary operations generally.

He spoke very intelligently and kindly of the missionaries; "But," said he, "they cannot succeed, because they lack confidence in themselves, in their own methods, and in the natives."

"Now, you have been to many of my meetings, and have learned much about our doctrines, methods, and spirit: can we succeed?"

"Yes, we can; and I am anxious to begin, and tell them what a great salvation I have found."

I spoke to him about being baptized.

"I think I should be baptized by a native minister."

I perceived that the said native minister had been labouring with him, as he had with Krishnā.

I reasoned with him; and he then said, "I'll leave it all to you."

I said, "No; you must face your own responsibilities, and voluntarily act upon your own convictions."

He seemed joyous in having accepted the Saviour; and said he would consider what I had said about being baptized.

Sabbath, 19th.—On my way to Colāba, I met Trimbuck, with the said native minister, on their way to the service of his missionary. I had a few words with him, and he said Mr. —— had been talking to him till midnight about being baptized by him or his missionary.

It had been arranged that Krishnā should be baptized at our eleven a.m. service at Frāmji Cawāsjī Hall; but they had been labouring with him till he was inclined to postpone. He called on me in my room, before meeting hour, to advise with me, and know if it would not be better first to write and consult his uncle.

I said, "In matters of conscience towards God, we must find out His will, and do it. To make our obedience hinge on the dictation of man is to ask God to defer to man. You know the mind of your uncle now as well as you can know it after writing him; and to provoke his prohibitive order, and then act in opposition to it, will be interpreted into direct disobedience, and greatly complicate your case."

He saw it all at a glance, and then kneeled down and prayed to God for courage to obey His plain command to be baptized. He is naturally a timid man, but now he became strong to do or die for Jesus. I preached from Isaiah xl. 4: "Every mountain and hill shall be brought low: and the crooked shall be made straight, and the rough places plain." Then, in the presence of our congregation, I baptized him. He spent the afternoon with us, and attended the evening service. He said, "I never was so happy before, as I have been since I was baptized. I have received Christ as I did not before, and feel unspeakable joy in my soul."

Monday, 20th.—Early this morning Krishnā came to my room in great distress.

"Brother Krishnā," said I, "what is the trouble?"

"Well, after I left you last night, I met Rev. —— and his wife; and she said, 'Krishnā, where have you been all day?'

"'I have been in the right place; I have become a Christian.'

"'Yes; but you are not baptized yet.'

"'Yes, I am: Mr. Taylor baptized me to-day.'

"'Why did you not consult me?' said the pādrī.

"'In matters pertaining to God and my conscience I don't follow any man.'

"'But did you not consult Mr. Taylor and Mr. Bowen?'

"'I got instruction from them in regard to my duty to God; but when I saw my duty, I did it unto God, and not to any man.'

"'Why did you not let us know?—and I would have had all our native Christians there to witness the ceremony.'

"'Mr. Taylor doesn't want any show and parade about such things.'

"God gave me words of wisdom to reply to all his questions," added Krishnā; "and he was quiet for some time.

"Then he said, 'Krishnā, your uncle will be down upon you like a shot. You must leave his house instantly. Your life is not safe there; and I cannot stop any longer in this neighbourhood: I must take my family away from here, and you must go with us. I will give you a home and protection in my house.'"

I love the said native pādrī and his missionary, and do not mention these things in a complaining or unkind spirit, but simply for the truth of history, and as illustrative of the principles of my Mission in contrast with those of older Indian Missions.

Poor Krishnā, knowing so well the positive character of his Hindū uncle, yielded to fear, and lost his peace; and now came weeping, and saying, "What shall I do?"

"Do that cowardly dodge, and you will bring disgrace on our cause that we cannot wipe off in months to come; and it would be an insult to your uncle that you never could explain away. It would be saying in effect, 'My uncle is such a bloody monster that I had to run for my life, and hide in a Mission compound.' Go right home, my brother, and write your uncle, and tell him that you have received Christ and become a Christian, and that you are stopping in his house, and with his permission will remain there. If he shall come and drive you out, you will find plenty of room outside; but don't go out till ordered out by your uncle. Go to your business to-day as usual. Do your duty to God and to man; receive and trust Christ, at all times, for everything you need, and never fear what man can do to you." I then prayed with him; and he received Christ as his strength, and went and did just as I advised him to do. Meantime I asked George Miles, who had known his uncle, to write him, and put in a word for Krishnā. He wrote accordingly, and gave Chowey a general account of the great work of God in Bombay, and how he and many of his old friends in this city, whom he mentioned by name, had received Jesus, and had been saved from sin; that though called Christians when he knew them, they were not real Christians then, but now had got hold of the right thing; and that he was happy to inform him that his nephew, Krishnā, had become one of his Christian brothers, and was very happy.

Captain Winckler called on Krishnā, and read Miles' letter to him, greatly to his comfort. Brother Andrew Taylor also met him, and spoke words of comfort to him.

Thus, while we have no rupees to offer, and no compounds in which to hide away native converts, we give them all the moral support we can, to help them to stand firmly in their home relations, and fulfil all their home duties. I am sure we are right, according to apostolic precedents and principles.

22nd.—Visited Krishnā and his brothers. Had a serious talk with Trimbuck and Anā, and prayed with them. Preached at half-past seven, but no definite result. Arranged for a series of prayer-meetings, specially for the conversion of the heathen—that is, to pray for wisdom and willingness to work "together with God" in the fulfilment of His purpose concerning them.

Saturday, 25th.—Rev. Narrainsheshādrā called at our place to-day, and I arranged with him to join me in an out-door service for English-speaking natives next Monday, at five p.m., near the Queen's statue. He said there were hundreds of educated natives leaving office at that hour, and we could take them on the wing.

A glorious fellowship band at our place this evening. Brother Krishnā told a good experience. He says he is ready to die for Jesus now; indeed, he would glory in dying for Jesus, if He should so order. I am sure he would—not from natural courage at all, but from heart-loyalty to God, and the martyr-spirit inspired in him by the Holy Ghost.

Sabbath, 26th.—At eight a.m. preached at Umercārry, and led Brother Coen's band. At eleven a.m., in Frāmjī Cawāsjī Hall, Brother Bowen preached,

—transparently and sweetly, as he always does. I preached there at six p.m., and administered the sacrament to ninety-two communicants. Our circuit is seven miles long; so that only about half of our members can get there.

As we came out from the meeting, I saw Krishna's tearful, smiling face in the moonlight, as he exclaimed, "Oh, I have received my blessed Lord Jesus; and I would not give Him up for ten thousand worlds like this!"

He had given up all hope of his earthly inheritance, but now found that, as an heir of eternal glory, he was rich beyond compute.

Monday, 27th.—Preached in the open air, near the Queen's statue, at six p.m. Had about 150 attentive, English-speaking native hearers. We had the moral support of Sisters Raitt, Morris, Ainsworth, the Misses Miles, and other sisters; and a number of our brethren.

Led the soldiers' band at Captain Christian's, and appointed Brother Durant in place of Captain Winckler, who is booked for Aden. So Aden and Winckler's name are put down together on our Plan. He is an earnest worker, and ready to be used as God shall appoint. He goes under engagement to take charge of the coal depôt in Aden. He speaks half a dozen languages, and will surely find a chance to speak for Jesus through some of them.

Tuesday, 28th.—Preached again at Queen's statue at six p.m., to about 150 hearers. After explaining the "Word of God," I called for "the testimony for Jesus" from a few of our witnesses.

Brothers Morris, Boyd, and John Fido told their experience. John Fido works in the Government Mint. After telling how he had verified the truth of God's Word, and got the demonstration of the Spirit that Jesus is a living Saviour, he appealed to a Parsee who works in the same department with himself, saying, "Dhanjībhāī, you know what a swearing, bad-tempered, drinking, abusive man I was before I received Christ, don't you?"

"Yes," replied the Parsee; "I know it well."

"Now, Dhanjībhāī, if you have seen one act of my life, or heard one word from my lips, not in accordance with the testimony I here give, that Jesus Christ has saved me from sin, and is daily preserving me from sinning, then proclaim it before this congregation."

The Parsee responded, "All that Mr. Fido has said is true. Everybody in the Mint sees and speaks of the change in him."

I then summed up the evidence, and added,—"You all know the nature of testimony, my friends: what a man thinks, or hopes, or believes, is not testimony. Let any witness in court begin to tell what he believes, or thinks, or hopes, and the judge will stop him at once. Nothing short of a plain statement of facts within the knowledge of a credible witness will be received as testimony. That is precisely the character of the testimony just now given. You know these gentlemen: you know that their testimony would stand in any court in the empire. You observe they have not said one word about their opinions, hopes, or beliefs, but have made a plain statement of facts which they know to be facts. With some circumstantial variety in regard to outlying incidents, they all essentially agree on the real point at issue. You are therefore, bound, gentlemen, to do one of two things: either to impeach the testimony of these witnesses, by showing that they are fools, and don't know whereof they affirm, or liars, making a false statement; or, admitting their testimony, to accept the fact it proves,—viz., that Jesus Christ is alive, and the available Saviour of guilty men."

Rev. Narrainsheshādrā then followed, with an exhortation in Mārāttī. He is an eloquent speaker; but made some cut that offended a Parsee, who was becoming boisterous and wanted to debate.

I said to him, "My friend, if you wish to talk, come to my house, or invite me to yours. Or if you want to explain your religion, appoint your time and place, and I will come and hear you, and will not disturb your meeting. We cannot allow any discussion here."

At seven p.m. we had a prayer-meeting for the native work in the "Old Home." Krishnā prayed in public for the first time—tremblingly, but plainly, and well.

Wednesday, 29th.—About 150 at the out-door service; and deepening attention. At the evening prayer-meeting Krishnā prayed again.

Thursday, 30th.—Had over 300 at our out-door service. Brothers Christian, Shaw, and John Fido followed with their testimony.

Rev. Dhanjībhāī also spoke; but while speaking in Hindūstānī a Parsee flared up, saying, "I know you: it's all humbug,"—and went on with abusive words, till Brother Bailey, inspector of police, took him aside, and said to him, "You would not allow us to disturb your gatherings for worship: why disturb ours?"

Supposing that Bailey was going to arrest the disturber, there was a rush of the Parsees, composing about half of our audience, to the spot.

I started a hymn, and all our party joined in singing,—

> "God is my strong salvation:
> What foe have I to fear?—
> In darkness and temptation,
> My Light, my Help is near.
> Though hosts encamp around me,
> Firm in the fight I stand:
> What terror can confound me,
> With God at my right hand?"

In a few moments we had them all back, and many more. It was upon the whole a very good meeting; deep attention by many, and some in tears. Good prayer-meeting in the evening.

Krishnā is growing nicely, but Trimbuck is getting into sad complications. The native pādrī can't get him over to his church, but is keeping him out of mine. His Hindū friends, reckoning him as one of themselves, tell him "what a fool Krishnā is to give up his inheritance and wife, and all his prospects, for nothing!"

Friday, 31st.—Visited Krishnā this morning. Found him sick with heavy cold, fever, and toothache,—a little discipline, tempered by the Master. He is sweetly resting in Jesus.

Saturday, June 1st.—Attended two fellowship bands, and read the "Rules." Captain and Sister Winckler sailed to-day for Aden. I hope they will put up a lighthouse on that dark Arabian coast.

Sabbath, June 2nd.—Preached in Frāmjī Cawāsjī Hall at eleven a.m., on "Watch and pray that ye enter not into temptation." Also in the evening, on "A new commandment give I unto you, that ye love one another." About a score of Hindūs present. One young man was converted to God.

Monday, June 3rd.—Had about 300 Hindūs and Parsees at the out-door service. I gave them an exposition of the moral law, and illustrated by the experience of a Būdhist doctor in Ceylon. Several brethren witnessed for Christ.

4th.—Held fourteen family services this morning. Preached in the open air at half-past five p.m., to over 300: deepening attention.

5th.—Out-door service about the same as yesterday.

Thursday, 6th.—A little late in getting to out-door appointment, being detained in the prison service. Coming in sight of the place, I saw a large crowd, and supposed that some one was talking to them; but on arrival I found that they were quietly waiting for me—some 300 Hindūs and Parsees waiting for the preacher to come. God is giving me favour with this people. The heathen of Antioch in Pisidia besought Paul and Barnabas to preach "the same words to them." Here are ancient mountains and hills unscathed and apparently impregnable; but God is true, and "every mountain and hill shall be brought low."

Our people are praying for power; I believe they will not cease till they get it, even if years shall intervene. The Saviour's whole ministry was mainly devoted to preparing workers for the Pentecostal harvest. This is but our commencement in Bombay.

Sabbath, 9th.—Preached to soldiers in Colāba, at nine a.m. In Frāmjī Cawāsjī Hall, at eleven, Brother Shaw preached a very good sermon on the "cloud of witnesses." Shaw is a Dublin Irishman, served his time as a draper, and had good business prospects, but took a "go-fever," similar to that which carried off the Prodigal Son to a far country; so he enlisted as trooper, and went to India. He had been a Wesleyan in his youth, and knew the Lord; but had been suddenly thrown off the track by an extra pressure of steam in the form of a hasty temper. On his voyage to India, however, falling in with a godly fellow-soldier, he was reclaimed. He did not long remain a trooper, but became an earnest worker among soldiers in the capacity of an army Scripture reader. He went as such in the expedition to Abyssinia, where he suffered much, wrought hard, and got some valuable experience. As Scripture reader he had a good position in Colāba—the military cantonment of Bombay. He was offered ordination in the regular line of "apostolical succession from St. Peter," but respectfully declined.

As soon as we organized in Bombay, he joined us, and is a very effective preacher, and an indefatigable worker.

Tuesday, 11th.—Doctor Vitters kindly tendered his large upper room for native meetings after the out-door preaching, where we invite all serious ones to go with us indoors. It rained this afternoon, causing our meeting to be late; but about a dozen Hindūs went to Dr. Vitters' room, and we had a good talk, and a prayer-meeting.

Wednesday, 12th.—Over 300 at out-door preaching. One Parsee and a few Hindūs at the after-meeting.

13th.—Out-door work about the same as yesterday. The Editor of the *Bombay Guardian*, in a notice of our out-door preaching, makes the following observations about our English agency:—

"The writer has been preaching for twenty-four years in the vernacular in the open air in Bombay; but it is a new thing to preach with a body of Christians, ladies and gentlemen, European and native, giving the moral force of their presence and prayers, uniting occasionally in singing, and ready to bear their personal testimony to the value of a true faith in Christ. It is not easy to overrate the importance of this kind of demonstration. Many of the natives have the idea that the majority of Europeans would scorn to identify themselves with the missionary, and that he has not their sympathy in the work of preaching the Gospel to the people of this country. They are much impressed by the evidence now furnished that there are many who profess to know Christ as their personal Saviour, and under the influence of their faith in Him have a sincere desire to welcome them, the people of this country, as brethren and sisters in Christ. The audiences generally listen with interest and respect; though it sometimes happens that there are some present of the 'baser sort' mentioned in the Acts, who delight in jeering and derisory shouting, and sometimes proceed to violence. This only helps to test the faith of those engaged in this work. The open-air preachings are followed by a prayer-meeting, in-doors, to which all disposed are invited."

14th.—A young Parsee wrote me a letter yesterday, addressed to the "President of the Esplanade Preaching Society," asking my name and address. He came to-day to my room at Major Raitt's,—this being my home when in Byculla, as Brother George Miles' was my home when working in the Fort and Colāba. The young Parsee was not much awakened, but interested in the preaching, and much struck with the testimony of so many witnesses, and wanted to learn. I gave him two hours of instruction, and he said he would come again. He had been a student—went up for matriculation, but failed; and was now an apprentice in a mercantile firm.

I heard Brother Christian preach at Mrs. Miles to about sixty persons. He is developing well as a preacher. Took cold to-day, weary and worn with excessive work: not weary *of* the work, but *in* it. God is my strength; but He will have me give closer attention to His physical laws—especially His sabbatic provision of rest for body and mind. My great weakness is to overtax my strength.

Saturday, 15th.—Two Parsees called to-day as enquirers after truth, and listened attentively, but are not deeply awakened. About 400 at the outdoor service. Slight diversion by a drunken Hindū; but I believe we carried our lines nearer the base of the mountain. "The morning cometh." Glory be to God!

Sabbath, 16th.—Krishnā dined with us, and had a long talk with a Hindū prisoner. The young Parsee—Nourosjee—came again to-day. I instructed him, and Krishnā told him his experience. A solid little man, named Flint, was saved to-night in Frāmjī Cawāsjī Hall. Trimbuck, too, was greatly moved, but I learn was kept back.

Tuesday, 18th.—Good meeting on the Esplanade: about 300; and about a dozen at the after-meeting at Dr. Vitters'. One young Hindū seemed under awakening, and opened his mind freely.

Wednesday, 19th.—As I was preaching on the Esplanade to-day, a large Hindū placed a stone about six feet from the one on which I stood, and mounting it, stood facing me. I paid no attention to him, and preached on as though he had not appeared; but as soon as our varied exercises were over, he opened a quiet, but very bitter abuse of the Bible, and held up a book which he said "exposed the contradictions and the demoralizing teaching of the Bible." Then he tried to offset the testimony of half a dozen respectable men who had testified to their personal knowledge of Christ as a Saviour from sin.

I asked him what religion he wished to offer to the people; and found that, though nominally a Hindū, he was an infidel in the broadest sense. Several young Parsees then joined him, and wanted me to answer foolish questions, and debate,—about half a dozen of them talking at the same time.

I said, "This is an illustration of one of the reasons

I gave you for refusing to debate from the beginning. Here are five or six of you, representing different religions, all vociferating at once. If any of you wish to ask me questions, or to talk to me, come to Major Raitt's house, where I live, or ask me to yours, and I'll talk to you by the hour if you wish; but I won't have this at all."

I then sang a hymn, our people joining heartily, till all became quiet, and dismissed the congregation. I saw, however, that a majority of the crowd sympathized with the infidel Hindū. The truth was getting hold of many of them; but his defiant attitude, and blatant infidel thrusts, stirred up their pride and prejudices.

21st.—Rained heavily last night, and frequent showers to-day. Brother Coen told me of John Lewis, engineer of the steamship "Delhi," who is very ill in one of the Peninsular and Oriental Co.'s buildings. I found him very low, but sensible, and in great distress about his soul. I watched, and talked, and prayed with him for over an hour and a half; when he received Christ, and said, "Oh, I am so happy—so happy! This is the happiest moment of my life. I have been seeking the Lord for years, but never found Him till now."

I sang one or two hymns, which he seemed to enjoy, but did not know them. I then sang "I do believe," and "Come to Jesus just now." Those he knew, and joined in singing; and said at the close, "Oh, so beautiful! Hallelujah! hallelujah!"

'Tis said he leaves a wife and five children in England. I was afterwards told that he died happy an hour after I left him. Brother Coen had written his will and attended to his temporalities before he sent for me.

Preached to the prisoners at three p.m. When I went to my out-door preaching-place, there stood the infidel Hindū on his rock, waiting.

I said to him, "You may have observed—or I can tell you, and these gentlemen will bear me witness—that I have not abused any man, nor attacked any man's religion; and our meetings were orderly till you came to make confusion. If I should attack your religion, and abuse your gods, then you might have provocation for reply; but I have not done so, and don't propose to do so. I come to speak in friendship and love to all who wish to hear, on what I know to be true, and of vital importance to every one as well as to myself. If any do not wish to stop and listen to me, the road is open to them; and it is open to you, if you don't like my words. If you have any communications for the people, set your time, and I'll promise that I will not disturb your meeting."

After a little cross-firing for about ten minutes, he said, "It was clear yesterday that the people were more anxious to hear me than to hear you; so we will let the people decide who is to speak here to-day."

He was going to shunt me clean off the track by a vote of the people. Though he had displayed no power of sound reason or common sense in anything he had said, he showed great impudence and some cunning.

He proceeded to put the question—saying, "Let all who wish to hear me instead of this man, hold up their hands."

A shabby-looking vagabond began to put up his hand, but seeing no others go up, he suddenly pulled it down; so the Hindū got but one half-vote of one hesitating hand.

"That settles the question, gentlemen," said I; and proceeded at once to preach to them. I had a very attentive audience of about 400. I observed among them more middle-aged and elderly Parsees than before.

Near the close of the sermon, a drunken Afghān pressed his way to the front, and wanted to open a debate,—throwing his arms about, reeling from side to side, and vociferating incoherently.

I said, "Whose champion is this? What party does he represent? Who claims him?"

Different parties said, "He is not our man."

"Now you see, my friends," I said, "how impossible it is to keep order, if we allow debate. Any irresponsible drunken man may join in, and it must end in wrangling and confusion; so I say again, we will have no debating here."

I followed my sermon with my testimony for Jesus, sang, and gave out my appointments for Sabbath and next week. The Hindū remained firmly on his perch, looking daggers at me all the time. As soon as I had done, he and a young Parsee wanted me to read and answer questions which they had written out on paper. I refused to look at them—saying, "I have said all I have to say on this occasion. If any of you wish to listen to my friend in the opposition, do so. Salām! Salām!"

The Hindū commenced to talk, but the mass of the people followed me, and cheered vociferously as I entered our carriage and drove away.

God turned the tide in my favour, and I had the sympathy of the crowd. A few returned, as I learned, to hear the Hindū—who seemed greatly confused.

Walter Winckler said to him, "Go on, and say what you had to say."

He tried to recall something I had said; and Winckler said, "*Kya bolā?*" (What did you say?) The people laughed at his discomfiture, and he left.

Sabbath, 23rd.—Regular services as usual; very good meetings.

24th.—Hindūs and Parsees now call frequently to talk in a friendly way. God is beginning to move among them. We cannot see a week ahead, as to our plans of work; but He is leading us.

25th.—Pouring rain; could not go into the streets.

26th.—Raining same as yesterday.

28th.—Had "Leaders' and Stewards' meeting" at Major Raitt's; and seventeen persons who had fulfilled their term of probation were recommended by their leaders for admission to full membership in our Church.

Sabbath, 30th.—I preached at Colāba at nine a.m. In Frāmjī Cawāsjī Hall, Brother Shaw at eleven a.m., and I in the evening; after which I received from the probationers' list into full membership, according to our "Book of Discipline," the following

14

persons:—James and Julia Morris, Major and Rosalina C. Raitt, W. A. E. Boyd, William and Eliza Ashdown, George Miles, Matilda Miles, Dorathea, Emily and Alice Miles, Mary and Julia Cassidy, C. W. Christian, Captain Joseph and Eliza Winckler. The following were admitted on their previous standing in other churches:—William J. Coen, James Shaw, Joseph and Mrs. Powell. Altogether twenty-one: the first full members in our new Mission. All this was novel and impressive to the congregation. We then called for seekers,—when a Scotchman and a Parsee came forward. The Scotchman got "the assurance of faith."

I spent seven hours and a half the other day in opening the Scriptures to Nourosjee. After we prayed, he said, "I feel very jolly now"; but he had not received Jesus.

Monday, July 1st.—Had Quarterly Conference at half-past five p.m. at Mrs. Miles', and love-feast in the evening, in the large hall of her new residence in Falkland Road. She tenders us the use of this hall, thirty feet by ninety, without charge—except twenty rupees per month for lighting and attendance. The Quarterly Conference recommended Brother James Shaw for licence to do duty as a local preacher. Hall crowded at the love-feast. Brothers Morris, Shaw, and Christian professed to be "sanctified wholly"; and the speaking was, as usual, clear, short, and to the point, and no time lost in waiting for one another.

A Parsee who had been twice to see me for instruction, and was under deep awakening through

TRIMBUCK CANAREN.

[Opposite p. 211.

the agency of Brother Jurain, stood up and told us that he had just received Jesus, and had got his sins forgiven.

At the close of the sacramental service, George Mann, and Arājee, the said Parsee, came forward and were baptized; after which Arājee again spoke, and said he was very happy, and asked the people to pray for him. The Parsees have been hitherto more inaccessible than the Mohamedans, but I believe many of them feel their need of a Saviour, and that God will lead them into the light.

Our meeting closed at ten p.m.; and after many had gone, as I was passing out, I saw Trimbuck and Anā, Krishnā's brothers, lingering at the door in deep distress. I warned them of the danger of delay, and said to Anā, "If you wish, we will go back into the room and pray for you; and if you will submit to God, and accept Christ, you will get forgiveness of your sins to-night. Will you?"

"Yes."

"If you get the pardon of your sins, is it your wish also to be baptized to-night?"

He hesitated, and declined to answer.

I then made a similar appeal to Trimbuck, and he consented. He had lost his peace, as before explained, and was now extremely unhappy.

With twenty-five or thirty sisters and brothers who had not gone away, we had a prayer-meeting for about half an hour,—when he obtained peace with God. After testifying to the fact of his pardon, he added, "Now I want to be baptized. I want to be baptized to-night, for I know not what may be to-morrow." So I baptized him. As soon as I said "Amen," he started off in haste, I knew not whither, till I saw him sit down by his brother Anā. Very soon he "brought him to Jesus." We then prayed with Anā till he got rest for his soul; and at his own request I baptized him. I then administered the Lord's Supper to them. What a blessed night! All glory to God, the Holy Trinity!

The Parsee is a mechanic in the Great Indian Peninsular Railway works, and has a wife. The two Hindūs are single men, in the Custom-house service,—sons of well-to-do parents, and pretty well educated.

Some say, "Ah! it is a small matter to get them converted, after they are educated."

But the educated classes, including the thousands from Mission schools, are, above all others, the most difficult to lead into the kingdom of God. Knowledge without the grace of God "puffeth up," and they get too wise to be taught, and too much inflated to get through the "strait gate." In the few cases of conversion among educated natives, their education, of course, is a blessing to the churches to which they belong.

Tuesday, July 2nd.—Commenced a series of lectures for natives, in the General Assembly's Hall, on Scripture history and geography, illustrated from my large map of Egypt, Arabia, and Palestine. Had a fair congregation—principally of Hindūs; and good attention. I want to help them to study the Bible, and become acquainted with "the record of God concerning His Son."

3rd.—Not so many at the lecture as last night; but very attentive.

4th.—About the same as last night; but many of them are students, and but few merchants.

5th.—Spent two hours with Krishnā, Trimbuck, and Anā, singing, praying, and expounding the Scriptures. The Holy Spirit is teaching them, and they are progressing encouragingly. Heavy rain; but about the same number at the lecture as the two preceding nights. The Esplanade is now so covered with water, on account of the rains, that we cannot have open-air preaching. The wet season will continue for several months.

Saturday, 6th.—Dined with Brother Morris. Nourosjee came here to see me. His awakening has been gradually deepening for some weeks. He said at different times, that his mind was so disturbed that he often took the wrong street, and wandered off out of his course. I was getting fearful that, if he did not get rest in Christ, he would go mad. To-day he came in great distress; and I, with Brother and Sister Morris, Brother and Sister Ashdown, and Sister Alice Miles, prayed for him and instructed him. He received Jesus, got peace with God, and I baptized him.

Sabbath, 7th.—Preached at Frāmjī Cawāsjī Hall on "perfecting that which is lacking in their faith." This afternoon Trimbuck took me to see an old Hindū sceptic. Trimbuck got two days' leave of absence from business, after his baptism, and spent the time in visiting his Hindū friends, to tell them what a dear Saviour he had found: different from the old plan of this country—of hiding a young convert, to keep the Hindūs from killing him! Trimbuck spent six hours on this sceptic; who expressed to me his gratitude to the young man for the interest he had manifested on his behalf, but remains unmoved.

At six p.m. Brother Bowen preached, and I exhorted: a Mr. Bennett was saved. Krishnā, Anā, Nourosjee, and Arājee all stood up voluntarily in turn, and testified for Christ. A number of Hindūs and Parsees were listeners; and some of them, I am told, were spies, and will give trouble to our native converts.

Monday, 8th.—As I was retiring, at ten p.m., two Parsees brought a letter and handed it to me, and hurried away. It purports to be from Brother Arājee, expressing regret that he had been baptized. I know it was not written by him; and if the signature (which is in quite a different hand) is his, I am sure it was not his own voluntary act. His wife is at her father's house, and but two days since gave birth to her first child. Arājee told me that his wife was favourable to his being a Christian, and would come with him to our meetings as soon as she should recover. The persecuting wretches have, no doubt, in her low, nervous state, driven her into hysterics; and under the terror of her cries and their taunts, forced him to do, to save her life, what he never would have done to save his own.

Tuesday, 9th.—Had but few Hindūs at our lecture to-night, but a good gathering of our own people. Met Brother Jurain this afternoon, and enquired about Arājee. They work in the same shop.

He said, "A messenger came yesterday afternoon in great haste for Arājee, saying that his wife was dying. Arājee said to me, as he passed out of the shop, 'Brother Jurain, pray for me, and go to Mrs. Miles', and ask them all to pray for me. I shall be beaten, and perhaps killed. If they beat me, I'll bear it; if they kill me, I'll go to Jesus."

10th.—In addition to our own people, we had not more than a dozen Hindūs.

11th.—About the same number at the lecture to-night as last. It is a drawn battle, if not a failure. There is a terrible combination against us just now. An official member of a church, and one of the trustees of this Hall, sent a bitter protest to all the members of the Board against allowing me to lecture in it. One good old man wrote on the protest circular, that it was a pity for them, as Christians, to refuse, when the Parsees allowed us the use of two of their halls—one for rent, and the other free. A majority concurred in that sentiment, and so we got the Hall; but there is a strong counter-current, perhaps from the same quarter, which is felt among the natives,—and, on the other hand, the baptism of two Parsees and two Hindūs within less than a fortnight, frightens the natives in some quarters, and provokes terrible opposition in others.

Friday, 12th.—Called to see Brother Jurain, to enquire about Arājee. He said, "For several days he did not return to business, but has been there the last day-and-a-half, guarded by three Parsees to and from the shop; and is closely watched whilst he is at work. In all that time I only got about a minute's talk with him ; and he said, 'My wife was dying. I was imprisoned for three days, and threatened with death, and now you see I am under guard. What can I do?' "

Saturday, 13th.—Nourosjee came; and I read with him eight chapters of the Gospel by Mark. He is quick to learn. We prayed together. He prayed intelligently, and in beautiful simplicity.

Sabbath, 14th.—Prayer-meeting with our native brothers at Major Raitt's, at three p.m. They pray with great earnestness. Nourosjee had been besieged by infidel Parsees and Hindūs. They showed him a great many infidel books, and insisted on his reading them. To quiet their clamour, he brought one away with him, entitled "Absurdities of Christianity"—an octavo volume printed in the Guzerāttī language. He had also written down a number of infidel questions for me to solve. I showed him how absurd and fallacious they were. One was about Ezekiel cooking "his food with man's dung."—They assumed that it composed part of his food. I said, "Nourosjee, you know that nearly all the food eaten in India is cooked with cow's dung ; but Ezekiel foreshadows a famine which shall destroy the cattle, cut off that kind of fuel, and bring on the dreadful scarcity thus indicated."

"O yes ; I see," he replied ; and tore up his papers. He left the infidel book in my room, and read it not.

Nourosjee said, "It was laid upon my soul this morning to find Brother Arājee, and if imprisoned, to get him out. I know not where he lives, but was going along praying and hoping that I might find him, when all of a sudden I met him in the street, guarded by three men. Arājee told him the same sad story related to us by Brother Jurain.

"Who are troubling you now?" enquired Nourosjee. "Are these the fellows who are threatening you? You should stand up like a man, and die for Jesus."

He says, "Poor Arājee has succumbed, and lost his courage."

Arājee subsequently stepped aside with Jurain, and said, "Brother Jurain, sing softly about the bleeding Lamb"; and Jurain sang in a low tone,—

"My Saviour suffered on the tree:
O come and praise the Lord with me.

He bore my sin and curse and shame,
And I am saved by Jesus' Name.

I know my sins are all forgiven,
And I am on my way to heaven."

Chorus (between each couplet):

"The Lamb, the Lamb, the bleeding Lamb!
I love the sound of Jesus' Name;
It sets my spirit in a flame:
Glory to the bleeding Lamb!"

When his guards saw him with Jurain, they came and ordered him away. About fifty men in the shop—Parsees, Hindūs, and Mohamedans, led by a few so-called Christians—with dreadful curses and threats made a set upon Jurain for getting the Parsee to "change his religion"; but Jurain witnessed for Jesus, saying, "You know what a vagabond I was before I received Christ; and you have been with me here every day since, and have seen the change in me. Jesus Christ saves me from all sin, and preserves me from sinning, and has taken away from me the fear of death. You can kill me if you like: I am ready." They sneaked off, and left him.

Monday, 15th.—This afternoon Trimbuck brought a Parsee to see me, who spoke to me last night after the meeting in Frāmjī Cawāsjī Hall,—Ardesheer. I talked to him for two hours. He said he was so distressed on account of his sins after our meeting last evening, that he could not sleep. He says he has been studying Christianity for several years, but is not attracted by the Missions in Bombay; and told me many things about their operations, which I partly knew before. I prayed for him; and he said he would seek from that hour till he should find Jesus.

CHAPTER XVII.

INVITATION TO POONA.

I SAID to some friends at Major Raitt's, "Suppose I go to Poona a few weeks during these heavy rains?" It was quite a casual remark. I had no serious thought of going soon, for I knew of no friends there to visit, and could not see my way to leave Bombay in the midst of so interesting a native work as was opening up daily. A few minutes after this remark was made, Brother Henry Bailey, Inspector of the E Division of Bombay Police, came in and said, "I am going to get two months' leave of absence, and take my family to Poona,"—and invited me to go there and stay with them, and take a little needed rest.

I considered the matter prayerfully, and on the 16th of July went second class (119 miles) to Poona.

Brother Bailey met me at the railway station, and drove me to his house.

Wednesday, 17th.—Went with Brother Bailey to market, and afterwards spent several hours at an auction, where over 3000 rupees' worth of household stuff was bid off. I had been worked nearly off the hinges; the change of scene was rest, and the earnestness of the auctioneer refreshing.

18th.—Brother Bailey drove me out to make a few calls. We called first on Doctor Fraser. His little daughter had been taken ill, and his wife had gone with her on a voyage to Scotland. It was said in Bombay that the Doctor would oppose me. The leading points in his history, as told to me, are—that he is descended from a noble family in Scotland, was born in America, graduated in a New York University, and went to Scotland to become a minister of the old Scotch Kirk, which required him to take an eight years' course in the University of Edinburgh. Meantime the disruption took place, and he went with the Free Church. He was for some time the minister of a church in France, afterwards came to Bombay, and was for some years pastor of the Free Church of Scotland on the Esplanade. He resigned that, and became a professor in one and then in another leading institution of learning, and finally a Government magistrate in Poona, on a good salary. He continues to preach sometimes in the Free Church in Poona, but is not closely identified with any church. I found him very affable and kind, and had a season of prayer with him.

We next went to see Captain Jacob and family. He said, "Rev. George Bowen wrote me that you were coming to Poona; and Colonel Field and I have been to all the hotels in search of you." I had no thought that anybody in Poona was searching for me.

Colonel Field received us very kindly. He and Colonel Phayre, both earnest Christian men, led the expedition into Abyssinia. Colonel Phayre surveyed the war-path, 400 miles, to Magdala; and Colonel Field's forces made the road and led the van.

Two African youths, educated by Rev. Dr. Wilson in Bombay, showed them the way in.

We called on Rev. Mr. Ross, Scotch Kirk chaplain, and talked to Mrs. Ross's thirty-five native orphan girls. Called at the house of Rev. Mr. Watson, the eloquent but sceptical Church chaplain; but he was not at home. Called at the "manse" of Rev. J. Beaumont, minister of the Free Church of Scotland: he was not in, but sent me a note inviting me to conduct their Thursday evening service in his church—which I did, and had an interesting time.

Friday, 19th.—Conducted a Bible class at Colonel Field's; at the close of which Mr. and Mrs. Beaumont invited me to come next week, and give a lecture to their native students and friends in their Institution Hall in the city, and conduct the Thursday night service again; and if I could arrange for special services, all the better; and said that I must put up with them. Thus my way was opened for a return visit.

Poona is high and healthy,—nearly 4000 feet above the sea. It is a large military station, and an old Mārāttī Brāhman city of 100,000 population.

Back in Bombay for Sabbath and Monday and Tuesday appointments, and returned to Poona on Wednesday the 24th of July, accompanied by Krishnā, who got four days' leave of absence from his work, and paid his own travelling expenses, that he might tell those Brāhmans about the Saviour he had found. I put up with Rev. J. Beaumont, and

Krishnā put up with Brother Bailey. On the evening of our arrival, I lectured in the Institution Hall, to about 200 Brāhmans, on the experimental evidences of Christianity. Rev. Vishnu Punt added some remarks in Mārāttī, and Krishnā witnessed for Christ by an account in detail of his awakening and conversion to God. We sang two hymns, which seemed to please the Brāhmans. All listened till the close with deep attention.

Thursday, 25th.—Preached this evening at six in the Free Church, which was well filled.

A lady in Bombay told Krishnā of a vagabond young native in Poona, whose father was for many years, till his recent death, a native minister of the Society for the Propagation of the Gospel Mission; and giving Krishnā his name and address, requested him to hunt him up, and try to get him saved. So this morning Krishnā found his house, and called at his door.

The response was, "Who's there?"

"My name is Krishnā Chowey, from Bombay."

"What do you want?"

"I have come by request of a friend to see you."

"Go away from my door: I don't want to see you."

"I promised my friend that I would see you, and I must see you."

"Well, I tell you to go away. You shall not come into my house."

"I am not going away till I see you. I'll sit down here at your door, and wait till you come out, or let me in;" and down he sat.

After a little delay he was asked to enter. He

showed the man a card on which his name was written by the friend in Bombay, and enquired, "Is that your name?"

"Yes: sit down."

Krishnā then opened up a friendly conversation with him, and gave him a history of his own life as a Hindū, and an account of his conversion to God.

By the time he had finished his narrative, his hearer was weeping bitterly, and exclaimed, "There it is: you were born and brought up a Hindū, and now you are a child of God—a Christian in deed and in truth; I was born and brought up a nominal Christian, and now I am worse than any heathen. Oh! God of my father and of my mother, what shall I do?"

Krishnā wept with him, and they kneeled together and prayed. Then the same day he brought him to me at Brother Beaumont's. I preached to him for an hour, and then the three of us went into my room and prayed till he gave his wicked heart to God, and accepted Christ.

Many months afterwards a person in Poona told me about this young man,—how wicked he had been, what an unaccountable change had come over him, and that he was then an earnest catechist in his father's church: the same individual whom my Hindū had dug up, as I have stated. Ordinary workers can't succeed in India.

On my return to Bombay, I went to stop again with Brother George Miles,—his wife and family having returned from England.

Glorious meetings at Frāmjī Cawāsjī Hall. On

Sabbath night, sacramental service; and several persons converted to God.

Monday, 29th.—Went to Egutpoora; stopped with Brother Pearcey, permanent railway inspector,—who, mostly with his own funds, had built a chapel there about twenty-six feet by forty. He was a Primitive Wesleyan local preacher. We had some encouraging meetings, but it was raining so heavily, and my time so limited, that no special result was manifest; but I visited all the families accessible, and sowed much seed, and prepared the way for future operations.

I wrote Brother Beaumont in regard to intended special services in Poona, and proposed to do what I might be able, to help him build up his own church; but that the many beyond his lines whom we hoped to get saved at our meetings should be at liberty, without any after-claps or reflections, if they in their judgment and conscience should so elect, to organize themselves into a Methodist Church, as so many had done in Bombay. He, after consulting Rev. John Wilson, D.D., of Bombay, wrote me, fully concurring in my proposition—saying, "If I can see people brought to repentance, they may become Methodists, or whatever they like."

Sabbath, August 4th.—A young Parsee—Shārpūrjee — who had been to many of my meetings, came to Brother Miles' this afternoon; and as I taught him the way of the Lord, and prayed for him, he professed to receive the Saviour, and a knowledge of forgiveness of sins.

After the evening preaching in Frāmjī Cawāsji Hall, Ardesheer came forward as a seeker, and after a season of prayer, in which many earnest souls participated, he found peace, and stood up before the congregation, and made a good confession; but he wished to defer his baptism till he could get his wife to receive Christ also, and then they would be baptized together. He said that he had spoken to her about it, and she was quite inclined to become a Christian. This he said quietly to a few of us who sat near him. I warned him against the danger of delay; and he so far yielded the point, that I believe if I had pressed the matter he would have consented, and I could have baptized him and Shārpūrjee also, that night. That would have put them across the visible bridge which spans the gulf separating Zoroastrianism and Christ's kingdom. But as it was getting very late, and no water easily accessible, I said, "Come to-morrow night to the meeting at Mrs. Miles', and I will then baptize you both."

They assented; and we hoped it would be all right.

But upon reflection, I said, "Nothing is right that comes short of apostolic precedent. If Paul had not baptized the Philippian jailer that night, even after midnight, the probability is he never would have done so. If these dear Parsee brethren had not been well instructed, and given clear testimony to their change of heart, of course I should not have mentioned the subject of baptism to them. Natives have come to me, and begged me to baptize them; but I have never yet baptized one of that sort. On examination, I found that they were not reliable. But an honest native, who knows, according to our teaching, that he "must go home to his friends" and endure persecution, naturally shrinks from baptism; for that is the first question that his suspicious friends will ask, and they will never consider him a Christian till he is baptized : hence, in St. Paul's day, baptism marked its subjects as targets for the persecuting archers; they were "baptized for the dead." Thus to enter the Church of Christ was to become a candidate for the regions of the dead.

In sorrow I seemed to realize the struggle and failure of Ardesheer. His father is a physician, and hence the family is of some note. Spies will go in advance, and lay the persecuting train to blow him off the track. When he gets home to-night, his friends in angry excitement will say, "Well, you have gone off from your nation, and scandalized your family."

"What is it all about?"

"Oh, you know very well what you have done."

"What have I done?"

"You wicked hypocrite!—are you going to try to conceal your shame, and deceive your friends, whom you have disgraced?"

"I have not disgraced them."

"You lie; you think we don't know about your scandalous conduct,"—half a dozen yelling around him at the same time.

Now comes the temptation to dissimulation.

"You all think that I have been baptized; but it is not true."

"You are lying. We know you have been baptized; you think we don't know that you publicly denounced your nation and family, and declared yourself a Christian."

"I don't know what you have heard; but I declare to you that I have not been baptized."

Three weeks after, when I was in Poona, he came to Mrs. Miles' with a Parsee witness, and stood up in the meeting, and gave expression to a few sentiments in favour of Christianity—sentiments that he had avowedly entertained for years—but stated that he had never been baptized, and did not see any use for such a ceremony. We learned afterwards, that the struggle I anticipated was substantially just what he passed through; that he had been starved for days, affirming that he had not been baptized, and they would not believe him; and he took the plan I have named to convince his friends of the truth of his statement. The apostles guarded their converts against the danger of such a well-circumstanced temptation by their baptismal initiation into the visible church of Christ. Thus indentured to God, and abiding in Jesus, they were ready to suffer anything that God would permit.

If I could have remained in Bombay the week after his conversion, I might have helped him. The poor fellow called at Major Raitt's to see me, but I had gone. When a Hindū, Parsee, or Mohamedan, thus lays himself open to the charge of becoming a Christian, he is bound, within a fortnight or less, to come out fully on the Lord's side, and confess Him before men, or purge himself of the suspicion by denouncing Christ. Every soul-saving man among the heathen ought, therefore, to be empowered to put a convert into his right relation to the visible Church of God. A man of God who can bring a heathen to Christ, and secure to him, by faith, the baptism of the Holy Ghost, and yet with no authority to apply a little water to him, and enrol him as a soldier for Jesus, is a man not "throughly furnished unto every good work." To be sure, we want all our lay men and women to be soul-savers; but there should be a sufficient supply of ministers available—which has been a painful lack in some parts of our Mission in India. In regard to Shārpūrjee, I did not entertain very much fear; but I did not see him again for two years. The day after I should have baptized him, a catechist got hold of him, as I learned afterwards, and represented to him that "Taylor is a mere adventurer and foreigner, and can do nothing for you, but here is the venerable Rev. ——, who can do everything for you;" and before the week was out, he was secured in the compound of the said Rev. ——. Then, as usual, there was a great furor among his friends about "the outrage of stealing a man away and hiding him," and a plan for his recovery,—of which they have many. So two Parsee gentlemen drove up in their carriage before the said Rev. ——'s door, and enquired for the young man Shārpūrjee. On learning that he was there, they said to the Rev. ——:

"His father is dangerously ill with cholera, and is most anxious to see his son before he shall die. Will you not allow him to come and see his dying father?"

After a little hesitation, the Rev.—— said, "If you

will allow me and Rev. Mr.—— to accompany him, we will consent to his going."

"O yes; of course you and your friend can come."

The two good ministers, who were acting in good faith in the whole transaction, took him between them in their carriage, and drove to his father's house. The young man was ushered in, and the ministers were told "This is a Parsee's house; you cannot be allowed to come in." So they had nothing to do but go home; and the young man was sent away from the city.

If I had baptized him, he would have gone home and stood his ground, without stirring up the old feud growing out of this "compound system." There are difficulties enough, in any event, but the only safe way is to follow strictly the precepts and examples of the Book. [I have to say, however, for Shārpūrjee, that a few months since (1875) he was baptized by the same good minister, and is under his protection now.]

Tuesday, August 13th.—Took the train for Poona at ten a.m. Brothers James Morris, Walter Winckler, and Nourosjee accompanied me, to help in the work. Lectured the same night to a large congregation of Brāhmans in the Institution Hall, Poona City. Brothers Morris and Nourosjee testified for Jesus after my lecture. It was a good meeting. I stopped with Colonel Field, Morris with Brother Beaumont, Nourosjee with Brother Bailey, and Winckler with Mr. De Sauza, of the "Great Trigonometrical Survey."

CHAPTER XVIII.

THE SIEGE OF POONA.

WE commenced operations at six p.m. on Wednesday the 14th of August 1872.

Brother Morris had to return to Bombay early in the following week; but, during his short stay, God used him to lead about a dozen of the native young women of the Scotch Orphanage to Jesus, and he taught them to sing some our hymns. They became the leaders of the congregation in that important part of worship.

Saturday, 17th.—I presided at a lecture on the immortality of the soul, delivered by Narrain, an educated Hindū. About two years ago a mutual improvement society for natives was got up—principally through the agency of a Jew. This society has a public lecture nearly every Saturday night. On this occasion over 100 persons were present,—mostly Hindūs, with a few Parsees.

The lecture to-night was of a superior order—in philosophy purely European, in religion orthodox. The lecturer gave some telling illustrations from the dying experience of French and English infidels. Any stranger hearing him would have set him down as a Gospel minister, and it was astonishing to me that he could remain a Hindū; but he is just like millions in England and America, who believe the Bible to be the Word of God, but are held by their carnal lusts, and the fear of man, fast bound in the service of sin and Satan.

In my application at the close of the lecture, I described a few triumphant death-scenes of the children of God, as Narrain had done of the infidels.

Sabbath, 18th.—Preached morning and evening in the Free Church, to about 150 hearers.

Monday, 19th.—Bombay reinforcements (Brothers Shaw, Krishnā, and Jurain) arrived; and the work went on vigorously. Among the "firstfruits," outside of the Orphanage, were Angelo De Sauza, James Cristie and his wife and her sisters, the Misses Mulligan, and their cousins William and Arthur Wright. These, with a host of others, have all become earnest and effective workers for God. [My limited time and space preclude my diary notes of daily details.]

Dr. Fraser attended our meetings from the commencement. His sick daughter died on the voyage homeward, and he was now in deep bereavement.

He wrote me during the second week of our work, and referred to one of my illustrations defining the difference between the good works of a formalist, however sincere, and the living fruits of the Spirit in the life of a true child of God. The illustration was this:—"Passing through the cocoanut groves of Ceylon, I frequently saw four little cocoanut trees standing at right-angles, forming a square. The trees were only about fifteen feet high; but each one, from the ground up, was loaded with cocoanuts, and ornamented with leaves and flowers. Any superficial observer would have given judgment in favour of the little trees before all the trees of the forest—'These are the trees! so full of fruit and so easy of access! Those stately trees have only a few bunches of cocoanuts hid away among the long leaves in the top, nearly a hundred feet up; but a small crop, and hard to gather.' What were the real facts of the case? The four fruit-bearing trees, so much admired, mark the spot where a dead man sleeps. When the Singhalese Būdhists bury a man, they plant down four rootless stems of trees, and tie on all the fruit and foliage from the outside: it is all 'put on.' That is a dead Christian—'ignorant of God's righteousness, and going about to establish his own.' Examine the live cocoanut tree, and you will find no redundancy nor needless display of fruit, but only in proportion to its real fruit-producing power. It gets none of its life or strength from its fruit, but from the soil, air, water, and light which God gives it—not a cocoanut 'put on' from without, but the result of real vital properties within. That is the true Christian." The Doctor in his letter said he had been in the Lord from his youth, but had got mixed up with the world, and though keeping up the form of godliness, the most of his works were cocoanuts "put on." He read my book "The Election of Grace," got his mind entirely cleared of certain kinks of his old creed, carefully studied the simple doctrines I daily set forth from the Word of God, and got into clear and blessed union with Jesus.

I had to spend every other Sabbath in Bombay; but Brother Bowen alternated with me, and the siege of Poona was steadily kept up. Many soldiers and civilians professed to find pardon at our meetings, who did not become members of my church. It is a principle with us not to persuade, nor directly to ask any one to join us. Those voluntarily unite with us, who are convinced that it is their duty by the force of our Bible teaching and the leading of the "Spirit of truth." In fact, we are a "sect so much spoken against," in India, that no one would think of joining us, except from a clear conviction of duty, and the martyr spirit of self-sacrifice—in the development of which they pass through a sifting, testing process, which deters all who do not imbibe fully our doctrines and spirit. Thus we secure a homogeneous body, "perfectly joined together in the same mind and in the same judgment; and all speak the same thing."

When unsuitable candidates chance to drift in among us, our "six months' probation" gives them the opportunity of finding out their mistake; and those who are "not of us go out from among us."

The church in whose house of worship our meetings were held did not share so largely in the fruits of the work of God there as we sincerely hoped, because several of their leading families declined to co-operate, or even to attend the meetings. It was a great pity; for I am sure God had a great blessing in store for all of them, and they might have built up a powerful spiritual church, as many in connexion with my work have done in different parts of the world. Rev. Mr. Lindsay, a Free Church minister in Launceston, Tasmania, brought his people to my meetings, by his own example got them into the work, had more than 100 of his congregation saved, and built up a strong working church; and the next year they built a large church edifice to accommodate their increasing working force. Rev. Mr. Ketley, Congregational minister in George Town, Demerara, British Guiana, did a similar thing, and added over 130 new converts to his church; and Mr. Dalglish, of the London Mission in New Amsterdam, Berbice, got over 100 in the same way. The people will not do it unless their minister shall lead: he cannot do it unless his people will concur. I think I understand this matter thoroughly; I have seen it in so many places, and in such a variety of phases.

Saturday evening, September 28th.—We held a fellowship-meeting at the house of Brother De Sauza. Over thirty young converts spoke very clearly of the saving power of God in their hearts. I had not decided in advance to bring up the question of church organization to-night. Several had mentioned it before; but I wished them to have sufficient opportunity, by our daily preaching and work, and our weekly fellowship-meetings, to know their bearings properly, and to form an intelligent judgment as to their duty and privilege in the matter. But at the close of the speaking I was convinced that it was the will of God that we should wait no longer. So I explained that I had all through desired to build up the church in whose place of worship, kindly tendered us, they had been brought to God; and "that no member of that church would feel it his or her duty to join my church. But, according to the written agreement with their minister, I was at liberty to give an opportunity to any saved outside of his lines, to be organized into a Methodist church if they should so elect." I explained briefly what would be required of them as members with us, and reminded them of the persecutions they might expect, and that they must be fully persuaded as to their duty, and if not clear on that point, take further time to consider it. Brother De Sauza brought paper and ink; Brother Winckler took down the names—which were distinctly announced, without any personal prompting. Dr. Fraser stood up first, and gave in his name. Thirty-seven names were recorded that night. Others took further time for consideration.

Having secured a place of worship for our own church and congregation in Poona, we had our first sacramental service on Sabbath evening the 13th of October. We had about 130 hearers and sixty-four communicants. The *Deccan Herald* of the next day states that the like was never seen in Poona before.

Churches had been established there for forty years; but those who attend say, "The number of communicants in any one, at any one time, is from five to fifteen." This is God's doing,—the work of a two months' siege. Brother Fraser became a clear, powerful, local preacher in our church; Colonel Evezard, saved a few months later, another. Brother Seale, from the British army, became a successful worker as a local preacher also. The church in Poona has from the first to the present been a living, working, growing church, and has a thrifty branch at Lanowlī forty miles to the north-west, where they have built a commodious chapel, and paid for it. When Her Majesty's 56th Regiment was transferred from Poona to Synde, beyond the Indus, our converted soldiers were accompanied by their minister, Rev. D. O. Fox, and laid the foundations of a witnessing, working church in Synde. Brother Seale afterwards went and helped to develop it; and now (in 1875) Rev. Frank Goodwin is our missionary there, devising liberal measures for extending the work westward.

[I have anticipated the order of events, to fill up a hasty summary.]

CHAPTER XIX.

MISSIONARY RECRUITS.

ON the 15th of November Brother James Shaw resigned his appointment of Army Scripture Reader, and became an itinerant preacher in our Mission, unquestionably called of God to this responsible position. He comes to us with a good wife to help him—a native of Bombay.

About the same time Rev. George Bowen joined us. He came to India over twenty-five years before, as a missionary of the American Board of Foreign Missions. After a couple of years' service he became convinced that to succeed in establishing a Native Church in India, on a sound, healthy basis, would require greater self-sacrifice, and a closer assimilation to native life on the part of missionaries, than had been generally supposed to be necessary. He embodied his views in a small pamphlet, which he respectfully submitted to most of the missionaries in India at that time; but failing to get any of them to concur in his views, he felt it his duty to give his principles a tangible form in his own example. He resigned his connexion with the American Board of Foreign Missions, and proceeded in his missionary work on the self-denying, self-supporting principle. He did not propose to set up a new Mission, but became a helper of all. He gave a few hours daily to a few pupils in a private family, and thus earned a living. For more than twenty years he has been the Editor of the *Bombay Guardian*—an able, outspoken, religious weekly: for many years also Editor of the Mārāttī publications of the Bombay Book and Tract Society, and agent of their Tract Depôt. All the people of this region, high and low, European and native, know George Bowen, and set him down without debate as a saint. He is a learned man, an author, a clear thinker, a transparent preacher of great humility and usefulness, a good musician,—a John the Baptist, to prepare the way for the Lord's coming to establish the self-supporting Indian Mission of which he has now become a member and minister.

On the 22nd of November, 1872, Rev. W. E. Robbins, a deacon of the Indiana Conference, arrived. He is a graduate of the Indiana Asbury University, was three years in the Federal army during the Rebellion, commenced his ministry in California, but on account of the death of his father returned to Indiana and joined that Conference. He read my "Call for Preachers"; and not falling in with a Mission secretary, or bishop, came on his own account, and paid his own expenses to Bombay. He learned to preach in the Mārāttī language before he was a year in India. If the Lord has any more just like him, I hope He will send them along.

On the 1st of December, 1872, Revs. Albert

Norton and Daniel O. Fox arrived in Bombay—also in response to my "Call," but appointed and sent by the Missionary Board.

They are both graduates of the "North-West University" and of the "Garratt Biblical Institute." Brother Fox had a few years' experience in the itinerant ranks in the Michigan Conference—which, with good preaching abilities and earnest spirit of work, suited him well for the development of our young Mission in Poona; and he was accordingly appointed as preacher in charge of Poona Circuit. He has proved himelf a "workman that needeth not to be ashamed."

Brother Norton is a young man of great earnestness; and, though peculiar in some points, we rejoiced greatly in the power and spirit he displayed as an evangelist.

January 1st, 1873.—Had a glorious love-feast and watchnight service last night. At our Quarterly Conference, in the afternoon, Brothers Morris and Christian were recommended for license as local preachers.

On Tuesday of next week, after holding a Quarterly Conference in Poona, with the concurrence of all concerned I am to start for Calcutta. Brother Bowen will be preacher in charge of Bombay Circuit, and have with him Brothers Shaw, Robbins, and Norton. The circuit embraces Thannā, Callian, and Egutpoora: the latter is eighty-three miles distant. Since the rains have ceased, we have resumed outdoor preaching to English-speaking natives four days a week on the Esplanade, and have opened a new place for preaching in the native languages four days per week, at the Fountain, near the head of Falkland Road. Brother Bowen superintends the latter.

I am very sorry to leave Bombay, for we are certain to have an advance in the native work. God gave me favour with the natives in Africa and Ceylon, and thousands were led to Jesus; and He is giving me favour with the natives here, and I am sure I could lead many of them to the Master. I love them, and I know God loves them. I have confidence in God and in His glorious Gospel; and I have confidence in man—no matter what his nationality, colour, or condition. This is the kind of faith which Barnabas took with him to Antioch.

But we have the work well organized, a new Plan made for the ensuing quarter, and the Circuit well manned. This work is no experiment in regard to the natives; we must sooner or later succeed, as certainly as that the Word of the Lord is true. God may prefer to develop these young workers without me; and we must extend, so as to have other churches growing up in other great centres of this vast empire. Brother Bowen remarked on this point: "We can't wait to see the full growth and fruit-bearing of one tree before we plant another, but must go on planting."

We have all been sadly chastened by dear Major Raitt's illness. The doctors ordered him home to Scotland on Thursday, and the following Monday, the 23rd of December, he and Sister Raitt left in the Peninsular and Oriental Co.'s steamer "Tanjore."

Brother Robbins and I, who had our home at Major Raitt's, came by invitation to stop at Mrs. Miles'.

I may anticipate my dates, and add here, that on the voyage the Major seemed to improve a little, but upon arrival in London grew worse, and died in the Lord, and went to his home in heaven.

Sister Raitt returned to India, and consecrated herself wholly to our Mission work—of course without financial remuneration; and the Lord is greatly blessing her.

CHAPTER XX.

PROGRESS OF NATIVE CONVERTS.

BROTHER MIRZA ISMAEL is not a married man, but continues to live, the same as before his conversion to God, in association with his people. An old Moulvy comes to see him sometimes, and wants to know why he gave up Mohamed for Jesus. He replies that he accepts Mohamed for all that he was, but he did not profess to be able to save sinners from their sins: Jesus came professedly for that very purpose, and has always shown His ability to do what He engaged to do, and therefore he has accepted Him as his Saviour. He is a quiet man, regular in his attendance at his band or class-meeting, and stated public worship, but not a very aggressive worker. We all love him, and he is happy.

NOUROSJEE has had a hard fight. His father storms at him, and orders him at once to leave his house. Nourosjee replies kindly, "Father, sit down and write an order dismissing me from your house, and I will go. If I go without that, people will say that because I became a Christian I ran away from home."

Then his mother begs the father to wait and see: "perhaps he will turn and be a good Parsee yet."

The Parsee papers took up his case, and warned their people against "the dangerous young man." A committee was appointed to compel him to return to the religion of his fathers, or force his parents to expel him from their house. To tell of the various methods employed to draw or drive him from Christ, would be too long a story. Old men came and entreated him to go with his mother to Surāt, and spend six months with his uncle. Then young men came and tried to lock him up in his own room, to be kept on bread and water for three months; failing in that, they threatened his life if they found him out at night. That evening I said, "Nourosjee, if you think it unsafe for you to go home to-night, you can stay here till morning, and go in the daylight."

"No," said he; "if I begin to yield to fear, there will be no stopping-place. I'll go, if they kill me."

One afternoon I was sitting in the house of Mrs. Miles; and heard a great shouting of a mob in the street. Our people were just returning from the service at the Fountain. We had seen the stoning of some of them before, by the Mohamedans, and were always on the look-out for squalls; so now I suspected foul play,—when in through the gate came Nourosjee as fast as he could run, and took refuge in the house. A stone had struck into the side-pocket of his coat, but he was not injured.

Some of our sisters were going to drive to the Fort, past where Nourosjee lived; and said to him,

"Come, get into the carriage, and we'll drive you home."

"No," he replied; "I have not been to a prayer-meeting to-day, and must attend the meeting to night."

A few minutes afterwards he passed over the same road where he had been mobbed, on his way to "the prayer-meeting." When he went with me to Poona, with his father's consent, heg ot a telegram saying "that his father was dying with cholera, and wanted to see him." He went by first train, though he did not believe it was true; and so it turned out. He lived at home, and endured hardness as a good soldier for a year and a half. But having been dismissed from business by his so-called Christian master because he had "changed his religion," and being a long time without employment, he went into a small trading business, and got into debt, and lost ground in religious life; and as our Mission has no financial inducements for ministers (for he had his heart set on becoming a minister), he was open to the proselytizing baits of the Bishop. He finally got into disgrace with us, and joined him. He is now in the "Bishop's College" in Calcutta, studying for the ministry. He has written to me frequently, confessing his faults, and professing to be restored to God's favour; and recently (February 1875), on my visit to Calcutta, he attended my meetings, and begged an interview with me, and gave me an opportunity to invite him to come back to our Church; but I told him that he had better go on with his studies in his present church relation. He came six miles to see me off by the train, at eleven p.m., on my leaving Calcutta. The Lord bless the lad!

KRISHNĀ CHOWEY has never wavered for one minute. The day after his conversion he went on with his work in the Customs; and after enduring much persecution there for a few weeks, he was transferred to another department, and put with a lot of very bigoted Brāhmans. He was trembling with apprehension when he told me of this change in his work, and feared that he could not stand against them. I said, "Go, my brother, and do your duty. What you most fear is just the discipline your Father sees that you need, and has hence sent you to hold out your light to those Brāhmans. Never fear. The Lord Jesus hath said, and had it written, that when brought even before governors and kings, you have no need to take thought beforehand 'what ye shall say; for the Holy Ghost shall teach you in the same hour what ye ought to say.' He will give you the right words for those dear fellows, who don't know our Jesus."

He went, distrusting self and trusting God. The Brāhmans badgered him fiercely for about a week. Then they gathered round him, and said, "Krishnā, what does all this mean? We never treated anybody so badly as we have treated you. We have tried every way possible to exasperate or intimidate you. You have shown no fear, nor ill-feeling, nor resentment. We can't understand it."

"Oh, my dear friends," replied Krishnā, "I show no fear because I am not afraid; I have quite made up my mind to die for Jesus, if He shall so appoint:

I show no ill-feeling, because there is none in my heart: I show no spirit of resentment, because I have none. The religion of Jesus is a religion of love. All this week I have been loving you, and praying for you. I love you all now, and want you to be happy, as I am."

From that day those young Brāhmans vied with each other in their attentions to Krishnā. A year afterwards, at the Esplanade preaching, when the mob beat Krishnā, and stamped upon him with their feet, and left him for dead, one of those very Brāhmans ran in, and taking him up in his arms, carried him away, and got water, and brought him round.

When Krishnā recovered consciousness, supposing himself to be passing through the gates of death, he said, "Thank God for the privilege of dying for Jesus! Oh, I am so happy to die for Jesus: He died for me!" The Brāhman stood over him, and wept like a child. Several of those Brāhmans came to the meetings, and came to see me. One of them wanted to teach me the Mārāttī language without charge. I believe I should have led them to Jesus, could I have remained in Bombay. We shall get them saved yet. Will my Christian reader join me in prayer for Krishnā's Brāhman friends?

Some months after Krishnā's conversion, however, he was tripped. A prating Hindū came into the office where he was, and used very abusive language against him; he paid no attention to that, but endured it meekly. Then he dealt out some dreadful epithets against me, which cut to the quick—for Krishnā loves me because I led him to

Jesus; but he took it patiently. Finally the mad heathen began to utter the most vulgar and blasphemous charges against Christ. Krishnā could not stand to hear his Master belied in that way, and with evident temper replied, "You wretched man! You are worse than a brute to talk so." His friends looked sorry, and said, "Ah, Krishnā!" He confessed to them his sorrow that he had allowed his feelings to get the better of his judgment. Three days afterwards Brother C. W. Christian was driving home from the Bank, and saw a native walking before him, apparently weeping. Coming closer, he heard him sobbing, and wondered who it could be: a sight so unusual. On coming up, to his surprise he saw it was Krishnā, and exclaimed, "Oh, Brother Krishnā, what is the matter? Come, get up in the carriage with me."

Krishnā got in, and told him all about the unhappy affair that occurred three days before. Brother Christian took him into his own room, and they together pleaded with God till the light of His face again filled Krishnā's soul.

"Well," says one, "I often get into such a temper, and think but little about it."

But you don't often lead poor souls to Jesus. I am sure you could not win a heathen to Christ. "He that ruleth his own spirit is greater than he that taketh a city." It requires great men of that sort to do great things for God.

Krishnā's uncle Chowey, who was in the habit of coming to Bombay every year in May or June, delayed his coming this year for a couple of months;

and thus the three nephews had time to grow and gather strength. They finally heard that he was on the way, and were looking out for the vessel to arrive. They were at our Sabbath afternoon prayer-meeting at Major Raitt's when the ship was telegraphed. They went in haste, yet with trembling, to meet him before he should land; but when they reached the ship he had landed and gone. Then they went to his house, in which they lived. Not knowing what might happen, Krishnā went in alone, while the younger brothers remained without. After a little while, hearing no row, they followed. They stood mute in his presence, as in boyhood they were often obliged to do; and he looked at them some time before he uttered a word. Then he angrily charged them with neglecting to do some unimportant thing, and they explained away his point. Then he surveyed them closely, and in a softened tone said, "Why, you look just as you looked when I saw you last!" (He expected to see them dressed in European clothing, and looking as though they were foreigners from a far country—according to what he had so often seen.)

"Our missionary is different from any you know," they replied. "He don't require us to change any outward custom, but simply to give up all idolatry and sin." But little more was said then.

When he afterwards got Krishnā alone, he said, "Now, Krishnā, I am getting old, and not so well up to business as formerly. I want you to resign your situation in the Customs, go with me down the coast, take your wife, and settle in a good home of your own. I'll make over all my business to you, and the property will all be yours in the end."

Krishnā replied, "Uncle, if that means any compromise of Christian principle, I cannot touch it."

The uncle then got into a very bad temper, and abused Krishnā very much. Afterwards he hinted to Trimbuck, that if he would resign his place and go and take charge of his business, he would cut Krishnā off, and make him his heir.

Trimbuck, but two months out of heathenism, replied, "Uncle, if you are of a mind to give us anything, we will thank you; but if your offer means that I am to give up Jesus Christ, I look upon all your possessions as dung."

The uncle was evidently taken aback. His fortune—the accumulation of his life of toil—going a-begging, and treated, as compared with the despised name of Christ, as worthless *débris!*

He took a peremptory course with Anā, and said, "Anā, sit down here, and write your resignation before me, and come with me down the coast."

The young fellow, who had always before been dreadfully afraid of his uncle, modestly told him that he could do nothing of the sort.

The uncle had spent thirty years in Bombay,—a bitter enemy of Christianity, but otherwise a fine man, and had many friends. The young men expected his friends to stir him up against them; but to their surprise, so far as they could learn, all except an old teacher of theirs—to whom the uncle would not listen—took their part, and told the uncle what good nephews he had.

An old Hindū living opposite said, "Chowey, you ought to be the happiest man in the world, with three such nephews. I have three nephews: I spent 10,000 rupees in marrying one of them, 8000 another, and 5000 another; and they spend my money and provoke me, and I don't know what to do with them. I sit with my wife at our window and watch your nephews. At early morn we see them by their windows at their books till the hour for business; then they are off: after business hours we see them back, and promptly at their books again. We often see gentlemen going in to teach them good things; and I say to my wife, 'Oh, if we had such nephews as Chowey, how happy we should be!'"

The uncle stopped with them in the house for about two months. Some days he was in a bad humour; and then the young men were very quiet, and watched the ebb of his temper—when they would bear witness for the truth. Sometimes he would argue with them, till Trimbuck would get the better of the argument; and then he would say, "Oh, you are a lawyer: I can't afford to take any more of that." Thus it went on, while many were praying for them and for him. [I have only given the substance of what I learned from day to day as these things were transpiring.] Finally he was taken ill, and they waited on him very tenderly, for they really loved him; and his prejudices broke down. He said, "Now I see that you are indeed my kindred, and that you love me. I am glad that you have become Christians —true Christians; and I want you to go on in the right way. I want all your kindred to become Christians. I am too old; it is no use for me to try now." So he parted with them in friendship, and left them in his house.

If Krishnā had hearkened to the false alarm of the native pādrī—"Your uncle will be down upon you like a shot"—and gone in mortal dread, and hid himself in the pādrī's compound, what would have been the result? If his uncle in such a case had not killed him, he would have cherished toward him the deepest contempt, and toward his missionary the bitterest enmity.

TRIMBUCK had many a battle, but the Lord helped him. A Hindū came into the office one day in the presence of a crowd of his kind, and jeeringly said, pointing to Trimbuck, "Ay, here's the fellow who went to a pādrī, and had some water sprinkled on his head: ha! ha! ha!"—and got up a general laugh at Trimbuck's expense. He was taken aback for a moment, but soon recovered, and said, "Now, friends, listen to me, and I will tell you all about it. I have been an ignorant Hindū, but I will tell you how I got light. I read our books, and found out the character of Ram,"—and he went over a list of the principal gods of the heathen, and gave his reasons for not worshipping this and that one: "According to our own books, this is their character;" then he delineated them, and said, "Are they worthy of my confidence as objects of worship? and am I to bow down and worship an idol made by some wretched man, not as good as myself? It is monstrous that you should expect a man of my intelligence to do such a foolish and wicked thing!" His assailant, overwhelmed and confounded, ran out of the office, and no one there dared to reply. Trimbuck had spiked their guns.

ANĀ is a quiet, meek, but brave young soldier for Jesus; but is in very delicate health. He went down the coast on furlough for his health, and lived for several months among his heathen kindred; and so far from being moved, he moved some of them—who came back with him, and have since been converted to God and baptized.

CHAPTER XXI.

CALCUTTA.

THIS great capital of the Indian Empire was not primarily a native city, but commenced as a trading post of the East India Company. The English flag was first hoisted there on the 24th of August 1690. It was in 1702 that "they directed their attention to the building of the town of Calcutta, and gave minute directions regarding its streets and houses. They completed the fort, surrounded it with an intrenchment, and mounted it with cannon." It, however, remained long in a poorly defended state; for it was in 1756 that it was taken by Serājā Dowlah, a Mohamedan nawāb, with 50,000 troops. It was by his order at that time that the celebrated "Black Hole" tragedy was enacted. One hundred and forty-six persons were thrust, at the point of the sword, into a room not twenty feet square, "in one of the hottest nights of the most sultry season of the year. The wretched prisoners soon became frantic with suffocating heat and insufferable thirst. The struggle to reach the window and catch a breath of air proved fatal to many. At length they began to sink one by one into the arms of death; and the few who survived that awful night owed their lives to the more free ventilation obtained by standing on the bodies of their deceased companions. When the door was opened in the morning, only twenty-three came out alive—the most ghastly forms ever seen." It was recaptured by the English in the following year. It is now called "the city of palaces." The more prominent among these are the Executive Mansion, the Treasury, the Town Hall, the General Hospital, the Government University, for the education of natives, and the Cathedral; with numerous superb business houses and family residences. Calcutta extends along the Hoogly, an arm of the Ganges, for seven miles, and is in parts rather more than a mile wide, "and covers a space of exactly eight square miles."

The English quarter occupies the south end of the city, on a beautiful plain a mile and a half long, leaving nearly six miles covered by the native city. The population of Calcutta is not much short of three quarters of a million—comprising all the nationalities of the East. The English, German, Armenian, Greek, and East Indian population denominated as Christian, is set down at 30,000. There are nine Episcopal churches—most of which, with their chaplains, are supported by the State; one Armenian, one Greek, and six Roman Catholic churches; one Church of Scotland, one Free Church, two Congregational, three Baptist, one Wesleyan, and now one Methodist Episcopal Church, with widely extending "societies."

The Mohamedans have a college in Calcutta, but in population number only about one to four Hindūs the city "contains 167 Hindū temples—all small buildings, which simply enclose a shrine. About twelve festivals are celebrated by the Hindūs at large every year, and some of them occupy two or three days." The whole Hindū population bathe in the Ganges, believing that its holy waters will wash away their sins.

Before going to Calcutta I wrote to Rev. John Richards, the Wesleyan missionary there, with whom I had laboured in South Africa, and whom I had often met in England, and proposed to give him a week of special services; but after that I should be free to follow Providential leadings beyond his lines, and if God should give me a people in Calcutta, as He had in Bombay and Poona, to organize them into a Methodist Episcopal Church. In his reply he said, "Of course I accept your offer of a week's services. When I wrote to you before, you were strictly an evangelist ; now you seem to have changed your plan. Well : if you can come, and through God's blessing be the means of creating some healthy religious excitement among us in Calcutta, I shall greatly rejoice. Come and welcome ; and I will work with you to the utmost of my ability."

Dr. Moffatt, of Cawnpore memory, had, by removal of Her Majesty's 14th Regt. to Calcutta, become a resident in this city, and had invited me also.

I commenced my services for Brother Richards on Sabbath the 12th of January 1873. His chapel is a neat Gothic structure—nave and transept—to seat about 300 ; with a large mission-house adjoining. At the morning preaching we had over 100, and in the evening about 200 hearers. We invited all who wished, when the evening congregation was dismissed, to remain for a prayer-meeting. A large number stopped ; and a student of the Jesuit College by the name of Jefferies, and a young woman, stood up as seekers, and professed to find peace with God.

Monday, 13th.—At seven p.m. we had about 100 hearers. Several native Christians, and one East Indian, declared their desire to find Jesus, and afterwards professed to be forgiven.

14th.—A Sabbath-school picnic at Barrackpore took most of my hearers away. They got back late and weary : about sixty came to the meeting. One woman, and a Singhalese medical student, professed to find Jesus.

15th.—Took a long walk before breakfast, to measure city distances and learn the lay of the land ; and prayed, "Lord, I am a poor blind man in this city. I pray Thee to show me the way into it. Thou wilt lead me."

I have no idea how the ministers here will treat my Mission. I apprehend they will be puzzled to know what course to pursue—especially those who are liberal and good. To labour with them purely as an evangelist would involve a collision with their more wealthy and worldly members ; but coming with an avowed purpose (D.V.) to establish a church, they will find it difficult to receive me : yet, seeing that God is with me, they will not feel like refusing. God bless them, and give them wisdom and patience, and lead me in the right way !

The interests involved are so momentous that the

obtrusion of personal considerations would be a great impertinence; and for me to defer to a human conventional principle of non-intervention, when God is guiding me, would be treason against my Sovereign. I am naturally very unobtrusive, and with Christian love added, I would not on my own account cross the feelings of any man,—much less a minister of the Gospel; but in a matter of duty to God, involving the salvation of souls, I have no alternative: I must obey God, and not man.

16th.—Went with Sister Richards at eleven a.m., and preached at "The Home." The poor women wept much as I explained to them the way of salvation. At the evening service, in the Chapel, a lady professed to find pardon. Received a letter from Rev. J. M. Thoburn. He had just returned from the great Missionary Conference at Allahabad. He says: "We had a delightful time at Allahabad. The only thing which we did not like was a resolution against going into territory preoccupied by other Missions. I think we might have defeated it; but Brother Harding begged very hard that I should keep quiet, and pledged his word that it did not refer to such work as you proposed. Mr. Fordyce also referred to your work, and was cheered when he expressed the hope that you would extend it. We all concluded that silence might be best—especially as we knew that you would not regard their resolutions in any case." Of course I will walk after the Spirit. If He forbid my going into Asia or Bithynia, I must not go. If He lead me to Troas, and to Macedonia, no matter who has been there before me, I must go, and do whatever work He gives me to do,—and if I get into tribulation, bear it; but it is a significant and pleasing fact, that while the Conference prescribes limits to every other Mission, it bids me to go forward without any limitations. They all know that I have no money, and that I don't want any of their native Christians, and therefore cannot antagonize, but may help them. Brother Harding, by that Conference resolution of non-intervention, was evidently seeking moral support against the encroachments of the Bishop of Bombay.

Friday, 17th.—Good congregation this evening, but no observable advance.

Saturday, 18th.—Attended the Minister's Bible Class this evening, gave them an address on the study of the Scriptures, and invited seekers. Mr. B—— and Lawyer H—— received Christ, and gave a clear testimony. The latter had been forward as a seeker for three evenings. He will make a valuable member for Brother Richards.

Sabbath, 19th.—Preached again in the Wesleyan Chapel morning and evening, and to their Sunday School at half-past four p.m. The largest congregation in the evening we have had. Several seekers came to the front, and two professed; but Brother Richards dismissed the meeting before I had time to speak to half the seekers—ten minutes before nine p.m. I said to him afterwards, "As it is so hard to get fish into the Gospel net in these waters, it is a pity when we are making a good haul not to secure them." No such an ingathering of souls as the outward conditions would lead us to expect.

Monday, 20th.—Dr. Moffatt drove me to see Mr. Brown, who showed us some halls in Bow Bazār for services; but none of them suited our purpose. Called to see Rev. Mr. Welland, whom I had met in Bombay; but he was out. Also upon Rev. James Ross, Congregationalist minister of Union Chapel. He was cordial, and candid,—very sorry that I was not purely an evangelist, as formerly. He was a pastor in Stirling, when I laboured in Edinburgh in 1867, and knew about my work. I explained to him how for sixteen years I had laboured as an evangelist in existing organizations, and how, in Bombay, God modified my commission, and, for India, laid upon me the additional responsibility of organizing churches; and gave him many details of facts about my work since that time, confirming me in my new position. He seemed much interested.

Had a family prayer-meeting to-day, at Mr. Jefferies', 142, Dhurramtollah Street. In the evening, no particular advance.

Tuesday, 21st.—Small prayer-meeting at Jefferies' at seven a.m., and a family service at half-past eight a.m. at the "American Home" for the ladies of the American Zenana Mission, employing about a dozen hard-working, earnest young women. They had about thirty of their native orphan girls present at our service. I asked the Lord this morning to open a way for services on a new line for next week, but never thought of a place in this "Home." But after our family service, the lady in charge said to me, "We think of offering you our large hall here for your services. It was suggested by the strictest

Episcopalian we have here, and the one that I should have least expected to propose such a thing."

I requested them to pray about it, and I would do the same, and call again on Friday; then, if we all see alike the Lord's leading in that direction, we will decide accordingly.

I attended, this afternoon, the annual meeting of the Bengal Bible Society, auxiliary to the British and Foreign. General Dorman was in the chair. Rev. Dr. Murray Mitchell, and Rev. Messrs. Nailer of Calcutta and Williamson of Allahabad, delivered earnest addresses.—"Bible now in 202 languages and dialects; copies issued by Bible Societies in sixty-eight years, 115,000,000.

Mr. Nailer said: "Eighty years ago John Thomas came to India as a surgeon, and became a Baptist missionary. His reports brought Carey." He then read the following extract from John Thomas's journal: "I would give £100,000 for a Bible in the Bengālī language for this people."

Had a large congregation at the preaching-service this evening; three men seeking, but none professed to find the Saviour. A deeper awakening, and a greater power of resistance manifest in many. Our workers are weak, but improving.

Thursday, 30th.—Preached in the Wesleyan Chapel nightly for two weeks. About twenty persons publicly sought and professed to find the pardon of their sins. Most of these were members of the congregation, and will probably join Mr. Richards' church. On my arrival, his English-speaking church consisted of eighteen members, according to the books. Their numbers and their working effectiveness have greatly increased.

Besides the English work, Mr. Richards has a small native church, several native preachers and teachers, and a few interesting native schools. On the third Sabbath—the 26th—I preached his annual missionary sermons, and made good collections, and on Monday night we had the regular public missionary meeting. General Litchfield, American consul, presided; and the meeting was put down as a decided success. This closed my labours for Brother Richards. I advised him to gather in his new recruits, organize his workers, and go on with this work in his own lines. So on Tuesday, the 28th, Rev. Brother Fentiman, Wesleyan minister from Lucknow, preached in the Wesleyan Chapel. They had invited all their members by special circular to be present, and after preaching they organized four praying bands, to hold prayer-meetings in four different places weekly. I urged the people of that congregation to stand by their colours, and help their ministers. I am very desirous that they should go forward, and develop a strong working force under their own flag.

I accepted the kind offer of the Zenāna ladies, and held my first service on Tuesday evening, the 28th. The Wesleyans had a good congregation; and so had I, without drawing one of them; so we have split fairly, and on the most friendly terms. Sister Richards and Brother Fentiman both tried to persuade me to limit my labours in Calcutta to their Church. I explained to them our principles:

to the effect that, as our doctrines were the same, when we found the Wesleyan organization adequate to the demands of the country, wheresoever established, we should not feel at liberty to organize on the same ground; "but here in Bengal," I continued, "there is a population of 66,000,000, and this little church is the only representative of Methodism in this great Presidency. You have been working here for nine years, and you now see what you can do and what you cannot do. The style of agency necessary to secure a great work of God, adequate to His purposes, is also necessary to conserve and extend it. It is not the work of a passing evangelist, simply, but requires the enlistment and combined struggle of millions of martyr spirits for a hundred of years." They felt the force of my argument, and gave in,—but not without manifest regret; and I was very sorry that I could not yield to their wishes.

I preached at the "Home" four nights. The congregation went up from about eighty to 150 hearers, with deepening interest. I did not call seekers; for I felt that I ought to get them well instructed and truly convicted of sin before I could move in that direction, and hoped to have gone on there long enough to secure a harvest of souls,—but found that our services were a greater inconvenience to our Zenāna sisters than was supposed; so it was arranged that for the next week they should be held in the Union Chapel Hall.

Sabbath, Feb. 2nd.—Preached at half-past ten a.m. in the Union Chapel; after which Rev. Mr.

Ross administered the sacrament of the Lord's Supper. Thirty women and fourteen men, besides ministers, partook of it. At half-past four p.m. I preached to their Sunday School; and at six p.m. to about 400 in the Chapel: aisles crowded.

Monday, 3rd.—At six p.m. commenced our services in the Union Chapel Hall. About 100 hearers—but few of the same we had at the "Home," and many of them very thoughtless young lads and lasses. Some young men behaved so badly that Dr. Moffatt had to go and speak to them, and Mr. Ross publicly reproved them.

So we have to begin breaking fallow ground again. I am learning the ways of the people; and God is doing the best He can with them. I have abstained from visiting the Wesleyans at their homes, as I don't want to draw them after me, nor appear to do so; and not having an opportunity to make the acquaintance of others, I am still a stranger in the city. I believe the Lord will confer a great blessing on all these formal churches, by planting, and maintaining in their midst, in vigorous organic life, the simple type of revived apostolic religion—"Christianity in earnest"—by which He aroused the churches of England and America a hundred years ago.

Many people say, "We have churches enough in Calcutta: most of the church edifices in the city are three-parts empty every Sunday."

But I learn that twelve years ago they were all crowded every Sunday, and that large numbers of educated natives then came regularly to learn about the Christians' God: now where are they? Their education convinced them of the absurdities of their own systems of religion; and they came to these churches to get light, and did not get it—or, if they did, it had not sufficient heat and attractive power; and they have gone back, some to the dismal depths of heathenism, a few to the Brahmo Somāj, and many to blank infidelity and unbridled licentiousness.

I gave several addresses to natives in the Cathedral College; and one day, after a lecture, I enjoyed a season of prayer in a private room with the professors,—after which one of them, pointing through the window, said to me, "Do you see that large house across the street? Twelve years ago a wealthy Hindū lived there; and for a long time he and eighteen of his Hindū friends met together weekly, to read the Scriptures and pray together to the God of the Bible; but after a time he gave up his meetings, and again became a most bigoted Hindū, and so lived and died. Then we had many educated bābūs regularly at service in our churches; but now it is a rare sight to see them in the house of God."

Now if God shall raise up another organization, wholly of newly-converted people, untrammelled by any of the embarrassments which fetter these older churches, to reflect light upon them from Him, provoke them to love and good works, and help them to rescue the fruits of their patient educational toil from the power of Satan, should not all good people say Amen? Of course they cannot believe at once that He has such designs in this movement; and I am quite willing that the work be subjected to all fair tests necessary to demonstrate it to be God's work.

About a year ago I wrote my patient wife that I should probably be detained in India beyond the time I had appointed to return home, and desired her to consult the boys, and give their mind about it with hers.

Two or three days after writing, I received a letter from her, written two months before, anticipating my question,—saying, "As you have laboured sixteen years as an evangelist, helping to build up other churches, if God has given you the opportunity of demonstrating in a heathen country the saving power of the Gospel from the foundation, you should take time to do it. We are most anxious to see you, but we will wait. Don't hurry on our account."

Last Friday I wrote her again on the same subject, saying, "I am here in Calcutta, the Paris of India. If God shall open this city to me, and give me a church, as in Bombay, I shall have to man it before I leave. That will detain me some months. Then I could go home for a couple of years, and return: but what shall I say for my dear wife and boys, whom I so long to see? Tell me what to do." This is the first time I ever wrote them about the probability of my return to India.

Yesterday, Feb. 2nd, 1873, I received a letter from her, in which she says, "I have never yet dared to call you home. It is likely you are too poor to come; and we are not able to help you: but if your work will allow it, we would wish you to do so, if but for a year. Perhaps your people will give you leave of absence, and money for a trip." God bless the dear woman!—He is manifestly leading her as He is her husband. This is another Providential pointer, indicating God's will concerning Calcutta and further extension in India.

Tuesday, Feb. 4th.—Preached a second time to-night in Union Chapel Hall, to about 100. I received an invitation to-day to call at Mr. Harris', the druggist's. I went, and met Mrs. Harris and Miss Purchase. They said they had stood up as seekers at my meetings in the Wesleyan Chapel; were members of the Church of England nominally, but having been brought to the Lord through my preaching, they wished to join my church; and Mr. Harris tendered the use of their house for any meetings I might wish to appoint. Thank God! He will give us places for our fellowship bands, and people to put in them.

Saturday, Feb. 22nd.—Our special services in Union Chapel Hall are over. I preached fourteen nights, to an average of from eighty to 100 hearers. They have learned to sing many of our hymns and tunes, and take an interest in the meetings; but the real fruits, in the way of soundly converted men and women, are but limited. Captain Jones, who was converted to God at my meetings in California, and was a member of my church there over twenty years ago, came to these meetings, and got revived, and is an earnest helper. Mrs. Forbes, Mrs. Patterson and her daughter Alice, Mrs. Thomas, and a few others, were brought to God there, and will bear our reproach and stand by us, I believe. A number of young women from the Calcutta Girls' Orphanage came often to the meetings, till one night about ten of them professed to find the Saviour, and were prevented from ever coming again. As many as seventeen seekers came forward last Wednesday night; but before I could speak to half of them, they got up and returned to their seats, and I could not learn much about their state. I have taken great pains to instruct them properly; but they are "dull of hearing," and so afraid of the opinions of their friends, that it is hard to make solid Christians of them; but I will not be discouraged. I have organized these few in a general fellowship band at Mr. Harris', which meets every Saturday night.

I stayed with Rev. Brother Richards while I was labouring for him; and he and his good wife asked me to make their house my home as long as I liked: and so I did. But I did not like to eat his salt when I ceased to work for him; and hence, on the 6th of February, I took apartments at Mrs. Schœnerstedt's, 65, Lower Circular Road, and paid for my board and lodging.

I accepted all the invitations I got to preach in the churches on the Sabbath; and accordingly preached one Sabbath each in the Union, Cooly Bazār, and Lāl Bazār Chapels. Then the people were enquiring of me, "Where are you going to preach next Sunday?" I said, "It is not arranged yet." I had no place in view, but expected the Lord to lead the way.

On Thursday, Feb. 20th, I returned the call of Rev. Mr. Kerry, Baptist missionary of Intally. He is the principal of an institution for the education of natives, and also superintendent of a number of native pastors and churches in and about the city. After showing me his school, containing over 200 lads, and Mrs. Kerry's girls' school, he conducted me into his native chapel, forty feet by sixty, and said, "I don't know what this chapel was built for, except the anticipation of getting many of the native students to become Christians—which, I am sorry to say, has not been realized. We have a small native congregation and church which worship here Sabbaths at seven a.m. and four p.m. Beyond that we have no use for it; and if you can make any use of it you are welcome to it." I thanked him for his kindness, but did not accept it at once. It was out of the way, in a narrow street,—well situated for its purpose as a native chapel, but not well suited for an English-speaking congregation. I considered the matter; no other place seemed available, so I concluded that God had opened that as the best to begin with; and we made quick preparations, advertised extensively, and opened regular services there the following Sabbath (Feb. 23rd, 1873), and kept them up in that chapel for about a year. Rev. Brother Kerry exerted himself on all occasions to advance our work. The first Sabbath, at ten a.m., we had about forty hearers; about eighty at night. It did not increase much for six months. We held special services there for more than a month: often with great promise, but with very little permanent fruit.

The congregation gradually grew, till the house was filled; and we got a few saved there who became earnest, but not very powerful workers. In visiting the converts and seekers, I became acquainted with the people, and established a line of family services which soon extended to over forty families, in each of which I held a service weekly,—besides public preaching, and the after-prayer and penitent meetings daily. The family services occupied from half an hour to an hour, according to the time the members, or myself, had to spare; and consisted of singing a few of the beautiful hymns and tunes in our book, compiled purely for this Indian work, Scripture lesson, exposition and exhortation, closing with prayer. Most of these were East Indian families—a very interesting people, but born and brought up among the heathen, and though comparing well in education and general intelligence with the middle classes of any other country, greatly needing plain Bible teaching and spiritual light. These services, being very simple and social, were made a blessing to very many, and prepared the way, I believe, for a harvest much more extensive than was really gathered in while I was among them. The family services, I may add, were usually held from half-past five to nine a.m., and from four to six p.m.,—before and after business and school hours; so as to have parents, children, servants, and neighbours who could come, all present. The hour and minute being a matter of regular appointment, I always found them ready; and so none of my precious time was lost through the ladies' toilet delays, which are often a hindrance to pastoral work. Of course I did the general duties of a pastor as well.

The hardest work of my life, I believe, was here in the streets of Calcutta, under the greatest discouragements. For months it seemed very doubtful, by all outward indications, whether we could raise a working force at all. I became more and more convinced that a great work of God was what Calcutta least desired and most needed, and that a more convenient season would never come; so I determined, as the Lord should lead, to push the battle and win, or die at the guns.

From all that I can learn, there has never been in this city, nor anywhere in Southern India, what could be called a revival of the religion of Christ. Except a few very valuable imports from other countries, in the form of earnest missionaries and lay men and women,—glimmering beacons scattered widely over this great empire of darkness, and leading a few, here and there, to Jesus,—there has been nothing to revive. We have to lay the foundations of a spiritual Church.

Sixty-six millions of perishing souls in this Presidency! Most of them have heard of Jesus, and hate His name immeasurably more than they hate the name of Satan. They won't listen to what His friends have to say in His favour, but drink in foul, blasphemous lies against Him, from the lips of Mohamedans and infidels. The books of French and English infidels—most of whom are now realizing the realities of Bible truth in the regions of the dead—are more extensively read, I believe, by educated natives in India than anywhere else. Tom Paine's "Age of Reason," for example, sells for a shilling in India; and nearly all the wretched infidel fallacies which, in Christian countries, have been refuted a hundred times, are now being sown broadcast here, with no antidote in the form of refutation. The many who have accepted these fallacious imputations against Christianity won't listen to anything that can be said on the other side, nor read the Bible itself. Worse still, the example of the mass of the people called Christians in India has so scandalized the name of Jesus, that in public discourse to the natives they will listen an hour to anything that strikes them as interesting, till you mention the name of Jesus,—when many will clear out in a minute, muttering blasphemously as they go away, and some will collect a crowd outside and proclaim against Christ.

"Why do the heathen rage, and the people imagine a vain thing? The kings of the earth set themselves, and the rulers take counsel together, against the Lord, and against His Anointed, saying, Let us break their bands asunder, and cast their cords from us." This is just as true of all the Indian rajāhs, and the great masses of their people, as it was true of old Pilate and Herod, and the murderers of our Lord's human Person. Though the case is desperate, God's resources are adequate and available; but where in all India is the agency suitable for such a work?

God has sent me here to organize at least one body of witnessing soldiers for Jesus, who will "endure hardness"; and by the power of the Holy Spirit I must succeed, or die in the trenches of the enemy. God help me: it is all for Thy glory, and the salvation of these poor perishing millions in love and pity for whom my Saviour died!

About the 9th of April, for the first time in Calcutta, I gave an opportunity for the converts who were attending our fellowship meetings to enrol themselves as candidates for membership in my church; and thirteen gave in their names. A very small beginning, after two months of so hard work: but, thank God! it is a germ of His planting, and will become a banyan, with branches and trunks innumerable, and millions will yet repose at the feet of Jesus under its shade.

Soon after this we got the use of the room in Bow Bazār belonging to the Young Men's Christian Association, for Sabbaths at seven a.m. and two nights weekly. Within a couple of months the Lord gave us about forty converts there: Brothers Curties, Tixeira, Ashworth, Tinley, Sharp, and their families, Brothers Bates and Martin, Sisters Freude and Rigordy, and a little host of witnesses besides—a number of whom were Roman Catholics; and we organized a fellowship band at the house of Philip Bates, and appointed Brother Frederick Curties leader. Now I began to feel the support of workers ready for any call of the Master. Unfortunately for the onward progress of the work, we had to give up the use of the Hall in which God so blessed us, and could not get another till we built one in Zigzag Lane, in the same neighbourhood. A dear brother in Bombay offered 10,000 rupees towards the erection of a Methodist preaching hall in that city; but as we have large bungalow halls there suitable for our present purpose, and none such here, our dear friends in Bombay said, "No,—give it to Calcutta"; so it was sent to a bank in this city subject to my order, for the purpose of building a Methodist Hall here. But we were in need of a place at once; and hence found it necessary to put up a temporary hall for the extension of the Bow Bazār work, while a more permanent chapel was being constructed,—requiring all the funds our people could give, in addition to the liberal gift from Bombay.

From about the first of September I was absent from Calcutta a month, holding quarterly meetings in Poona and Bombay.

CHAPTER XXII.

PROGRESS OF THE WORK IN BOMBAY AND POONA.

EARLY in my Calcutta campaign I became so absorbed in the struggle, that, though making history daily, I had no time to write it: I cannot, therefore, promise very definite dates, nor extracts from my diary,—for I kept none for the rest of my term of service in India; but my facts from memory, so far as I may give them, will be substantially none the less reliable.

Our quarterly meeting in Poona was, indeed, an occasion long to be remembered. The quarterly conference was held on Saturday night, just before a public preaching service, and was composed of a score of humble, valiant men of God, instead of three, as when we organized it, eight months before. Our brethren and sisters from Deksall, about 100 miles south-east, and from Lanowlī, forty miles north-west, had come in force to attend the quarterly meeting—representing churches which had meantime grown up in those places. At this meeting a building committee was appointed to put up a Methodist chapel in Lanowlī; which has since been completed and paid for. Brother Geering, one of our converted railway men there, paid 1200 rupees towards its erection.

MANEKJEE MODY.

[Opposite p. 275.

Our love-feast was on Monday night. The speaking was superb. About eighty persons in the space of an hour witnessed for Jesus. Brother Fox, our minister there, on that Sabbath baptized two Hindūs, cultivaters from a village ten miles out; and, at a later period of our services that week, two Brāhmans, both school teachers—one in a Government, the other in a private school. I spent a week in Poona on this trip, and had a few new cases brought to God.

I then spent a week in Bombay. During my absence of eight months, the work of God in that city had wonderfully developed and extended. In addition to a large increase of English and East Indian members, over a dozen Hindūs, and three Parsees, had been saved and baptized. Meantime, Brother Norton had opened up a new work in Bhosoual, 276 miles east of Bombay. All these converted Hindūs and Parsees were abiding among their people, according to the avowed principles of St. Paul's mission, and ours as well.

"What are those principles?"

"You will find them fully exemplified and illustrated in the Acts of the Apostles."

One of our Parsee converts—Brother Ruttonjī Merwanjī Metta—is now (1875) planting a Mission in Khandwa, Central India.

Another is in Christian work with Narrainsheshādrā, in Jālna.

Another was Brother Manekjee Mody. His higher social position, and his bold testimony for Christ at our out-door services on the Esplanade, exposed him to great persecutions. In his boyhood he went for a short time to a Sunday School in the Kirk—which made it easier for him to come to a Christian place of worship; but he remained a staunch Zoroastrian till awakened at our meetings.

His testimony, which he repeated again and again, in different languages, to the masses at the out-door preaching, was substantially as follows:—

"Friends, you know me. You know what a sincere zealot I was for the Parsee religion. After the death of my wife, I got up at three o'clock in the morning, and, with my incense and sandal-wood, went, in those dark hours of the night, to the Tower of Silence; and there, near the bones of my ancestors—where my own father and my own dear wife had been given over to the vultures—I burnt my sandal-wood, and in the odour of my incense offering mingled my prayers and groans and tears, from a broken heart. Let no man doubt my sincerity: I was sincere. Every morning at three o'clock, when you were all asleep in your beds, I repeated this daily for two years; but found no rest for my sin-burdened soul. I have no quarrel with my nation, and I don't abuse our great man Zoroaster; but he was not a Saviour. Our Parsee religion has no Saviour to offer to our dear struggling people; hence I could find no relief from it. Then I was led to examine the claims of Jesus Christ. From the records of the Bible, and the testimony of His people, I became convinced that He was indeed the Saviour sent by God to deliver poor sinners from their sins. I sought Him; and in Forbes Street Hall I submitted to Him, and received Him as my Saviour;

and at once He delivered me from my sins, and gave rest and peace to my soul. Now I know that I am a child of God, and that the Lord Jesus abides with me, and preserves me from sinning, and sustains me under all my trials and persecutions."

The open-air services I had established on the Esplanade and at the Fountain, the year before, had been kept up four days per week, except when disturbed by heavy rains. During all this time, "as Jannes and Jambres withstood Moses," so the Hindū infidel who withstood me at the early opening of the Esplanade services had withstood Brothers Robbins, Shaw, and their fellow-witnesses, all the way through, in a most abusive, insulting manner. At the Fountain also, nearly the whole time, Brother Bowen and his native preachers had been annoyed by a Mohamedan. During the week of my visit to Bombay, the opposition on the Esplanade culminated in mob violence. As there were many Parsees engaged in it, it was believed that, according to previous threats, the object was to crush or destroy Brother Mānekjee. He and I intended to go to the service in company; but, worked nearly to death, I lay down in the afternoon to rest, and dear Mānekjee sat beside me talking—till, before we knew how time was flying, we found it was too late for us to do so.

Meantime, while Brother Shaw—a grand out-door preacher—was proclaiming the Gospel, the mob commenced knocking down and stamping in the dust some of our native brothers. A dear young Parsee brother was nearly killed. Brother Krishna, as before related, was also left for dead. Brother

Robbins seized the fellow who knocked one of them down, and delivered him over to a police Sepoy; but the Sepoy, evidently a party to the murderous business, or under fear of the mob, immediately released him. Robbins, a big strong Westerner, who had been three years in the Federal army during the Civil War in America, seized the fellow again, and insisted that he should be taken in charge. Robbins had drawn the mob from the preaching-place; so Shaw finished his discourse to all who remained to listen, and then, coming to his help, saw him holding the man, and the crowd pressing around him. All of a sudden the prisoner fell down, apparently lifeless. The brethren thought he was shamming at first, but soon found that he was indeed insensible, and helpless; so they let him go, and his friends carried him off the field. The two ministers came in for a few strokes from the mob; but, though Robbins lost his hat and umbrella, and both got a few scratches, neither was seriously injured. They remained on the spot till all the people dispersed. They learned from an eye-witness, meantime, how the prisoner got back so suddenly what he had given. A desperate fellow attempted to kick Robbins in the stomach, but in the crush of the crowd missed his aim, and the prisoner received the kick designed for the preacher.

The next day the Commissioner of Police held a court of enquiry to investigate the affair. Brother Samuel Page was called on for evidence, and gave a full statement of the facts in the case.

One of the officers enquired, "What sort of people are these Methodists?"

"Well," replied another, "they are a curious people. I heard Taylor tell of one who got his sins forgiven in a quarter of an hour."

"Bosh!" rejoined another.

Then said Page, "Well, gentlemen, you know I would not tell you a lie: though I was long under awakening, it was not till the 21st of last September that I came out as a seeker; and then in less than a quarter of an hour I received Christ and got all my sins forgiven."

"Very well, Mr. Page," said the Commissioner; "we will not discuss that subject. Why don't these Methodists appeal to the law for protection?"

Page replied, "They don't disclaim their legal rights; but under all ordinary wrongs, and this opposition to their work, they prefer to suffer rather than appeal to the law."

"Why, they have no spirit!"

"O yes; they have the spirit of Christ their Master. They are not cowards. You will find them preaching in the same place to-morrow, quite undismayed."

"Why, they might get killed!"

"Oh, they would not mind that at all; they are not afraid of death. They are a people who wish only to know their duty,—and that they will do, or die in the attempt."

"Well, then," said the Commissioner, "we must protect them."

The Court then decided that without partiality they would protect any orderly person who wished to preach in the streets—Christian, Hindū, Mohamedan, or Parsee; but, for the sake of order, they must

BOMBAY AND BENGAL MISSION,

(WILLIAM TAYLOR,

FIRST QUARTER, 1875.]

PLAN OF

Meeting Places.	January.																	
	S 3	M 4	T 5	W 6	T 7	F 8	S 10	M 11	T 12	W 13	T 14	F 15	S 17	M 18	T 19	W 20	T 21	F 22
FALKLAND ROAD HALL.																		
FALKLAND ROAD.																		
Preaching each Lord's Day, at 11 a.m. and 6 p.m.	1						9						2					
	1						8						2					
Marātti Service at 3 p.m.	14						25						7					
Thursday, 7·30 p.m.					6						7						8	
Sunday School, Sabbath, 4 p.m. (No. 9).																		
Prayer Meeting, Monday, at 7·30 p.m.		19						20						21				
Marātti Service on Tuesday, at 7·30 p.m.			15						10						13			
Fellowship Band every Saturday, at 6 p.m. (Sister M. Miles); and at 8 p.m. (No. 4).																		
THE FORT.																		
FORBES STREET HALL.																		
Preaching each Lord's Day, at 11 a.m. and 6 p.m.	2						8						5					
	2						1						8					
Marātti Service, at 3 p.m.	12						1						15					
Thursday, at 7·30 p.m.					8						9						2	
Sunday School, Sabbath, 4 p.m. (No. 23).																		
Prayer Meeting, Monday, at 7·30 p.m. And on Wednesday at 7 a.m.		28						26						27				
Marātti Service on Wednesday, at 7·30 p.m.				2						11						14		
GEORGE MILES'. Fellowship Band every Wednesday, at 6 p.m. (Sister Morris); and Saturday, at 8 p.m. (No. 5).																		
JAMES MORRIS'. Fellowship Band every Saturday, at 8 p.m. (No. 16.)																		
MAZAGON.																		
Preaching every Lord's Day, at 11 a.m. and 6 p.m.	7						2						1					
	6						2						1					
Prayer Meeting, Monday, at 7·30 p.m.		16						17						18				
Service every Thursday, at 7·30 p.m. (No. 4).																		
Fellowship Meeting every Saturday, at 7·30 p.m. (No. 17).																		
BYCULLA.																		
AINSWORTH'S. Fellowship Band every Friday at 7·30 p.m. (No. 28).																		
GEORGE AINSWORTH'S. Fellowship Band every Saturday, at 8 p.m. (No. 7).																		
PEREIRA'S. Malayalam and Tamil Service, on Sunday, at 11 a.m.																		
English Service every Wednesday, at 8 p.m.				11						21						10		
Marātti Service on Friday, at 8 p.m.						7						24						12
Fellowship Meeting *in Marātti*, Saturday, at 8 p.m.; and Sunday, at 10 a.m. (No. 11).																		
HENRY BAILEY'S. Preaching Service every Tuesday, at 7·30 p.m.			8						2						7			
Fellowship Band every Saturday, at 7·30 p.m. (No. 8).																		
JOHN CHATTEN'S. Fellowship Band every Saturday, at 7·30 p.m. (No. 10).																		
COLABA.																		
REGIMENTAL SCHOOL HOUSE.																		
Preaching each Lord's Day, at 9 a.m.	4						19						8					
Fellowship Band every Wednesday, at 7 p.m. (No. 18).																		

Open Air Services at the Fountain, at 5 p.m., and at three places on the Esplanade, at 5 p.m., Monday Tuesday, Wednesday, and Thursday of each week.

FIRST Quarterly Meeting, or Love Feast, 1st April, 1875.

Sacrament of the Lord's Supper to be administered the last Sabbath evening of each month, at

METHODIST EPISCOPAL CHURCH,

Superintendent.)

BOMBAY CIRCUIT.

January.							February.																							
S 24	M 25	T 26	W 27	T 28	F 29	S 31	M 1	T 2	W 3	T 4	F 5	S 7	M 8	T 9	W 10	T 11	F 12	S 14	M 15	T 16	W 17	T 18	F 19	21	M 22	T 23	24	T 25	F 26	S 28
1						2						4						1						2						5
1						2						4						1						2						1
1						2						11						13						15						1
				9						1						6						7						8		
	23						26						27						22						16					
		11						7						24						1						14				
4						1						2						6						1						4
4						1						2						8						1						4
25						12						2						24						1						15
				6						7						8						9						5		
	16						16						17						18						19					
			24						15						13						10						7			
8						6						9						2						4						1
8						7						5						2						4						9
	19						20						21						23						26					
			1						9						19						20						21			
					13						14						1						11						10	
		8						4						2						6						7				
5						4						7						8						19						6

Ministers.

George Bowen .. 1
W. E. Robbins .. 2
Geo. K. Gilder (*Baroda*).
William Curties (*Jubbulpore*).
F. Pearcey (*Egutpoora*).

Local Preachers.

James Morris 4
George Miles 5
Wm. Boyd 6
*George Ainsworth .. 7
Sydenham Smith .. 8
Thomas Glover .. 9
*John Chatten .. 10
*John Pereira .. 11
*Krishna Chowey .. 12
*Rama Shunkur .. 13
*Namaji B. Powar .. 14
*Ruttonji Merwanji Metta 15

Prayer Leaders.

Albert H. Durant .. 16
William Bedford .. 17
John Fido 18
William Wright .. 19
Henry Bailey 20
Robert Waller .. 21
James Bapty 22
Joseph Fido 23
*Trimbuck Canara .. 24
*Manekjee H. Mody 25
Samuel Page 26
Anthony Cumming .. 27
Wm. Ashdown (*Rutnagherry*).
J. Legg (*Budlapore*).
W. Wilcox, Arthur Lynn } (*Baroda*).

Falkland Road Hall, and the first Sabbath evening of each month at Forbes Street Hall (excepting on the last and first Sabbath of the quarter, when it will be administered, on the evening of the Love Feast, in Falkland Road Hall.)

* Preachers in Marātī and other native languages.

have their preaching-places half a mile apart. If a Mohamedan establishes a preaching-place, no Christian will be allowed to open one within less distance than half a mile. The Hindū who has for nearly a year and a half been giving so much annoyance on the Esplanade must be arrested at the next meeting. He must not be punished at once, but warned; and if then he repeat it, punished. The same warning must also be given to the Mohamedan at the Fountain.

This order was faithfully executed; and, after patient suffering for a year and a half, our out-door preachers got protection unasked, but none the less appreciated. Since that, two other places on the Esplanade have been opened for preaching four days per week; so that we have sixteen out-door preaching services weekly in Bombay, and three or four in-door Sabbath services, for the natives, in most of the different native languages spoken in that great Babel of the East. Brother Manekjee now stands often alone, and proclaims the Gospel on the Esplanade, and does his full share of the out-door preaching in English, Mārāttī, Guzerāttī, and Hindūstānī.

The preceding list of preaching-places and names of official workers, according to the Plan of the Bombay Circuit for the first quarter of 1875, will furnish an index to our missionary work in that city. Brothers Bowen, Robbins, and Ainsworth preach in both English and Mārāttī. Eight others, as seen on this Plan, preach only in Mārāttī and other languages of India,—especially Guzerāttī, Hindūstānī, and Malayalam.

Krishnā's wife was sent to him by his uncle. He got her well instructed, converted to God, and baptized; and then they were united in Christian marriage. Her likeness is marked No. 2 in Krishna's group (*see* Frontispiece). He is now a licensed local preacher in our Church, and believes that he is called to devote his life to the work of the Christian ministry. I believe so too; but as yet he is pursuing his business in the Customs, and devoting his leisure to study and active soul-saving work. He has had eight of his kindred saved and baptized, and hopes soon to get all his family connexion into the kingdom of God. Trimbuck preaches well, and was recommended for licence at our District Conference a few months ago; but, wishing a better preparation, begged the Conference to let his case lie over till their next meeting.

The number of native converts in the Bombay Circuit—mostly from Hindūism—is now about sixty. The great break in their lines has not come yet; but a grand preparation of the field and of the workers is daily progressing, and God will give these heathen to Jesus for His inheritance. I expect to see many thousands of them brought to God before many years shall have elapsed.

On my way back to Calcutta, Brothers Krishnā, Trimbuck, Manekjee, and other native brethren, accompanied me eighty miles, to Egutpoora, where we held a number of services. At a general fellowship-meeting there, Krishnā gave us some facts in his experience which I had not heard before; and as they illustrate a principle in our Mission—in regard to taking stumbling-blocks out of the way of the natives by getting the nominal Christians of India converted to God—I will here insert the substance of his narrative.

"I read the New Testament when quite a young man, and was deeply impressed with its doctrines, and especially with the example of Jesus and of His disciples. I thought, Surely this is God's book, and these were God's people. I studied their characteristics closely, and felt a desire to know whether or not there were any such people now living on the earth. So I met an English gentleman in the street, and said to him, 'I have been reading a very interesting book.'

"'What book is that?'

"'It is a book called the New Testament.'

"'Yes; that is indeed a good book.'

"'I was very much impressed by the example of Jesus and of His disciples, and feel a great desire to know if there are any such people living now.'

"'O yes; there are many Christians living here in Bombay.'

"'Indeed!—will you kindly show me one?'

"'O yes: come along with me.'

"I went with him a little way, and we met a man; and my guide said, pointing to him, 'There is a Christian.' I followed the said Christian straightway, and sought his acquaintance, and became intimate with him and others who were said to be Christians. I studied them as best I could in their social life, religious assemblies, treatment of their servants, and business transactions. I compared their lives with the lives of the apostles, and could not find a single point of cor-

respondence. The example of those Christians paralyzed my understanding, and I became an atheist. I remained nominally a Hindū, but practically an atheist, till I came to Brother Taylor's meetings last year. There I saw scores of the people who passed for Christians stand up publicly, and with flowing tears confess that they were miserable sinners. They went down upon their knees, and were instructed and prayed for, and afterwards testified to the people that they had accepted Jesus Christ as their Saviour, and that He had taken away their sins and given them a new heart. I again read the New Testament, and got a fresh impression of the characteristics of Jesus and of His apostles. I then studied these people who said they had found Jesus. I closely observed their conduct towards their servants, their social life, their business habits, and their religious exercises; and found a complete correspondence. I found in them the same patience, meekness, truthfulness, honesty, love, and sympathy, that I had read about in the lives of Jesus and His disciples; and I came clearly to the conclusion, 'After all, this is God's book, and these are God's people.' Thus I was awakened, and became a Christian."

The living example of a holy church in India is the only argument that will ever convince the natives that Jesus is the Christ, or that the Bible is the book of God. Education has been unduly relied upon by very many good earnest missionaries and their patrons; and now they are reaping bitter disappointment in seeing the thousands whom they have educated turning their own guns upon them,

and allying themselves with the heathen, Mohamedans, infidels, and the Brāhmo Somāj, in combination against Christianity.

Many, to be sure, who have been educated in Mission schools are personally friendly to the missionaries; but not one in a thousand of them receive Christ, and but very few have the moral courage, in the presence of their heathen friends, to say one word in His favour. Indeed, those who are educated in Christian schools are, of course, most liable to the suspicion of being tainted with Christianity; and they feel it incumbent on them to purge themselves of all grounds of suspicion by denouncing Christ in the presence of the heathen, while many of them will assent to everything the missionary says if alone with him. If mere literary education had any regenerating power in it, then the educated people of Europe and America would be model Christians. But what has their education done to cure their spiritual maladies? I would not say that the natives should not have been educated, nor under-rate the Christian knowledge they have thus obtained; but it is a well-known fact that mere knowledge in the head, without the grace of God in the heart, tends to pedantry and pride; though with a regenerated heart it is a grand instrument for good.

Brother Manekjee accompanied me as far as Bhosouel—276 miles from Bombay—where we had a couple of days of special services.

I spent two days, also, in special services at Allahabad, with Rev. Brothers Thoburn and Osborn.

My tour from Calcutta to Poona and Bombay, and back, involved 2972 miles of railway travelling—which by first-class ticket, going and returning, would have cost 267 rupees 15 annas. I went with the native masses, by third and intermediate class carriages, at a cost of 61 rupees 4 annas 6 pies. That may illustrate one of the ways by which we run a self-supporting Mission. Of course, the Mission has nothing to do with my own expenses. We do not oblige any of our preachers to travel third class, but my example makes it easier for those who wish to do so; and I believe all of them travel third class, except those who preach much to railway people, and have a first-class ticket given them.

Before I left Calcutta for this trip, we leased a lot in Zigzag Lane, and let out to contract the building of a plain chapel thirty feet by fifty. We had trustees, and a building committee; but as Sister Freude, a thorough business woman, lives near, the responsibility of superintending its erection was left with her, and she did her part faithfully.

We also bought a lot in the best centre of the city,—in Dhurramtollah Street, near Wellington Square,—for 4600 rupees, and let out the contract for building a permanent brick hall forty feet by eighty.

CHAPTER XXIII.

BACK AT CALCUTTA.

AT the opening of our new chapel in Zigzag Lane, the place (though at eight a.m.) was crowded, and God was with us. It was at this opening service that Koshenāth Boroosh, a high-caste Hindū from Assam, and a student of the Calcutta Medical College, was baptized. He was brought to Jesus during my absence in the following manner. Two Singhalese native medical students—Brothers Everts and Fry, who were converted to God at my first series in Calcutta—brought Koshenāth with them one night to a fellowship band. He was a bitter hater of Christianity. He had a young brother who had been a short time in a Christian school, but died at the age of fourteen years, and requested, when dying, that there should be no Hindū ceremonies performed over his dead body. No one knew why he made such a request. Well, Koshenāth sat down quietly in the fellowship class-meeting, and heard twenty-seven men and women tell that they had received Christ and had been saved from their sins, and that Jesus was with them, and that He was giving them power daily to resist temptation, and was preserving them by His own Almighty hand from sinning.

Koshenāth listened, and thus reasoned with himself: "These are intelligent men and women—not carried away by excitement, for they are all sitting quietly, and talking calmly; not to be heard by the outside world, but conversing with each other. They are not speaking about creeds or opinions, nor telling of things hoped for; but testifying to facts within their personal knowledge. These are credible witnesses, whose testimony would stand in any court of justice. They speak of Jesus, not merely as a historic character of the past, but a living Person of the present. They say, though invisible, they know Him, and have daily communication with Him. They say they received Him by faith: a thing which I have considered nonsense before; but how reasonable it seems to me now! How could they receive Him except by faith? That is just the way I received my father. I never could have known him except by faith. I received him as my father on the testimony of my mother; and he confirmed the fact by his fatherly care of me. This is the way I am required to accept Christ as my Saviour. There can be no other way of receiving Him but by faith. If I receive Him on the testimony of these witnesses, and if He saves me, then I shall have the certain knowledge that He is alive and is the Saviour of sinners, and my Saviour. I will receive Him: I will receive Him just now."

So he stated his case to the band, and asked them to show him the way to Jesus. Dr. Moffatt and others gave him words of instruction, and they all prayed for him; and before the meeting closed, he testified that he had then and there received the Lord Jesus as his Saviour, and that He had filled his heart with light, love, and peace. But emerging so suddenly from the darkness of heathenism, it appears that he needed further confirmation of the great work God had wrought in his heart; and that night, he says,—whether sleeping or awake, he is not sure,—his deceased brother's spirit appeared to him. "He looked as natural as when in life, but shining in a transparent beauty not to be seen in any body. He did not speak in audible words to my ear, but conveyed his ideas as distinctly to my mind as if brought to it through the medium of words. He said, 'Oh, Koshenāth, my brother, I am so glad that you have received the Lord Jesus. He is indeed the only Saviour of sinners. He saved me, and brought me to a glorious place, which I cannot describe to you. Cleave to Him, my brother, and He will bring you to the same home of bliss and glory, where we shall for ever abide with Jesus. I will appear to you again.'" Koshenāth, filled with joy, got out of bed, fell down on his knees and wept, and praised God for salvation in Jesus. About two months afterwards his brother again appeared to him in the visions of the night, congratulated him on his steadfastness so far, and urged him to watch and pray, and never look away from Jesus,—assuring him again that He would certainly bring him to the same glorious place which was now his home.

After I had been nine months at work in Calcutta, some one said to me, "Are you preaching for the natives in this city?"

I replied, "Except a course of six or seven lectures given to educated natives in three of the principal institutions of learning here, I have not felt prepared to look a native full in the face, or speak to one about Jesus and salvation. Christianity has been so scandalized here by so-called Christians, I have not the heart to go to the natives, till God in mercy shall clear the way, by taking up these stumbling-blocks, and sending them forth again as undoubted specimens of His saving power,—thus furnishing an argument that will have convincing power on the native mind. A man here the other day, seeing a bābū reading the Korān, said to him, 'Why don't you throw that book away, and read the Bible?' He replied, 'I have been observing these people who read the Bible, and I find that they are haughty, proud, overbearing, and cruel to their servants; that they cheat, tell lies, get drunk, and do so many wicked things, that I think the less I have to do with you, and your Bible, the better.'"

Thus the masses of so-called Christians of India are heathenising the heathen. Near the close of the year I had a few out-door services in three languages. I gave out the words of truth in English, Koshenāth translated them into Hindūstānī, and another native brother put them into Bengālī. We had good audiences, and good order; but my time in Calcutta was then too short to drive the native work up so far as we did in Bombay. Some months after my departure, during College vacation, Koshenāth made a tour of 3000 miles, visiting the Missions of the North-west Provinces and the Punjāb, witnessing for Jesus. We hope that God will use him for the salvation of many of his people. Pray for him!

We begged the Missionary secretaries to send us missionaries to supply the growing demands of our work in India; but this year they did not send us one. My Mission, and the principles which render it peculiar, have to pass, as I expected, a severe ordeal of criticism and opposition. Every new steam-engine or boiler has to be tested ere it can be trusted; and so with every other new thing—though like our Mission, having no novelty but the new application of old principles. The misapprehensions of friends on both sides of the world, the mis-statements of those not friendly, the fallacies of speculators, and the long letters written, would make up material for a very curious, but very uninteresting book, which I don't intend to write.

We heard of Bishop Harris's episcopal tour round the world,—holding conferences on his route in Japan, China, India, Bulgaria, Germany, Denmark, and Sweden; and we were awaiting his arrival with pleasure. Hearing that he was accompanied by Rev. Brother Waugh, who had been home on furlough, and Rev. Brothers Spencer and Houghton, who were making the tour of the globe on furlough from home, I arranged to have them all stop with me, while in Calcutta, at Mrs. Shœnerstedt's, in Lower Circular Road. When the Bishop stopped at

Ceylon, he telegraphed to Rev. Dr. Thoburn in Lucknow to meet him in Calcutta; so Brother Thoburn came in advance of their arrival, and gave us valuable help in our work. I was told, afterwards, that the good Bishop had an apprehension, from the many things that were rumoured about my Mission, that I was going to set up a new sect—a thing entirely out of the question from the first, both with myself and all my people—and thought he might need Thoburn's advice. Every document we had, and the trustees and deeds of our property in Calcutta, were all proofs of our entire loyalty to the Church of our choice, though refusing first and last to yield a single principle or plank in our platform as a Mission.

When the Bishop and his party arrived, I met them at the ship, and invited them to stop with me. Brother Richards, meantime, begged us to allow the Bishop to be his guest; and I was glad to yield my own preference to gratify my old friend, and so took the Bishop to his house, and the other brethren to mine.

As soon as we left the ship, and the Bishop and I got into a carriage alone, he said, "Now, Brother Taylor, we want to bring your Mission into a closer connexion with our Church; and we want you to become officially, and in name, what you are in fact—its superintendent."

I replied, "I received a very kind letter from Bishop Simpson, proposing the same thing; and at the same time a letter from Dr. Eddy, containing a similar request from you. I immediately wrote, in reply to Bishop Simpson and to yourself, stating that while I was not at all ambitious of any honour or official position in the gift of the Church, yet, as God had opened and organized this Mission through my agency, and had thus made me its superintendent, I should not object to your official confirmation of His appointment, provided there should be no interference with the peculiar principles on which our Mission was founded."

"I had left New York before your letter got there, and never received it," replied the Bishop; "but your principles are very clear and sound. Where the Missionary Society appropriate the funds of the Church, of course they are responsible for their proper disbursement; but where they give no money, as in the case of your Mission, what have they to do with its internal management?"

So the whole thing was arranged in less time than it takes me to write it. It was agreed, as a matter of convenience, that I and my ministers, until we could organize a Conference of our own, should join the India Mission Conference; but that the said Conference should not have an official relation to the Bombay and Bengal Mission, any more than the Baltimore Conference has with our Mission in Japan because Rev. R. S. Maclay, its superintendent, happens to remain a member of that Conference. Though we agreed to designate this Mission by the names of the two great Presidencies which span the Empire, it was a matter of specific stipulation and mutual concurrence that all that was meant by the second clause in the Mission Committee's "List of Missions" (viz.—

"INDIA: First, *The Indian Mission Conference,*
"Second, *India beyond*),"—

should be the legitimate sphere of the Bombay and Bengal Mission. The said Conference limits are defined in the "Discipline"; all India outside those lines belongs to our geographical field.

The Bishop preached for Brother Richards on the morning of the Sabbath he spent in Calcutta, and in the evening for my people; and presided at a general fellowship meeting for us on Monday night. The other brethren gave us some stirring sermons, and the grandest singing our people had ever heard.

At the ensuing Conference—in January 1874, in Lucknow—these arrangements were all completed; and contrary to my expectations, and to my great joy, Rev. J. M. Thoburn, D.D., resigned his work in the India Mission Conference, and joined my Mission. He had resigned his salary a year before, and had fully adopted the principles of our Mission. Brother C. W. Christian had resigned his situation in the Bombay Bank some months before, and become my assistant preacher in Calcutta; George Gilder, also of Bombay, and C. R. Jefferies, of Calcutta, had been duly recommended for the itinerant work; so that our lack of helpers from the Mission Board was being made up in part in India. Our members and probationers in Calcutta and Kidderpore now numbered over 100. The whole number in our Mission then was about 500; and our appointments, as announced by the Bishop at the close of the Conference session, stood thus:—

BOMBAY AND BENGAL MISSION.

WM. TAYLOR, *Superintendent.*

Bombay.—George Bowen, W. E. Robbins, James Shaw.

The Deccan (Poona, Lanowlī, Deksal, etc.).—D. O. Fox.

Central India.—Albert Norton, George K. Gilder.

Bengal (Calcutta).—J. M. Thoburn, C. W. Christian, C. R. Jefferies.

We had, at the same time, a cause developing at Secunderabad, through the agency of Brother Walter Winckler, a nephew of Mrs. Miles. Walter was in England when our work in Bombay began; and when he heard of the conversion of his kindred, he was very angry. He returned to Bombay soon after we organized our church there, and sat opposite to me at Brother George Miles' table, and looked fiercely at me for a week. Then his prejudices began to yield; soon he came to our meetings; and then the Spirit of the Lord came upon him, and after a hard struggle with Satan and self, he accepted the Saviour. When but four months converted to God, he gave us valuable help in the Poona siege, as before stated, and was then appointed by Government as a Civil engineer to Secunderabad, in the Nizam kingdom, to build a section of the Government railway. He arrived there an entire stranger, but soon commenced witnessing for Jesus to a number of soldiers in a cow-shed. Next he went among the civilians, and got some of them saved. Then he was taken ill, and Dr. Trimnell, the Civil surgeon, a good man in his way, came to see him; and by some sort of mutual improvement society the Lord used the doctor to cure Winckler's body, and used Winckler as a witnessing agent in getting the doctor's soul into the hands of the Great Physician, and he was healed.

As my time and space are so short, I may as well anticipate the order of events, and finish the outline of this story.

During the year 1874 Brother Bowen visited Secunderabad, and organized our church there; of which Winckler, under God,—daily hard at work making the railroad, and preparing the way of the Lord as well,—was the founder.

Later in the year Brother Shaw spent a few months there, and greatly extended the work. Later still I spent a few days there, and found a healthy, growing, working church of God, of more than 100 members and probationers, besides scores of converts who had not joined our body. We had 120 communicants at the sacramental service which we held among them. Dr. Trimnell, my kind host, told me that, becoming a Methodist—and hence a total abstainer from all intoxicating drinks—he has daily done two hours' more work than before, with less fatigue. He was what is called in many circles a temperance man, before,—"never known to be the worse for liquor"; but thought he could not get through with his excessive work without artificial stimulation—especially when up all night with the sick. Now he finds that he was quite mistaken before, and instead of loss, he has gained a greatly improved condition of nerve, muscle, and brain, with a clear gain in time of two hours per day. He gave me the testimony of a Mohamedan merchant concerning the work of God in Secunderabad, as seen and noted by the Mohamedans.

An army officer owed this merchant a bill, and seemed more disposed to lay out his money for drink than to pay it. The Mohamedan said to him, "If you will give up drink, like these Methodists, I'll give you the amount of your bill. These Methodists are all teetotalers. They are willing to pay a fair price for an article, with but few words about it; and always pay their bills."

Brother Wale, our recording steward there, gave me a similar testimony from a Parsee merchant, who has a very large general store in Secunderabad. The Parsee said to a man who came into his shop, "Have you joined the Methodists yet?"

"No; I have not."

"Well, I advise you to join them, for they are a very good people. They don't want an article for less than it is worth, and they always pay their bills."

"But," replied the man, "they are all teetotalers, and don't buy any of your wine and spirits."

"Yes, I know that; but, though I sell them to other people, I know the Methodists are right; and, moreover, spending no money for grog, they have the more to lay out for things of value to them; and I never have any trouble with Methodist bills, for they are always paid promptly."

It would be well for some Methodists of other countries to take note of these Indian Methodists, as represented by their religious enemies.

On my way to the said session of the India Conference in Lucknow, I called at Cawnpore to see my friend Dr. James Condon, M.D., Civil surgeon of that station. He has a brother in Madras, surgeon in Her Majesty's 21st Fusiliers—Dr. E. H. Condon, M.D. Doctor James has long been in correspondence with his brother about the work of God in connexion with my ministry; and now, when I went to his house, he read to me a letter he had just received from his brother in Madras, stating that for months he had been trying to get the missionaries of that city to invite me to go there; and that Rev. Mr. Barton, of the Church Mission, warmly favoured it, and brought the question of inviting me before the January meeting of their monthly Conference, but that it was not concurred in; and that he would invite me on his own responsibility; and deputed Dr. James to urge me to go, as the need of a stirring-up there was the greatest need of that city.

I replied to Dr. James Condon, that "having Calcutta on my hands, I cannot possibly promise anything, and certainly cannot go to Madras for months to come."

But when Dr. Thoburn joined me, and was appointed preacher in charge of our work in Calcutta, I suddenly found myself foot-loose, and told the Doctor to write his brother that (D.V.) I would go by the first steamship from Calcutta. Having hastily put Brother Thoburn into line, I sailed by the Peninsular and Oriental Co.'s steamship "Indus" for Madras.

I paid my own fare, first class: 100 rupees. I was nearly used up by excessive work; and the best accommodations were the cheapest for me. By the mercy of God, the voyage restored me.

Before sailing, however, I received a letter of invitation direct from Dr. E. H. Condon, asking me to make his house my home while in Madras; adding that Col. Goddard, Dr. Vansomeren, and Mr. Bowden were associated with him in asking me to come to Madras, and would back me to the utmost of their ability; but that he hoped I would not organize a church there.

I replied, "I will leave that entirely to the Lord's leading, as He may manifest it clearly, not only to me, but to you and your friends. I cannot certainly anticipate His will in the matter; but must leave myself entirely free to accept His decisions, and yield obedience to His will as He shall make it known to us."

CHAPTER XXIV.

MADRAS.

THIS city was a small Hindū village, in which a plot of ground was marked out by the Rājāh of Chundergiree as a trading post for the East India Company. They erected a factory in 1639—which, in the intervening centuries, has expanded into this great city. At that early period, to give confidence to the native merchants, a fortification was built, and twelve guns mounted upon it; and they named it Fort St. George. This is the Fort in which my Brother and hospitable host, Dr. Condon, his estimable wife, his sister, and two little daughters reside. I found my way to their happy home on Tuesday, the 4th of February, 1874.

The population of Madras, according to a recent census, is as follows:—

Europeans	3,613
Eurasians or East Indians .	12,018
Hindūs	330,052
Mohamedans . . .	50,964
Others	910
Total . . .	397,557

The Roman Catholics have been operating in Madras

and in many parts of Southern India for centuries; indeed, they claim that the Apostle St. Thomas was the pioneer missionary to plant the Gospel in Southern and Western India. It is true that the Syrian Christians of the Malabar coast of Western India can trace their origin, as organized churches of Christ, nearly, if not quite back to the period of St. Thomas's ministry; be that as it may, they have tens of thousands of people bearing the name of Christ, with numerous churches and regular forms of worship. These, however, are not Roman Catholics, but not very spiritual, nor hence aggressive in the work of God. St. Xavier and the Portugese East India traders planted Romanism in India. But it is a fact admitted by all parties acquainted with Indian history, that "whatever true spiritual Christianity there may be amongst the natives of India, it owes its birth and existence to the agency of foreign missionaries and Christian people" of the present century.

The Church of England, of course, has many spacious places ot worship in Madras, and a great monopoly of precious souls who know the English language. If they were saved from sin, living among the natives as they do, they would be blessed "leaven" in the great heathen "lump"; but unhappily, except the Church Mission—missionaries who are really spiritual and earnest in their work—most of their churches are very ritualistic. All the leading churches of Nonconformist bodies are represented there, and have some large schools for the heathen and Mohamedans.

The Wesleyans, under my friend Rev. Mr. Burgess, have a flourishing native High School, and numerous branch schools. My old friend Rev. James Jillings is chairman of the Madras District. My plan for an evangelistic tour in India put Madras as my starting-point, and the Wesleyan Missions of South India as my principal field for work. I was so intent on a grand advance of the kingdom of Christ among them, such as we had in Africa, that I brought a marvellous musician and singer from Tasmania to help me. The ministers were written to by Rev. Samuel Hardy of Capetown, and urged to open my way in South India, and help in the work; but by some means they did not respond, nor invite me to help them; and hence, after our campaign in Ceylon, I sent my man back to Australia, and went to North India myself, as before related. I am out of pocket over £80 on that enterprise in behalf of South India. That was my plan, humbly made by the best light I had at that time. "There are many devices in a man's heart; nevertheless the counsel of the Lord, that shall stand." I could not by any possibility anticipate God's plan—under which, instead of an evangelistic tour, and then off home to my family, I should have my commission as an evangelist so modified as to become an organizer as well, and be committed probably to a life-work in India; but all this came to pass before I arrived at Madras.

The Wesleyans have done a great deal of most important seed-sowing in South India, and have a great educational work, especially in Madras and Bangalore; but have not yet had so great success in

India as they have in other countries. Of course the difficulties are greater in regard to the heathen; but among a population of over 15,000 Europeans and East Indians, after a period of sixty years of work in Madras, to have but eighty-six English-speaking members, showed clearly that there was room for the Church which it has pleased God to plant there —not to antagonize, but help them in their great soul-saving mission.

On Thursday, Feb. 6th, Dr. Condon introduced me to all the Nonconformist ministers of the city, the missionaries of the Church Mission, and a few of the more liberal of the Establishment, in their own houses.

On Friday evening we attended the weekly Bible-class at Colonel Touch's; and by request I gave an account of the work of God as I had seen it in different parts of India.

Rev. W. Miller, of the Free Church of Scotland, gave us permission to use their Evangelistic Hall for our first series of special services, to commence on Monday night, the 10th of February. The following notice of his educational work I clip from the *Bombay Guardian* of a later date :—

"The Rev. W. Miller, of the Free Church Mission, Madras, is well known for his ardent devotion to the work of giving a high Christian education to the natives of India, and for his great abilities as a teacher. To show what a high position the Institution under his care has attained to, it is enough to mention that the Church Missionary Society now sends to the Free Church Institute those students from their different High Schools in the Mofussil who wish to complete their education in

Madras. The College department of this Institution had 78 pupils in 1873, 112 in 1874, and has now 139. The students in this department paid in fees last year 3400 rupees—about thirty rupees each per annum. The receipts from fees are only about one-fifth of the expense, but they are gradually rising. In December last thirty-eight students passed the Matriculation examination."

Saturday, Feb. 8th.—Preached my first sermon in Madras this evening, in the Union Prayer-meeting Hall, in New Town. They have preaching and prayer-meeting every Saturday evening; and Mr. Feuks, the secretary, requested me to conduct that service weekly as long as I could. The Lord was with us to-night, to quicken the faith and zeal of believers. The Hall was crowded, and there were many who could not get in—it being a small place; so their committee said that, with my consent to serve them, they would secure the use of the Baptist Chapel hard by, which will seat about 350 persons. They arranged accordingly.

Sabbath, 9th.—Having no appointment for preaching, I accepted Miss Condon's invitation to visit the Ragged School in Blacktown.

She said: "We have over 100 poor children there, who are taught for an hour, and then a breakfast is given them. They are greatly interested in the breakfast, but very dull as learners."

"Do you teach them to sing?"

"O no; they are too stupid for that; they don't seem to have any capacity, except for food."

"Well, I will engage to teach them to sing a hymn and tune in fifteen minutes."

20

So we went to the School, and found Dr. Vansomeren, his earnest Christian wife, two daughters and a son, Mr. and Mrs. Bowden, and others, engaged in this work. I was asked to address the school. I said, "I will first teach these children to sing. We can do that in fifteen minutes. Now these gentlemen can look at their watches, and see that these children can learn to sing in the given time. Now, children, I have said you can learn to sing in a quarter of an hour. Your teachers love you, and they have got a good breakfast ready for you out there; but they don't believe that you can sing. I am sure you can. Now open your ears, and I will put the song into you. Don't open your mouths till the song gets in; and when you feel it trying to get out at the ends of your fingers and toes, then open your mouths, and we shall all hear the song rolling out like little water-brooks after the showers of spring. Now we will begin :—

"'We are bound for the land of the pure and the holy,
The home of the happy, the kingdom of love:
Ye wanderers from God in the broad road of folly,
Oh, say, will you go to the Eden above?

Chorus—Will you go, will you go, will you go?
Oh, say, will you go to the Eden above?'"

I repeated this verse for about five minutes, and then said, "I see you are getting filled with song: now all of you open your mouths, and sing the chorus after me." They mastered the chorus in about two minutes, and the verse and tune in five minutes more; and before the fifteen minutes were out I was quiet, and the mass of children singing the whole thing themselves, to the astonishment and delight of their teachers. They soon committed to memory all the verses of the hymn; and for a number of Sabbaths I went and talked to them about Jesus, and taught them many hymns and tunes. About the third time I visited them I said, "We will sing 'The Eden above.' Let some one start it." In the corner a lot of little girls were huddled together on the floor—being too small to sit on the benches; and one of these little birds raised the tune on the right key, and they all joined and sang it through themselves.

In the evening, according to previous announcement, I preached in the open air, at the back of the school-house where I met the children this morning. After preaching, Dr. Condon and Colonel Goddard related their Christian experience, and we had one or two seekers. It was a good meeting of its kind.

Monday, 10th.—This evening we commenced our series of services in the Evangelistic Hall, which seats about 300 persons, and was packed with attentive hearers of all sorts, including twenty or thirty Hindūs. After preaching, I went with Dr. Condon to the monthly Missionary Conference, at the house of Rev. Mr. McDonald, of the Church Mission. The regular topic for the evening was postponed, and I was invited to occupy the time. I gave them an account of how God had led me in the organization of the Bombay and Bengal Mission, and of its peculiar principles of self-denial on the part of its ministers, self-support by its people, and the self-reliance of its converts. I gave them a number of examples of converted Parsees, Hindūs, and others — illustrative of the practicability of carrying out the Gospel principle of self-reliance, under which Jews and Gentiles alike were expected, when converted to God, to "go home to their friends and tell them what great things the Lord had done for them." In regard to men's relations in life, and the duties growing out of them, St. Paul says, "As God hath distributed to every man, as the Lord hath called every one, so let him walk. And so ordain I in all churches. Is any man called being circumcised? let him not become uncircumcised. Is any called in uncircumcision? let him not be circumcised. Circumcision is nothing, and uncircumcision is nothing, but the keeping of the commandments of God. Let every man abide in the same" secular "calling wherein he was" engaged when "called" by the Spirit of God. "Art thou called being a servant? care not for it: but if thou mayest be made free, use it rather." "And the woman which hath an husband that believeth not, and if he be pleased to dwell with her, let her not leave him." "But if the unbelieving depart, let him depart. A brother or a sister is not under bondage in such cases, but God hath called us to peace."—1 Cor. vii. 17-21, etc.

If a breach is made in any business or domestic relationship, it must not be by the converts, but by their persecutors; and they must for Christ's sake suffer the injustice of slavery or any form of persecution rather than break these relations; but if after all they are violently rent asunder, the child of God is released, and at liberty, under the leading of God's Spirit, to do the best thing available in the sad disruption of his relations in life. Thus we should never assume that a saved wife or child cannot go back after baptism, and "remain in whatsoever calling" or relation they sustained when called by the Spirit of God; but rather assume, on the authority of apostolic precedent, that they can; and so teach them from the start.

"But," replied one of the missionaries, "have not times altered since the days of St. Paul?"

"Yes, they have; especially here in India, under the life-sheltering wing of the British Government. If these principles could be carried out, as they certainly were, and sealed with the blood of martyrs innumerable, under the Roman Government, why can they not be carried out under the benign rule of a great Christian Government? I don't care to debate the abstract question; but we are daily demonstrating the soundness and feasibility of these great principles. Our Mission, but two years old, cannot claim practically to have solved this problem; but, so far, all our converts have gone home to their friends, and all remain, except two,—one a young Parsee, who was turned out by his uncle, and got a situation for self-support immediately; the other a young Jew, who was also cast adrift by his people, but in a few days got a place in the Mission Medical College as a student." I gave a number of cases, with illustrative facts concerning their Christian struggles in stemming the tide of persecution, and standing firmly in their home relations.

It was but a month before, that the same body declined to invite me to Madras: now I stood among them, as a sort of wonder; but they received me as kindly as they could,—some with real pleasure, and some in meekness, as they would other inevitable visitations. I had, upon the whole, a very good meeting with these dear men of God, and with their wives, who were present as well.

Tuesday, 11th.—Hall again crowded this evening, and a great awakening. I called for seekers to come to the front, where I could get access to them, to instruct them, pray for them, and lead them to Jesus. About thirty came—a large proportion of whom stood up afterwards, and testified that they had obtained the pardon of their sins and peace with God. These services were kept up four days in the week for three weeks; and preaching every Saturday evening for the New Town Prayer-meeting Committee, in the Baptist Chapel, for three months.

We went from the Evangelistic Hall to the Memorial Hall—built in memory of God's mercy in preserving Madras from any outbreak in the Mutiny of 1857. It is a fine hall, to seat about 600, centrally located; and is as the Exeter Hall of London, available for all religious and other popular assemblies. We had that Hall well filled four days in each of four weeks. We next got the use of the London Mission native chapel, in Pursewākum—a very populous district of this straggling city of Madras. We afterwards rented that chapel, and established regular Sabbath preaching services in it. Later, Dr. Condon and his friends built, seated, and lighted (at the cost of 1000 rupees) a "pàndal" forty feet by sixty in size, on the Esplanade. The city authorities would not give us permission to occupy the site for a longer period than three months; but it became such a place of popular resort five nights in each week, and productive of so much good, that they kindly renewed our free lease, to run on indefinitely. They of course can order us to quit; but unless some new heads of department come in who are adverse to our work, we may go on there (D.V.) for years. A "pandal" is simply a shed,—pillars of wood, stone, or brick, covered with thatch or tiles, and walled up on all sides about four feet. It is a fine institution for India. It lets a free Gospel out, and lets the fresh air in. It is a native institution; and it is easy to get them to come into it, and hear the Gospel proclaimed; and multitudes who will not come inside, stand within earshot outside, and hear just as well.

Each night of our services, I wrote down the name and address of each person professing to find Jesus; and next day, or as soon as possible, called to see them. Those whom I found to be connected with the Baptists or Wesleyans, or wherever they were likely to be well cared for and do good, I advised to remain, and discontinued my pastoral visits to such,—amounting to perhaps a couple of hundred persons; but all such as were not actual members of any church, or merely nominal members, especially of ritualistic churches, with not much probability of pastoral nurture such as they needed, I organized into fellowship bands in private houses—not at first church organizations, but bands for mutual edification and usefulness. Our first band was organized on Saturday the 22nd of February, 1874, at the house of Mrs. Elizabeth Mitchell, No. 20, Anderson Street, Blacktown. She, with her daughter and son-in-law, Mr. and Mrs. Wallace, found peace with God the first week of our services.

On Sabbath morning, the 23rd, Band No. 2 was organized, at the house of Captain Barton. He was formerly a ship-master, but then in Lloyds' Survey Agency. He had been a praying man for some years; but now received Christ, and for the first time got assurance of his acceptance with God. He became enthusiastically zealous, and testified on all occasions—in his office, on board ship, or railway, both to Europeans and natives, and urged all with whom he came in contact to be reconciled to God; but after a few months, during which time he believed he had led many to the Saviour—among whom was a Hindū woman employed in his family, whom I baptized, and who continues to abide in Jesus—our dear brother, Captain Barton, suddenly fell sick, and died in the Lord. Captain and Mrs. James, of the Madras army, also brought to God at our first series, became members of Band No. 2.

Band No. 3 was organized soon after, on Sabbath afternoon, at the house of Mr. Burr, in Pursewākum; No. 4 at the house of Widow Swain, in Chindarapet—to meet every Wednesday at seven a.m. She and her household, and Dr. Lynsdale, her son-in-law, and his large family, were brought to God at one of our Saturday-night meetings in New Town.

Band No. 5 was organized at the House of Mr.

Joseph Monk, in Parktown, near the Memorial Hall —to meet every Tuesday at seven a.m.; Band No. 6 in the house of Mr. Joseph Reardon, near Pursewākum Chapel—for Sabbath at five p.m.

Band No. 7 was organized in the house of Serjeant Ballantyne—to meet each Thursday at seven a.m.; Band No. 8 in New Town—for every Saturday afternoon. Eight bands organized within about a month of my arrival in Madras.

In addition to the special services six days per week in different parts of the city, I led these eight bands weekly myself for five or six months, till I could develop leaders for them from among our newly-converted men. After the number of converts in Madras had gone up to about 300, we convened a meeting of the dear men who had taken it upon them to invite me to come to that city, and who, with a few of their friends, had borne all expenses up to that time, including a horse and carriage for my extensive pastoral work; and who had requested me, as before noted, not to organize a church there. At this meeting, which was held in the house of my host, Dr. Condon, all the facts came in review before them, of which they were themselves the witnesses; and they unanimously advised me by all means to organize a Methodist Episcopal church, to conserve the fruits of this blessed work of God, and adjust this newborn agency to the soul-saving purpose to which He had called them.

Early in May Brother Bowen visited Madras, and gave us a few valuable discourses, both in the city and in Perambore.

Sister George Miles gave us a few days of valuable service. Soon after, Sister Raitt came, and helped us for six months,—organizing female prayer-meetings, attending the bands, visiting families and the sick, and in every possible way helping on the work of God. She works in a very quiet way, but very effectively for good. After I left Madras, Dr. Condon wrote me that Mrs. Raitt was worth her weight in diamonds. Brother Walter Winckler came and delivered a few able discourses.

Our first advance out of the city, early in May, was to Perambore—famed for its great railway works, and for the wickedness of the mass of its people. About twenty persons from there received Jesus at our meetings in Pursewākum, and walked three miles each Sunday afternoon to attend fellowship class at Brother Reardon's. The Wesleyans had a Wednesday night preaching-service, and four members there who attended class in the city; hence I would not go to Perambore till so large a portion of Perambore had come to me, and I could see clearly that God would have me organize in their own town, rather than have them walk three miles weekly to meet us in the city. They soon after bought a lot, and built a place of worship, and, with a little help from the city, paid for it; and there that beautiful prediction of Isaiah had another fulfilment—"The wilderness and the solitary place shall be glad for them; and the desert shall rejoice and blossom as the rose."

Mr. John James, of Salem, 207 miles from Madras, on the line of rail to Baypore on the west coast, who had formerly lived in Perambore when it was considered the very vestibule of perdition, hearing of the marvellous change in so many of his old friends there, came to see what it was, and found that the half had not been told him. While there, he submitted himself to God, and received Jesus as his Saviour. He returned to Salem, and opened his own house for meetings; and, though he was at first laughed at and jeered, within a few weeks he got ten of his neighbours converted to God, and now we have a living, growing church of God in Salem station.

About the middle of May, by invitation of Captain Grove, I went for a few week-days, eleven miles out, to Palaveram. Being a military station, the chaplain, who lives three miles distant, at St. Thomas's Mount, and who preaches each Thursday night in Palaveram, considered that I had no right to go there. So he called at Captain Grove's the day of my arrival, and said to me, "Why do you come here into my parish to preach?"

"I came by invitation of Captain Grove, backed by Colonel Gage and Colonel Grant."

"But, then, you ought to know that this is my parish."

"I have heard that you preach here once a week; but I was not aware that you had exclusive rights to the town; and the need of some additional ministerial help, as seen in the many drunkards about here, is manifest to all."

"But why did you not ask my permission?"

"I will answer that question by telling you a little of my experience in the city of Philadelphia a few years ago. A municipal order had been passed forbidding open-air preaching; but I went into the market-places, and preached Sabbath afternoons for three months to many thousands of persons who never went to any church. A minister said to me one day, 'How did you get into the markets to preach? I have had a burden on my soul for years to preach to these outside masses; and I applied to the mayor of the city for permission to preach in these markets, and he would not allow me to do it. How did you get in?' 'I got in just as St. Paul got into the market in Athens. I acted under my authority from God to "preach the Gospel to every creature," so far as I have opportunity; and, without stopping to consult anybody, walked in and proclaimed the tidings of salvation. If the mayor has any business with me, he can find me at No. 6, Catherine Street.'"

The chaplain softened down, and I preached to him for an hour. On the following Thursday night I went to his preaching, and was pleased to hear many of my statements of truth repeated by him to his people.

Palaveram is a military station especially for the residence of veterans, who, having fulfilled their term of service, have their choice to go home to England, or settle down in that place, and do light military duty, and receive rations and pay. Many, having married East Indian women, prefer to remain. So in a short time we had a great work among the veterans and their families. A large proportion of these converts remained in the English Church; but a number felt it their duty to join us, and so we have a society there. On the 21st of May, at that series, C. J. Haudin and his wife received Jesus, and at once became earnest workers; and opened their house at Mount St. Thomas, eight miles from Madras, and were used by the Holy Spirit in organizing a "church in their house." Brother Haudin is now a candidate for our ministry, and assistant travelling preacher of Madras Circuit.

To make a long story short,—in the space of seven months we had about 500 who professed to find salvation at our meetings. Many of these, who were allied to other churches, remained in them; many came in from other parts of the country and returned; but a large majority have enrolled themselves in church fellowship with us.

In sketching the record of this work in Madras, I am sorry to feel and know that I cannot, in my situation, do justice to the subject. I am in the midst of exhausting labours in connexion with Messrs. Moody and Sankey; and not having received my papers from Madras, I have nothing to assist my memory, and no time to write half of what is clearly in my mind. But among the many good men God has given us in Madras, I have to make grateful mention of Philip B. Gordon, Esq.—a Scotchman by descent, and successor to his father's law office and practice in that city. In addition to his successful attention to his legal profession, he has for thirty years been a diligent student of the vernaculars of Southern India. He received Christ about the 6th of July, and at once was drawn out by the sympathy and love of Jesus to devote all his leisure to preaching to the natives; and preaches with marvellous power in Tāmil, Telāgū, Canarese, Hindūstānī, and English: a most valuable worker for God.

In the month of June we bought a small lot for 271 rupees, in Pūdūpet Road, in Madras, and built a pandal at a cost of 250 rupees, forty-six by sixty-seven feet; the seats and lights made an extra cost of about 200 rupees. Brother and Sister Fitzgerald were the leading workers in getting up this pandal, and the native school in it—the banner school of our new system of education in India. It is simply a new application of an old principle—viz., the Sunday School principle applied to every day in the week except Saturday: voluntary unpaid teachers; school from seven to nine a.m., giving half an hour longer to all who wish to learn to sing Christian Tāmil lyrics. This school was organized just before I left Bangalore for the first week. Prior to my going we had four or five Tāmil singers. The Sabbath after my return I baptized a Hindū woman who had received Christ a few weeks previous: just before so doing I said, "You may sing a lyric in Tāmil"; when lo! a choir of over a score of good singers opened up, and sang with marvellous effect. They had been trained during my short absence, and consisted of Hindū boys and girls from our new school.

The pandal is covered over with about three inches of clean sea-sand. The little Hindū children sit down in it; and each one smoothing a little square in front of him, writes, as instructed by a teacher, in the sand with the forefinger.

Sister Duckworth has a class of usually about

thirty little ones, near the door. After she thus teaches them to write the Tāmil alphabet, and give the sounds, they graduate to a higher class. They learn to read the Bible in about three months. This school in a few weeks ran up to 125 scholars; some were poor East Indian children, but the mass of them Hindūs.

Soon a second school was opened, in the Esplanade pandal. Lawyer Gordon opened it with prayer. The first day they had more teachers than scholars; but before the week was out they had sixty-five Hindū and thirteen East Indian children, who had, in addition to the regular studies, learned the tune and words of a Tāmil hymn.

One day the singing teacher did not come; and Sister Raitt said, "Who will start the tune?" and up jumped a Hindū boy and led the choir.

During my absence at Bangalore, and other new fields, before I could appoint a minister to take charge of the Madras Circuit, it was worked for a period of over two months by their own lay agency, with Sister Raitt to use the circuit horse and carriage in visiting; and made steady onward progress in every department of the work. When all the members of a church are thus working for God, they have no time nor inclination for backsliding, and do not require much pastoral treatment.

Our work among the natives is just opening; and yet before leaving Madras I baptized six Hindūs who had publicly come out as seekers, and professed conversion to God.

CHAPTER XXV.

BANGALORE AND ONWARD.

BANGALORE is the capital of the native province of Mysore,—a large native city, and military station.

My first visit was about the first of August, in company with Lawyer Gordon, who owns property there. I was his guest in one of his houses, which he keeps furnished and occupied by servants, as a home for himself, his family or friends, when visiting that city. Brother Gordon having just received Jesus, is like a sponge ready for the living waters of truth fresh from God's Book; and I had a blessed sojourn with him for the few days of our stay in Bangalore. Meantime we called on nearly all the ministers in the city; and I preached once for the Wesleyans.

I found that St. John's Hill and Richmond Town were very populous centres, about two miles apart, and the only places of worship near either were high ritualists and Romanists; so I asked Brother Gordon to secure a lot for a chapel in Richmond Town, and my friend J. D. Jordan, Esq., to secure a lot on St. John's Hill. They each succeeded in getting a good church lot on reasonable terms, in very good localities.

The ministers were all kind, but regretted that I thought it necessary to organize. I explained to them how God had manifestly laid that responsibility upon me, and that while I was very sorry to antagonize their feelings, I had no option in the case; but that a true work of God cannot be injurious to anybody, and that they would all be sharers in the fruits in proportion to their investment of sympathy and co-operative effort. It was at that time raining daily; but as September is usually an open, fair month, between the two annual monsoons which fall upon that region, we selected it as the best time for special services. I deputed Brother Jordan to secure a hall and make arrangements. In due time he wrote me that Judge Lacey, of Mysore, had tendered us the use of Clarendon Hall, a mansion with a large central, and transverse front, hall, giving sittings for about 300 persons.

The rains continued to pour in heavy torrents through September, so that I did not return to Bangalore till about the 25th of that month. Brother Gordon and I arrived on Tuesday morning. Brother Jordan was confined to his house with illness, so that all arrangements for seating and lighting the hall had yet to be made. It was still raining, and the look-out was very gloomy; but we went to work, and before night we had borrowed seats, and bought lights, and had the hall all ready. Owing to the uncertainty of the weather, and other conditions, no announcement had been made of our services. Dr. Condon had some large posters printed for Bangalore special services, and we had them posted the first day; but they were torn off the walls, so that I never heard of but two or three

21

that were seen by the people who would be likely to come; so the first and second nights I had only twenty-four persons in attendance, but when the news of our services got out, we had our hall crowded. Up to Friday night we had more than twenty persons forward as seekers, and a few saved. Then I returned to Madras for the Sabbath—distant 216 miles. That was the Sabbath of our second quarterly meeting in Madras; and a glorious meeting it was. The love-feast was on Monday night, in the Esplanade Pandal. In an hour and thirty-five minutes 117 sisters and brothers gave a clear, distinct testimony for Jesus. No commonplace quotations, nor cant phrases, but a simple statement of facts: date and place of their conversion to God, and of the saving power of Jesus, by which they were daily preserved from sinning. Visited the Mount and Palaveram on Tuesday; and on Wednesday, accompanied by Brother and Sister Haudin, returned to Bangalore, and pushed the battle for five weeks. The first Sabbath night after my return I preached in the Wesleyan Chapel: a spacious hall, and a large congregation that night, but no conversions. The ministers of the different bodies are hard-working, good men—most of them engaged in teaching school; but, for reasons no doubt satisfactory to themselves, they did not co-operate publicly in my meetings. One of them came three times, another twice, and two others once each; but J. D. Jordan, Esq., stuck to us, and got a great blessing in his own soul; and his dear wife, for many years a consistent, earnest seeker and worker, and reputed to be a devout Christian, was at these meetings brought into the light and liberty of assured discipleship. Lieutenants George Rumsay and Jacob Hodgins, of Her Majesty's 18th Huzzars, and Lieut. Russell of the 9th Battery, received Jesus and salvation, and gave us great assistance in many ways; over thirty soldiers, with a number of their wives, also became soldiers of the Lord Jesus at those services; and large numbers of civilians,—the Laceys, the Barrows, the Stevensons, the Mershes, the Marshes, the Devereuxs, the Duckworths, the Brittons, the Barneses, the Margenos, the Palmers, and the Thomases (a Hindū family living with the Palmers), Mrs. Judge Gordon, Miss Martha Shaw, and many more,—numbering altogether 140 converts during the campaign of less than seven weeks, one hundred of whom united with us in church fellowship, and were organized into four fellowship bands: one every Wednesday at Dr. Barrow's; one on Tuesday at Mr. Marsh's, on St. John's Hill; one at Clarendon Hall, on Thursday; and one on Saturday at Mrs. Buchanan's, in Wood Street, Chuley. Sister Helen Lacy rendered us great service in spiritual work, and in raising funds.

Meantime the contract was let for building a cheap chapel on our lot on St. John's Hill, thirty feet by seventy. I appointed Rev. James Shaw, one of our ministers in Bombay, to the charge of this new circuit, and initiated him into the work before I left the field; and soon after, his wife and three children joined him. The preacher in charge, and his family, are all well provided by this new organization. The chapel has since been opened, and the work is progressing well. Dear Brother Shaw has the failing common to the preachers of my Mission—that of working too hard. He has worked himself nearly to death. I wrote him that, as we had no missionary appropriations, and as the moneyed resources of our people were but limited, we could not well afford to go home on furlough for rest, nor to the Sanitarium in the hills, nor even to pay funeral expenses ; and that we must, therefore, give close attention to the laws of health, and especially secure regular nightly and sabbatic rest for body and mind. He replied that he never expected to "go home," nor to go to the hills for rest, till his work was done; and he had no concern about his funeral expenses, as the municipality would see to it that after his death he should not be allowed to remain above ground beyond his time. His people love him and his dear wife, and will do everything possible for their comfort, and see that they shall lack for nothing which it is in their power to give them, living, dying, or dead.

From Bangalore I returned to Madras, and remained nine days, including two Sabbaths; and then, accompanied by Brother Haudin, spent a week on the Madras railway line, and organized a society at Arconam, another at Jollarapett, and another at Salem station (where John James laid the foundations),—distant respectively from Madras, 42, 132, and 207 miles. Thence we went to Secunderabad, and spent a few days in Walter Winckler's circuit, and had 120 sisters and brothers at the sacrament of the Lord's Supper. Thence Haudin returned to Madras; and I proceeded to Poona for a few days, and thence to our District Conference in Bombay.

As usual, we had a glorious love-feast in Bombay, as we had in Poona the week preceding; at each of which about eighty persons told of their trials and triumphs in the service of God. On this occasion, in Bombay, three more of Krishnā Chowey's kindred were saved, and I baptized them at the love-feast: Unūpren Cānnan, aged forty-two years; Sūnderī Buttī, aged thirteen, and Paidal Buttī, aged ten (Nos. 3 and 4 respectively in the Frontispiece).

These, I learn, are getting on well. Rev. W. E. Robbins, in a letter dated March 29th, 1875, says: "In the school where Paidal is going, a heathen boy a few days ago accused him wrongfully. Another heathen lad took his part, saying, 'Paidal is a Christian, and will not tell a lie'; and went on defending the Christian boy before the heathen school till they honourably acquitted him of blame or suspicion."

So our Hindū converts, old and young, stand their ground in the midst of their heathen friends and foes, and let their lights shine where light is so much needed.

Part of my business in Bombay at this time was to meet three missionaries from New York, sent us by our Mission Board. I expected to have returned to Bangalore and Madras, and thence, *viâ* Calcutta, to Shāhjehanpore, to the annual meeting of the Indian Conference, in January; but on account of delay in the arrival of our new missionaries, and a change in the time of Conference session (from the 14th to the 6th of January, 1875), I was unable to return south.

Our dear brethren, Revs. C. P. Hard, Frank A.

Goodwin, and John E. Robinson, arrived in good health, in the fulness of the blessing of the Gospel, the day after our love-feast; but we extemporized another, and had a grand rally of our people, who were greatly refreshed by the rich testimony of our new men, and their grand singing—all being good musicians and singers. They arrived on Friday, and left for their work on the ensuing Monday. Brother Hard was appointed superintendent of the Madras Circuit, Brother Goodwin of Synde Circuit, beyond the Indus, and Brother Robinson of Secunderabad Circuit—Brother Winckler, its founder, having been transferred by Government order to Mysore.

Soon after their arrival our new missionaries were saying to each other, "Now we must separate; but we shall probably see each other occasionally during the year." I informed them that Madras was 800 miles south of Bombay, and Kurrachee, Brother Goodwin's head-quarters, 821 miles north, so that when they wished to converse with each other, they would stand at the respectful distance of 1600 miles apart. Brother Robinson will be about half way between Bombay and Madras.

The brethren did not know how they would get to their work, as they, according to agreement, came to us "without purse or scrip"; but when the time came to start, each one found his bedding, new and clean, all strapped and ready, tickets for travel, and funds for the journey put into their hands by our stewards. The missionaries were so surprised by such things that they came and told me all about it, as news for my information.

In the spring of 1874, five of my members in Calcutta, belonging to the Government Telegraph—Brother Bates, and Brothers De Sylva and Snell and their wives—were sent to Agra.

While on this trip to Bombay I received a letter from Brother Bates, giving a detailed account of the work of God in Agra. On his arrival he found Brothers E. O'Daugherty and L. A. De Prazer, from Brother Osborne's church in Allahabad, and Brother J. Smith from Lucknow, and organized them, with the said members from Calcutta, into a fellowship band. Then, after a few weeks, they wrote for Brother Osborne to come and help them; and by his powerful preaching, under God, many were brought to Christ. Before his return to Allahabad he left an organized church of forty converted people in Agra, with no pastoral care, except from occasional visits by Brother Gladwin from Cawnpore; and they were anxious for me to help them, and send them a missionary. So I went from Bombay to Agra, preaching, on the way, two nights at Jubbulpore. I laboured a few days at Agra in company with Dr. Fraser, from Poona, and lodged at the house of his son-in-law, Captain Angelo. We had a few persons saved; I conducted their first watchnight service, and the infant church was quickened. But though my Calcutta members organized the first class, and though Agra territorially belongs to the Bombay and Bengal Mission, as the work had been developed principally by Brothers Osborne and Gladwin, I stipulated with them, and with Brother Mansell, their presiding elder, that for the present they might include it in their work, and supply it, provided they would conduct it on our self-supporting principles—which they promised to do; and at the ensuing Conference Brother Gladwin was appointed superintendent of the Agra Circuit.

From the Conference in Shāhjehanpore I went to Lahore, *en route* to Synde; but in helping my Presbyterian brethren, Brothers Forman and the three missionary Newtons, in special services, I was detained in that city till I received the invitation to come to London. The letter containing it, written in December, was sent to Madras, and had to be forwarded to me in Lahore, nearly 2500 miles distant; hence it did not reach me till the middle of February. I was so intent on pushing my work in India, that I did not for a moment entertain the thought of leaving at that time; but the next day I saw it was God's will that I should combine that with my visit to my family, and come away at once. The following, containing some confirmatory evidence from the pen of Rev. George Bowen in regard to our Mission, is clipped from the *Bombay Guardian* of February 27th, 1875:—

"The Rev. Wm. Taylor has received a letter from Mr. R. C. Morgan, Editor of the *Christian*, in which, after giving an account of the plan of Messrs. Moody and Sankey to carry on a preaching campaign of four months in London, he says:—

"'Mr. Moody has requested me to write to you, in the hope that the Lord may give you to hear in this invitation the cry, "Come over and help us." Of course all expenses will be guaranteed. I am desired by the Committee of the Noon Prayer Meeting to say that we must be responsible for these. I may remind you that London is the metropolis of the world, and that to move this mighty city as it never has been moved, is worth any effort which any number of men of God could put forth. . . . 'We fervently hope that it may be our Father's good pleasure to appoint you as one of His ambassadors in this great work.'

"It is seven years and a half since Mr. Taylor has seen his wife and children. His wife is a woman of kindred spirit to his own, taking the deepest interest in the work which the Lord has been accomplishing through him; nor has she ever once asked him to leave this work and come home, till now: in the last letter received from her she for the first time expresses the desire, not for her own sake so much as for that of his sons, now fast growing to manhood. Mr. Taylor had calculated upon taking a furlough next year. At present, however, the work in India, through the reinforcements recently received from America, is in such a state of development and organization that it can be left by him. He has been thus led to believe it to be the will of God that he should now visit England and take part in the great evangelistic campaign to be carried on there during the next four months. After this he will be free to visit his family in America. We do not anticipate that he will be long away from India.

"We do not suppose that Mr. Taylor has seen so many brought to the Lord under his ministry in India as he hoped to see before he came here. He has seen vast numbers converted under his preaching in the United States, Canada, Great Britain, the West Indies, Africa, and Australia. Formidable difficulties here presented themselves. From the beginning his desire was to be made useful to the natives; but he found the interval between India and his native land was not so great as that which separates Christians in India from the masses of the people. The Lord led him to see that the stumbling-blocks must be taken out of the way before the chariot-wheels of His salvation could go forward. The type of Christian life in India was too divergent from that of the Gospel; before the heathen could see that Jesus Christ was the Saviour of sinners, it was necessary that they who professed to believe on Him should show in their consecrated lives His saving power. During the last three years Mr. Taylor has given himself heart and soul to this antecedent and preparatory work of raising up, through the blessing of God, a witnessing and working Church, embracing men and women of all nationalities, but mostly using the English language, with this idea dominant in the hearts of all,—that they are commissioned of God to show forth His saving truth to the Gentiles among whom they live. In the development of this work nothing is more marked than the tendency to ramify. Men have been raised up in Bombay to become evangelists and pastors in many different parts of India; nor has Bombay suffered. With only two ordained ministers here resident, there are about *fifty services* held weekly, in English, Mārāttī, and other languages. One peculiarity of this work is that it is self-sustaining. It is not dependent upon the aid of any Missionary Society in England or America. The converts have been mostly among the middle or lower classes, yet there has been no lack of funds. Six missionaries came from America to join the Mission-work superintended by the Rev. Mr. Taylor; and the expense of their passage from America was all that the Missionary Society was asked to defray. We have before us the financial statement of the Bombay Circuit for 1874, printed for the information of members. The total disbursements amounted to 7733 rupees. This embraces expenditure, not only in Bombay, but in a number of places where the work was in its infancy. The receipts were 7042 rupees. A surplus at the beginning of 1874 supplied the deficiency. Of the receipts, 3291 rupees was collected in fellowship bands, 2735 rupees in the congregations, and 1012 rupees by subscriptions and donations. Mr. Taylor has taken nothing from the churches which he has been the means of raising up in India—not even his travelling expenses: just so far as these churches shall be animated by the same self-renouncing spirit, they may expect to accomplish the end for which they have been raised up."

CHAPTER XXVI.

LIGHT IN DARKNESS.

THIS chapter is from the pen of Miss M. E. Leslie, daughter of an old minister, deceased, of the Baptist Mission in Calcutta. Sister Leslie is a very earnest Christian worker, and successful teacher in charge of a ladies' high school, in which many native young women and girls get a good education in English and Bengālī. I held a series of special services in her school; and about a score of her Bengālī girls received the Saviour, and are making good progress in their heavenward journey. A number of our dear converts have gone from the Bombay and Bengal Mission to their home in heaven ; but as no details of the glorious triumphs which all of them experienced in their death-struggle have been given, I am glad to avail myself of the loving painstaking of Sister Leslie in noting the facts of this narrative, as illustrative of how God gives victory to our people in life and in death. Her account of my dear blind sister is as follows :—

It is with a glad heart that I take upon me a labour of love in writing a short account of one who has lately passed away from our midst into the immediate presence of the Lord Jesus Christ. I do it "to the praise of the glory of His grace, wherein He hath made us accepted in the Beloved; in whom we have redemption through His blood, the forgiveness of sins, according to the riches of His grace."

In the beginning of 1873 there was living in Calcutta a large family by the name of De Cruz. They were not rich in this world's goods; indeed, they were very poor. Three brothers and two sisters depended on the earnings of an elder brother,—who, being a child of God, uncomplainingly took upon himself the burden of his sisters and brothers. The eldest sister, Susan, was sorely afflicted. She had been paralysed, but had in a great measure recovered the use of her limbs. Blindness followed the stroke of paralysis. She could distinguish day from night, but very little else. Feeble, distorted, blind, she might have been deemed helpless; yet to her, as the eldest sister, all the rest of the family clung. From the time of her mother's death, in 1864, she had been as a mother to her younger brothers and sisters. To her they went for counsel and help; it was she who managed the household; she was indeed the centre of that family circle.

She was, however, in double blindness. The eyes of her body had been darkened, and the eyes of her understanding had not yet been enlightened. She was consequently not happy. But the loving Saviour, who when He was on earth showed so much pity for the blind, had thoughts of love towards her, and drew her to Himself, and laid His Divine hand upon the eyes of her soul. Very wonderfully was the change brought about. Her elder brother had often seen that much loved, much honoured servant of God, the Rev. William Taylor, pass his house; and he wished greatly to ask him to come in and speak to one of the members of his household. For some time he hesitated to do so; at last he resolved to speak to him, and watched several mornings for his passing by. At length one morning he saw him coming along, and stepped up to him and asked him to come in. From that time Mr. Taylor commenced holding meetings at the house on Monday mornings at half-past five o'clock. The word spoken by him entered into Susan's heart, and she began to feel uncomfortable. She told me that one Sabbath evening especially she felt the burden of sin lying very heavily upon her conscience. She was so distressed that she slept but little that night. The next morning—July 7th, I believe—Mr. Taylor came as usual. He used to make her sit close beside him, that she might distinctly hear the words of the hymns he sang. That morning he taught and explained the hymn beginning with,—

"Zion stands with hills surrounded,
Zion, kept by power Divine;
All her foes shall be confounded,
Though the world in arms combine;
Happy Zion!—
What a favoured lot is thine!"

She acknowledged she felt much, and wept very bitterly all the time; but said nothing till after the meeting closed, when Mr. Taylor rose to go, and then she could not restrain herself any longer. She stood up and said, "Oh, Mr. Taylor, I want to be saved." Ever ready in his Master's service, Mr. Taylor instantly knelt down beside her, instructed her, and led her to Christ. She said, "It was as if an angel spoke to me." She was enabled that very morning to receive Christ as her Saviour, and to rejoice in Him as a sin-pardoning and sin-cleansing Redeemer. The eyes of her understanding were now enlightened, and her soul grew full of light.

It was very sweet to hear her from time to time bear her testimony to the power of Christ to save. Few who were present at the first fellowship-meeting she attended will ever forget the scene. After hearing her blessed experience, with hearts full of joy, we sang the following verses :—

"Now, methinks, I hear him praising,
Publishing to all around,
'Friends, is not my case amazing?
What a Saviour I have found!

"'O that all the blind but knew Him,
And would be advised by me!
Surely they would hasten to Him—
He would cause them all to see.'"

Having found the Lord herself, Susan was very anxious that others also should find Him and rejoice in Him. About three months after her conversion she heard of a blind person who was still in spiritual darkness. All her warmest sympathies were at once excited, and she expressed a wish to speak to her. A meeting was arranged, and very lovingly and tenderly did she strive to lead her blind sister to Jesus by telling her what Christ had done for her own soul. Among other things, she told her that it seemed to her as if Christ were always sitting close beside her, and she had only to ask for what she wanted, and it was done. Before parting, she prayed very earnestly and touchingly for the blind one beside her. It was not long before that prayer also was granted: the blind now sees.

Soon after 1874 commenced there came feebleness and pain. With this feebleness temptations beset the sufferer, but through the agency of the same beloved servant of God the darkness cleared away. In February she had the first severe attack of illness. She was in great pain, and was obliged to go to the Medical College Hospital. There I visited her, and found her in perfect peace. Christ's presence brightened up even the dreary wards of the hospital. She desired to live, and requested prayer for life. It was not for herself that she wished it, but on account of the younger members of her family—especially for the sake of a young sister about ten years of age. On my first visit to her, thinking she was near the end of her journey, I said, "Would you like to send a message to Mr. Taylor?" "Yes, I would." "What?" "Tell him that my sickness is much worse than it was when he was here, but that my mind feels very nice. I feel much more peace and love than I did when he saw me. Give him my best regards and a sister's love. Tell him I thank him many, many times for coming to our house. If he had not come I should have remained in the same state of inward blindness. He led me to Christ. I may never see him in this world, but I shall see him in the next."

She recovered from this attack, and was soon able to go back to her house. But as this wave receded it left her nearer her heavenly home; the next was to lift her still higher; while the third was to carry her further still, and leave her safely landed on the other side.

On the 28th of May the next attack came on. She had suffered much from restless and sleepless nights, during which she used to solace herself with singing. "Oftentimes," her brother says, "at the dead of night her sweet voice would be heard singing hymns one after another, and when we pressed her to keep quiet, she would tell us that Jesus had told her to sing." The evening before she was taken ill she retired in her usual health, and during the silence of night sang as usual, only her voice was louder than before. Towards morning she became unconscious, and continued so all day. She was often spoken to, but returned no answer. About six in the evening her brother asked her if she knew Jesus, and to his astonishment she answered, "Yes." The night which followed was a wonderful night. She sent her brother for me, charging him not to return alone. I went; and never shall I forget the scene of triumph! I said to her, "You are now in the dark valley of the shadow of death: is Jesus with you?" "Yes; He is here." "Do you feel any fear?" "No." She asked me to sing "Over There." I sang the two first verses, and she joined me in singing,—

"In that beautiful land over there,
By the side of the river of life,
Where the tree of life blooms ever fair,
Is no sorrow, nor sighing, nor strife.

"The glorified saints over there,
They once suffered and toiled here below;
Now exalted, Christ's triumph they share,
Sin, nor anguish, nor death ever know."

I then repeated, "Let not your heart be troubled: ye believe in God; believe also in me." She responded, "I do believe." I went on, "In my Father's house are many mansions; if it were not so, I would have told you. I go to prepare a place for you. And if I go and prepare a place for you, I will come again, and receive you unto myself; that where I am, there ye may be also." I then remarked, "Jesus Himself will come to receive you to Himself. He will not send an angel." In a surprised tone she said, "But He is here!"—and pointed to the side of her bed. "Do you see Him?" "No; but I know He is here. Do you love Him?" she then asked me. "Yes; I thank God, I can say that I do." She seemed restless and in bodily distress. I softly sang,—

"My heavenly home is bright and fair,
Nor pain nor death can enter there.
We'll wait till Jesus comes,
And we'll be gathered home."

She joined in and continued the second verse herself. I spoke to her of the sufferings of Jesus, and said, "What did He do for you?" "He died for me," she answered; and at once struck up—

"My Saviour suffered on the tree:
Glory to the bleeding Lamb!
O come and praise the Lord with me:
Glory to the bleeding Lamb!

"The Lamb! the Lamb! the bleeding Lamb!
I love the sound of Jesus' name!
It sets my spirit in a flame:
Glory to the bleeding Lamb!"

I asked her what I should request from God for her. "Nothing in particular—only that Jesus may come and take me soon." I prayed accordingly. The scene was very affecting: paroxysms of intense pain and convulsive struggles, and in the intervals words of triumphant faith and verses of hymns. Her voice rose clear and strong—often joining with others in singing, often bursting out into song alone. On leaving her I said, "Have you any message?" She answered, "Write to my dear Father Taylor; give him my kind regards and love: tell him I shall meet him 'in that beautiful land over there, over there,' and we shall sing together again."

Early the next morning I went again. She was asleep; but woke soon after, and asked who were in the room. I said, "I am here." "Who else?" "Your brothers,—and Some One else." She said quickly, "Jesus." I stayed some time while she slept. When she again woke I came away, saying, "If we do not meet again here, we shall meet yonder." "Sure," was her reply.

In the evening I went with Mrs. Lish. At my request the next morning she wrote out an account of this visit.

"When we went in, the dear sufferer was moaning from pain. Miss L—— asked her, 'What is Jesus saying to you?' She replied, 'He is telling me to wait.' 'You must have patience and wait His time.' 'Yes.' She asked Miss L—— to sing. 'What shall I sing?' She replied quickly, 'Safe in the arms of Jesus.' Miss L—— began the hymn, and presently a low but clear voice joined hers; it rose higher and louder as the hymn advanced, and with great emphasis she sang,—

> "'Safe on His gentle breast;
> There, by His love o'ershaded,
> Sweetly my soul shall rest.'

"She was asked, 'Is Jesus precious to you?' 'Yes; He is precious: He is near me always.' 'Have you any trouble from Satan?' 'No.: O no!' she said triumphantly; 'He never troubles me; he never comes here. How can he?—Jesus is here, so Satan will not come; he is afraid, and trembles. Sing "I'll wait till Jesus comes";' and she again joined in the hymn with a clear voice. Miss L—— said, 'Jesus is fulfilling His promise to you. He is with you to the end.' 'Yes, He is with me; Jesus is with me'; and then she sang out,—

> "'O Jesus! Jesus! Jesus!
> My all-sufficient Friend!
> Come, fold me to Thy bosom,
> E'en to my journey's end.'

"Her heart seemed full—full of the presence of her precious Saviour; and every few minutes she sang out with a clear voice, but catching breath, a verse of some hymn telling of the love of Jesus. Miss L——

asked, 'Would you like to tell me something to convey to the unconverted?' 'Tell them that heaven is a beautiful place—a *beautiful* place; there is neither pain nor sorrow there. Tell them to seek Jesus.' At one time she said, 'I shall be with Jesus and *see* Him.' When about leaving, Miss L—— told her she had brought a friend to see her. That friend stepped to her bedside, and told her she rejoiced to see what the Lord had done for her. She said, 'Do you love Jesus?' 'Yes.' 'Do you love Him *very* much?' 'Yes; He is my precious Saviour.' 'Would you give Him up for all the diamonds and rubies the world contains?' 'I would not give Him up for the throne of England.' 'But the diamonds and rubies of the world are more valuable than the throne of England.' 'I would not give Him up for all the world contains.' 'And are you my sister?' 'Yes, I am your sister, and I love Jesus, thank God!' Miss L—— said, 'We may not meet again on earth, but we shall meet in heaven.' 'Yes, we shall meet each other in heaven,' was her reply."

I saw her again on Sabbath morning, May 31st. She was better, but wanted to go soon. I said, "You must wait patiently," and quoted,—

"Here let me wait with patience."

She took it up, singing from the last line,—

"Break on the golden shore,"

and continued through the chorus. I asked her if Jesus were still with her. She said, "He has not stirred from me for one minute." "What shall I pray for?" I asked. "Pray that Jesus may take me soon." I therefore committed her to Christ, and asked Him to do what was best, and to bless her testimony. I told her that perhaps Jesus was keeping her for a while that she might lead some souls to Himself; and I asked her if she would not be willing to stay. "Yes," she said; and quickly added, "Shall I ask Him to let me stay?" "No," I answered; "say only, 'Thy will be done!' What message shall I give your fellowship band?" I enquired. "Give them my love, and tell them that I am going before, and they must follow me. I will look out for them when I get home."

On June 1st I went again with Mrs. G——, the blind sister in whom she had felt an interest, and who during the interval had been brought to know the Lord. She was better, and told me she was willing to go and willing to stay; she asked me to sing "O bliss of the purified, bliss of the free," "I hear the Saviour say," and "Safe in the arms of Jesus." Never shall I forget with what an expression of unutterable content she said, as I finished the last hymn, "That is where I am resting." I asked her if she talked much to Jesus. "Yes," she said. "About what?" "I tell Him about my father, and ask Him to make him good; and He will do it. I also tell Him about our cookwoman. I have been talking to her this evening; and she cried." "And do you talk to Him about Mr. Taylor?" "Yes—about Father Taylor and Dr. Thoburn and Brother Christian, and the work." She spoke very sweetly to Mrs. G——, asking her if she loved Jesus, and telling her to love Him best of all, to keep close to Him, and to give up everything for Him.

I frequently visited her after this. Though she had rallied considerably, yet still she almost daily had attacks of fever. One day she said to me, "I think God has spared my life for some reason. I think He has some work for me to do. I want you to ask that God would show me what that work is, and prepare me to do it." "Are you willing to do anything for Christ?" "Yes." So we asked for this great blessing. Another day I spoke to her about the fulness there is in Christ—fulness for the supply of every want. I asked her what Christ had lately given her out of His fulness; she at once answered, "Patience."

In August the third severe attack of illness came on. She had strong fever; her lungs were evidently affected, for she had a cough, and was quite unable to sing; and rheumatism seemed to have laid hold of her whole body. One day I asked her where the pain was. She pitifully answered, "All over." It seemed worst in her poor sightless eyes. It was the last wave of trouble—the wave sent to carry her right home. One evening I went in about nine o'clock, and found her crying aloud with pain, the agony was so severe; almost immediately after I entered, the Rev. H. Mansell and some other friends came in. Her sufferings had made her very nervous, and almost every sound distressed her. Mr. Mansell spoke to her very tenderly and soothingly, and then asked her what we should sing. She asked for her favourite hymn, "Safe in the arms of Jesus." We sang it. She then asked us to sing "There's a land that is fairer than day." After this Mr. Mansell sang,—

"I will sing you a song of that beautiful land,
The far-away home of the soul;
Where no storms ever beat on the glittering strand
While the years of eternity roll."

The singing calmed her; her moans ceased, and she lay quiet. At last she spoke, and said tearfully, and in a way that none of us will ever forget: "I grieved Christ to-day. I said, Christ had forsaken me, and did not hear my prayers. Oh, I am so sorry!" She was most tenderly assured that the loving Saviour knew all about her intense sufferings, and had already forgiven her. She seemed to realize His forgiveness, and rested quietly on the Lord.

A few days after she spoke to me calmly and confidently regarding herself. She told me that if she had to seek the Saviour then in the midst of her sufferings she would not be able to do it. I said, "But it is all done; you can say,—

"'Tis done: the great transaction's done!
I am my Lord's, and He is mine;
He drew me, and I followed on,
Charmed to confess the Voice Divine."

I asked her again what I should request from the Lord for her. She said, "Ask that I may have relief from my pain; but that if it is His will that I should go on suffering, I may have patience."

On the 30th of August she was brought very low.

It was thought she could not survive an hour. I asked her if she felt Jesus with her. She could not speak, but nodded in assent. I repeated, "Though I walk through the valley of the shadow of death, I will fear no evil, for Thou art with me; Thy rod and Thy staff they comfort me,"—and said, "Do you fear any evil, dear sister, now that you are in the dark valley?" She shook her head. We sang softly, "O bliss of the purified, bliss of the free!" "My Saviour suffered on the tree," and "Safe in the arms of Jesus."

The next evening, August 31st, she was rather better, having rallied somewhat during the previous night. She asked me to sing "My Jesus, I love Thee; I know Thou art mine." After singing I said, "You can say this now, dear Sister Susan?" "O yes; I love Jesus very much—my Jesus!" "You feel Jesus nearer to you than ever, and more precious?" "Yes." Mr. Meyers then prayed with her, asking for her a calm, painless dismissal, with the presence of Jesus to the end.

I saw her once again, but she was asleep, and I did not like to disturb her. And thus ended all my visits—visits which had been sources of great blessing to my own soul.

On the 9th of September, about half-past six in the evening, she safely reached home. She had been very low for some days; but the end, after all, was rather sudden. God graciously led a dear brother, Mr. H. J. Meyers, to visit her a short time before she died. I give the account of this visit in his own words:—

"It is with unspeakable joy that I detail here the occurrences of a last interview that I was privileged to have with our dear departed sister Susan. It seemed to me that the Lord led me to the bedside of our dying sister in order that I might witness the glorious triumph of faith over all earthly pain and suffering and deprivation, and the power of our Lord Jesus Christ in keeping us near Him, and making us forget all our bodily sufferings when He sheds upon us His Divine influence and love.

"I found our dear sister in great pain, and under great bodily suffering; her extremities were icy cold. I spoke to her; she recognised my voice immediately. Being convinced that her end was near at hand, I asked her if she was fully prepared now to stand in the presence of God, and whether there was any fear lurking in her heart about her future eternity, upon the brink of which she was then standing.

"I shall never forget her reply; it has made an indelible impression on my heart—an impression which will remain until my dying day. She said, 'Brother, I am fully prepared; more so than I have ever been before. I look forward to the moment when my dear Redeemer will come for me, and guide me safely through the valley of the shadow of death. He was with me this afternoon, and I saw Him in all His Divine glory.'

"After telling me all this, our dear sister seemed more calm and happy than she was before. I sang to her that beautiful hymn, 'I will sing you a song of that beautiful land,' which seemed to increase her joy. I then sang 'Near the Cross,' and engaged in prayer with our dear sister. While thus engaged, it seemed to me that the room was filled with the glory of God. Jesus was indeed very near to us—nay, *with* our dear sister, whispering words of encouragement in her ears, soothing her last moments, and lulling her gently to sleep, whilst He in His dear arms would carry her safely over Jordan's stormy waters. I bade our sister a final farewell, and left the house, feeling that the Lord had indeed blessed me, and hoping and trusting that when my earthly course is run, my end may be like hers. She expired shortly after I left her."

The next evening we buried her. Before the removal of the body we met in the house around her dear remains. The Rev. H. Mansell conducted the service: we sang her favourite hymn, "Safe in the arms of Jesus," and tried to realize how safe she was —no fear of her ever falling away—*safe for ever.* Mr. Mansell read part of 2 Corinthians v., and then thanked God for all His goodness to her, and for having at last taken her safely home. And then, while her ransomed soul was rejoicing in light, the body was borne away and laid in the grave, there to wait until Jesus comes and calls His saints to rise and meet Him in the air.

The day had been very rainy—a dark, dismal, dreary day. But just about sunset, the time of her burial, the clouds lifted, and a bright flood of sunshine lighted up the whole scene. I thought of the darkened life, of its joyous close, and of the glorious fulfilment of that word of promise, "At evening time it shall be light."

"Unto Him that loved us and washed us from our sins in His own blood, and hath made us kings and priests unto God and His Father: to Him be glory and dominion for ever and ever. Amen."

CHAPTER XXVII.

SUMMARY REVIEW.

I.—*Calcutta Progress.*

OUR chapel in Dhurramtollah Street was opened by the superintendent of the Circuit, Brother Thoburn, about a fortnight after I left for Madras. The naked building cost about 8400 rupees—which, with gas fixtures, seats, etc., ran up to a total, including price of the lot, of about 16,000 rupees; and everything was done on the most reasonable terms. Having received 10,000 rupees from Bombay, it seemed to leave but little for our people in Calcutta to do; but their means were so limited, that it was a matter of great concern to know where the money was to come from—having already built and paid for the chapel in Zigzag Lane. It is a principle of our Mission not to go in debt. We are too poor for that; we cannot afford to pay interest, and do not believe in it. We have adopted Henry Reed's principles in regard to church building; which are as follows:—

"In undertaking to build a house for God, settle three questions in the premises, and from these deduce a practical conclusion as the principle of action; which, if properly worked, will build without debt:

"First, Does God want the house built?

"Second, Are we the people for whom and by whom He wishes to build a house for His glory?

"Third, Has His time come for its erection?

"Settle these affirmatively, and deduce the conclusion that God is able to build it without having His credit pushed into the market of money-lenders; that is to say, He has the resources, adequate and available, for such a house as He wants built in any given case; and these resources must, by united and believing prayer and praise to God, and by proper representations of the work and its claims to the people concerned, be drawn upon in the name of the Lord for His purpose."

So we built and worked in Calcutta; and I was filled with joy and gratitude to God on receipt of a telegram from Brother Thoburn, saying that the chapel was opened without an anna of debt, and that money was given at the opening, in addition, for a large Sunday library. The house would not contain the people; and souls were saved the first day. It was supposed—as the audience-room had capacity to seat 600 persons, and pack 700—that, after the excitement of the opening had passed, it would then be found sufficiently large; but such, happily, was not the case. Every Sunday night, after packing the aisles and all the standing space about the doors, hundreds had to go away for want of room. The soul-saving power of the Holy Spirit was manifested in the conversion of sinners every week.

Brother Thoburn, according to an engagement made before he joined my Mission, spent three months in Nyne Tāl, and had a blessed work there—that being the summer seat of Government for the North-west Provinces. The presence of Sir William Muer and his family added greatly to the religious influence of the place. Brother Thoburn got Rev. Henry Mansell, presiding elder of Lucknow District, to supply for him in Calcutta during his absence ; and well and efficiently he did it. Meantime the Lord gave us two additional preachers for the Calcutta work.

One was Brother Thomas Oakes, who felt that he was called to that work before I left. I said to him, "Your father has educated you to help him in mercantile pursuits, and greatly needs your services just now ; so you should be very clear in your perceptions of duty."

He replied, "I am clear that God has called me to devote all my time and energies to His soul-saving work. I am quite willing to remain a layman, and have no ministerial aspirations ; but I must follow the leading of the Holy Spirit of God ; and if He wants me exclusively for His work, He can take care of dear father and mother and my younger brothers and sisters. I dearly love them,—God knows I do, —and I would gladly do anything for them in my power ; but I must obey God."

Soon after I left he gave himself up wholly to the work ; and God has wonderfully blessed his testimony for Jesus—especially among seamen. Of all the seaports on the face of the earth, for drunkenness and debauchery among seamen, and the brutal treatment they receive from landsharks and native police, Calcutta has been noted as the worst. But God is lifting up a standard for His poor sailors in that city.

Scarcely a ship ascends the Hoogly that is not immediately boarded by Thomas Oakes; and the captain, mates, and all the crew come in for a share of his faithful but loving exhortations and testimony for Jesus; and they soon learn to value his visits, and give him a welcome. We have also two bands of brave, humble, loving women of God, of age and experience, who every Sabbath afternoon visit all the sailors' boarding-houses, and hold services in the bar rooms,—with singing, prayer, testimony to the saving power of Christ, and earnest entreaty with the sailors, for their own sakes and for the sake of their mothers and friends at home, to receive Jesus and be saved from their sins; and hundreds of them are thus brought to hear our ministers on Sabbath nights. My old friend Captain Jones was our pioneer in seamen's work in Calcutta. He brought others; and before I left the city we had Captains Curfy, Williams, Home, and about a dozen seamen besides, converted to God.

Now we have eight "societies" organized in eight different ships; five of them led by their captains, and three by subordinate officers. We believe this is just the beginning of a grand work among the seamen who do business in those waters.

The other preacher added is Brother P. Mūkūrjī, mentioned in connexion with Cawnpore. Owing to the long illness of his wife in Calcutta, he was obliged, with the consent of our brethren in the north, to resign his work in Cawnpore, and settle down in Calcutta. He became the assistant minister of the Bhawānīpore native church, in connexion with the London Mission. He had been educated and was baptized there; but had received Christ and become consciously saved from sin at a Methodist camp-meeting near Bareilly.

After the death of his wife, and the arrival of his old presiding elder, Dr. Thoburn, in the city, he resigned his charge, by mutual consent of all concerned, declined other offers of pecuniary advantage, and joined our self-sacrificing Mission. Being a Brāhman by birth, and having hence access to high-caste natives; and being well educated and deeply devoted to God, he gives great promise of usefulness. So we have four preachers wholly devoted to evangelistic and pastoral work in Calcutta: one an American, one an Englishman, one an East Indian, and one a Brāhman,—all one in Christ; working earnestly and successfully, without salary, yet lacking nothing. During the past winter, to accommodate our large and growing congregation in Calcutta, they rented a theatre at, I believe, 270 rupees per month, and had a regular congregation of about 1400.

As an index to the progress of the work in Calcutta, I will here insert in full a circular letter, issued by Brother Thoburn, when I was last in that city:—

"A STATEMENT AND APPEAL.

"FOR some time past the congregation worshipping in the Methodist Episcopal Chapel, Dhurramtollah Street, Calcutta, have been put to much inconvenience for want of a larger place of worship. When the present Chapel was built, it was not thought probable that a very large congregation would be gathered together, at least for some years; and as the members were few in number and limited in means, an inexpensive building was erected, intended to accommodate comfortably about four hundred persons. From the very first, however, the place has proved too small: so much so, that in the very hottest weather six hundred persons were crowded into it every Sunday evening, and often from fifty to a hundred stood by the windows outside. Among those who came were usually from thirty to fifty educated Hindūs; and it is believed that many more of this class would have attended but for the difficulty of obtaining seats.

"The very great inconvenience of worshipping in so crowded a place, together with the desire to find room for the scores who had to be turned away from the door, led to the resolution to engage the Corinthian Theatre for Sunday evening services. This was done with some regret, as many good people entertained conscientious objections to worshipping in a theatre; but the exigency seemed to justify the step, and the services held there have been signally blessed. The same difficulty, however, has again arisen: the place is found much too small for the congregation. The theatre is furnished with seats for more than 1100 persons—in addition to which 300 extra seats are put in every Sunday evening; and yet as many as a hundred persons have been turned away from a single service, owing to the want of room. Even if the theatre were larger, its use involves a large monthly payment for rent and incidental expenses; and if this difficulty were removed, the place would still be unsuitable in many respects for a permanent place of worship.

"We have thus been led, step by step, to consider the question of erecting a much larger place of worship—a church, or tabernacle, large enough to hold about two thousand persons—built in plain but substantial style, and adapted to its specific purpose as a place into which the surrounding masses may be gathered to hear the preaching of the Gospel of Christ.

"The proposal to erect such a building has been most favourably received by those best acquainted with the wants and condition of the congregation. Indeed, thus far not one person of those whose advice has been sought has hesitated to commend the enterprise, and to urge its immediate and vigorous prosecution. Many who belong to other churches, and whose personal interests are in no manner connected with this congregation, have expressed a warm interest in the undertaking—believing, as they affirm, that the best interests of our common religion will be greatly promoted by the erection of such a place of worship in the midst of the great city of Calcutta. In addition to the resident European and East Indian population, thousands of English-speaking Hindūs and Mohamedans are close at hand, hundreds of strangers from different parts of India may always be found here, while from one to two thousand sailors may always be found connected with ships in port. Many of these sailors have been converted in connexion with the recent services in the theatre; and the proposed tabernacle will, no doubt, be a great place of resort for them when it is finished.

"It is believed also that such a building would often prove a most convenient place for large religious assemblies such as have been held in Calcutta during the past year. At present there is no audience-room in the city suitable for such meetings. The Town Hall, the only room large enough, is very inconveniently situated, and has such bad acoustic qualities as to be practically useless. The churches are all too small; and a large audience-room like that proposed, in a central part of the city, and adapted to the purpose of public worship, would most effectually supply a long-felt want. Although retained as the special place of worship of the congregation who build it, and to whom it will belong, it would always be available for those large religious assemblies in which all the churches have a common interest.

"The probable cost of this building, including site, can hardly be less than 65,000 rupees, and may be 75,000. It is impossible to make an accurate estimate until a site is selected; but under the most favourable circumstances, it will be impossible to erect such a place of worship for less than 65,000 rupees. Such a sum can only be obtained by a general appeal to those interested in this special work, and to the many others who, scattered over India, are interested in *every* good work which seems to give promise of helping forward God's work in this land. It is believed that this is an enterprise in which Christian people in all parts of India may rightfully claim an interest. All the provinces of the Empire are represented here, and strangers from all parts of the country, not to say of the world, may here find an open door inviting them to enter and hear the Word of Life. It will be a place of religious resort for the masses who are unattached to any religious organization. The sailor and the soldier, the Hindū and the Mohamedan, strangers from the hotels and boarding houses, the careless hundreds who are in a large measure indifferent to the claims of religion,—will all be much more easily drawn to a place of worship of this kind than to an ordinary church or chapel. Indeed, the experience of the past few months abundantly proves that such people may literally be gathered together by hundreds, and many of them thus be brought to a saving knowledge of Christ.

"On behalf of the congregation engaged in this enterprise, the undersigned begs to appeal to the Christian public of Calcutta and of India to assist in erecting this place of worship. The work has been undertaken after much earnest prayer and careful watching of God's providential indications; and this appeal is made with a profound conviction that God would have us build this place for the preaching of His Gospel. The work is His, and to His people the appeal for help is made.

"J. M. THOBURN,

"*Pastor of the Methodist Episcopal Church, Calcutta*

"28, North Road Entally, Calcutta,
"*4th February*, 1875."

A month later, the following confirmatory bit of information appeared in the *Christian Spectator*:—

"In Calcutta the good work goes on among the English-speaking population, especially in connexion with the Methodists. It is proposed to erect a large chapel for the Methodist congregation. The Corinthian Theatre has been filled week after week on the Sunday evening; but the heat would be too oppressive to hold service there in the hot weather. Hence the desire to build a large chapel, that will seat 2000 or more persons; and which might also serve for large public religious meetings, for which there is no good place in Calcutta. The cost of the new chapel is estimated at 65,000 or 75,000 rupees; but, judging by the response which has already been given to the appeal sent forth, and the earnest zeal of the members of the Methodist Church to do all they can, it is hoped that the money may be raised and the building finished in the course of the year. There seems to be a special readiness to hear on the part of the sailors in Calcutta, and very many have found peace in Christ.

"The ladies who visit the sailors' lodging-houses in Lāl Bazār are still always well received, and evidently much impression is produced. Men of many nations are met with,—English, American, French, German, Italian, Spanish, Greek, Negro,—tracts are given to them, and they are urged to give their hearts to Christ. The sailors join in the hymns sung, and often listen with weeping to the words spoken to them; early religious impressions are revived, many of them are induced to attend the evening preaching, and not a few of them have found peace and joy in believing. The ladies referred to are our sisters Mrs. Lish, widow of a Baptist missionary; Mrs. Leslie, her daughter, and wife of Brother Leslie, the solicitor; Miss Leslie, the educator; Mrs. May, the wife of Brother Frederick May, the jeweller—a sister distinguished as a witness and a worker for Jesus; Mrs. Meyers, and others."

The following item, from the *Calcutta Daily News*, is an index to the subject of churches and Gospel hearers in that city. The said census was taken in January 1875.

"There are fifteen Protestant churches in Calcutta, of which seven are established. The attendance at all the churches, on a Sunday evening last month, was 4165. Of this number 2241 were at the non-established churches."

II. *Madras Progress.*

A Christmas Treat was given to our two day-schools in this city. The *Madras Daily News* has the following notice:—

"PŪDŪPETT BANNER SCHOOL.—This School, opened by the Rev. Mr. Taylor, has been very successfully worked by members of the Methodist Episcopal Church on the free system. The children, numbering 143 on the register, mustered at the Pūdūpett pandal at four o'clock on Saturday afternoon, to enjoy the 'Christmas Treat' which was got for them by the superintendent and teachers of the School. Among those present were noticed the Rev. C. P. Hard, Captain Newman, R.A., Dr. E. H. Condon, P. B. Gordon, Esq., and other members of the Methodist Church. The children sang two beautiful hymns: 'Shall we gather at the River?' and 'The Gospel Ship'; then followed the singing of the Grace, and the children sat down to a rich repast, to which they did ample justice. After this they sang 'We'll journey together to Zion,' and 'We are coming, Blessed Saviour!'—followed by the native girls, who sang two Tāmil hymns about the 'Birth of Christ,' and the 'Impenitent Sinner,' which did great credit to the School. A short address was then delivered to the children by Captain Newman, who spoke on happiness here and in the world to come.

"Dr. Condon then introduced the new pastor, the Rev. C. P. Hard,—who next spoke, congratulated the teachers on their success and the large attendance; and then giving the children as well as the teachers good and sound advice, urged them to go on steadily. Thirty other poor children of the neighbourhood were also treated to the dainties. Great thanks are due to Mr.

and Mrs. P. B. Gordon, Mr. and Mrs. Fitzgerald, and the teachers, for getting up this Treat. The Benediction was then pronounced by the Rev. C. P. Hard, which brought this delightful evening's entertainment to a close."

Concerning the second School Treat the *Madras Standard* says :—

"ESPLANADE PANDAL SCHOOL.—On Monday evening last, a Treat was given at the Methodist Episcopalian School Pandal, Esplanade, to about 130 European and East Indian children. The pupils attend school daily, and are carefully instructed. There are also about sixty native pupils attending the same school, and to whom a treat will be given in a few days. Addresses were delivered by Colonel Goddard, the Rev. Mr. Hard, and Mr. Wallace. During his address Mr. Wallace alluded to the approaching departure of Colonel Goddard, who had evinced the greatest interest in the improvement of the school, and in the Mission in Madras. Allusion was also made to the departure of Mrs. Raitt from Madras to Bombay. This lady assisted the Rev. Mr. Taylor during his stay in Madras, visiting the poor in the interval of time between Mr. Taylor's departure and Mr. Hard's arrival. The Methodist Episcopal Church has a permanent missionary in Madras; and Mission work is carried on at the Mount and Palaveram, and more than 200 miles along the Madras railroad. The number of members is stated to be four hundred."

The work in this city is developing and extending marvellously, as a few extracts from letters will show.

The first will illustrate the spirit with which my

men go into their work. I have not a man in my Mission that needs a spur; but all need to be held in, to prevent them from working themselves to death. Brother Hard, in a letter dated Madras, December 28th, 1874, writes :—

"DEAR SUPERINTENDENT,—Safe arrival, after joyous journey; crowds of friends—full salvation—good health—plenty to do——I need not complete the sentence, which started to tell you that I am very happy. Ten days in India have been a delight. Perhaps I should give a brief report of self and charge. Well, I preached at Lanowlī on Monday night; Poona, Tuesday night; Gooty, Thursday morning; Puddapah, Thursday night; Esplanade, Saturday night, and Sabbath morning at eight; Pūdūpet, Sabbath morning at eleven; Perambore, Sabbath afternoon at two; Pursewākum, Sabbath evening at six. A hundred stayed in a precious prayer-meeting at Pursewākum after the sermon. One fine young lady of Salem all broken to pieces; turned to the Saviour for the first time.

"I preach there to-night. We rally at the Esplanade pandal Wednesday and Saturday nights this week. Five watchnight meetings on Thursday, from nine to twelve p.m.: Jollarapett, Arconum, Perambore, The Esplanade, and Salem.

"The day-schools will be resumed after the holidays, January 4th. The Sunday School library is in a box at my feet.

"Our missionary collection taken in one place will be completed at the watch-meetings and reported to you.

"The pastor's study is nice. The pastoral administration of Sister Raitt has been admirable. She will stay some time. Brother Aitken is shut up in the sick-room.

Brothers Gordon, Goddard, and Condon are in good preaching trim. The two latter leave India for England in April.

"Quarterly Conference and love-feast on Monday evening, January 4th, when the licenses will probably be given as you named.

"Your Son,
"CLARK."

Eight days later, I received the following report of progress :—

"MADRAS, *Jan.* 4, 1875.

"DEAR SUPERINTENDENT,—I hope by this time you have received our new Plan, and that you are pleased with its appearance. All the workers respond with a wish to do all they can; and some want more work, and we tell them to dig it up. Brother Goddard is obliged by ill-health to omit a few of his appointments (six or eight) in the three months. We are joyful in these days; and the only reason we do not have thorough public meetings by ourselves this week (week-days) is, that we go into the gathering of all 'the saints' during the week of prayer, beginning to-night at six o'clock in Memorial Hall. Brother Somerville is expected. Our forces are in line of battle. Excellent Sister Raitt is ready to take the carriage at any hour; and we give double pastoral supervision wherever we go. She may remain quite a time yet, I trust. We should like to keep her, at least till you come: as you wanted two pastors for Madras. The Lord makes me glad in the work; and has in the eight days just passed permitted me to preach eleven sermons, lead five fellowship bands, make pastoral calls four hours per day, see the Plan through the press, review the leaders' books, prepare and write the church register of members and probationers, address three Sunday Schools and one day-school, revive the Tract Society, sell some dozens of books, hold one watch-meeting (and arrange for four others), hold three love-feasts, administer the sacrament of the Lord's Supper three times, receive twenty-one into full membership, and sixteen on probation out of the twenty who have been converted within these eight days—most of them being men.

"Your son,
"CLARK."

The following despatch, one day later, will speak for itself:—

"MADRAS, *Jan.* 5, 1875.

"DEAR SUPERINTENDENT,—Memorial Hall was full last evening, the Methodists being there. The Quarterly Conference, at eight p.m., in the Esplanade Pandal, was good. Licenses were granted to Brothers Gordon, Haudin, and Peters—as I said you had proposed their names. Brother Peters is to teach me Tâmil three times per week, from twelve to two p.m. Brothers Haudin and Peters are to be students in my theological seminary!

"The register of the church now made up shows that our Circuit has—

(In Madras)	Full Members . .	205
,,	Probationers (previous).	50
,,	,, (this week)	16
Band at	Salem	25
,,	Jollarapett . . .	12
,,	Arconum	15
,,	Mount	20
,,	Palaveram . . .	7
		350

"We were delighted with the Pūdūpett school this morning: 105 scholars. Five sought the Lord at Jollarapett watchnight service.

"Brother James writes me that he held a good watch-meeting at Salem; and they have four meetings per week.

"Col. Goddard's physician has forbidden his preaching at all.

"In the missionary money which your work gives to the India Conference treasury, you may put in Report, 'forty rupees from Madras,' and I will send you draft if you order it, or to the treasurer whose name you will send me. With the love of all,

"Yours,
"CLARK."

Another war despatch from Brother Hard:—

"MADRAS, *Jan.* 18, 1875.

"DEAR SUPERINTENDENT,—Though your letter to me has not yet come, still I write, as I suppose a dutiful son ought, and as I love to do. Mrs. Raitt and I have been busy most of the time since I last wrote to you; and we have enjoyed the work of the Lord. She has been pressing on in her ever bright and useful way. We have been in good health. The Lord has permitted me to preach fifteen times during the last eight days, and lead as many prayer-meetings for seekers of 'salvation' (not 'religion'). During the last seventeen days, sixty men and women have presented themselves in our midst as seekers of God, and two-thirds of them have been born again. Thirty have joined us on probation.

"At Otary we have established a weekly prayer-meeting, where ten have sought the Lord with strong crying and tears. At each of the four preaching-places conversions have occurred.

"At Palaveram two were converted and four reclaimed in our meetings of last Tuesday night and Wednesday morning.

"We organized a Sunday School at Pursewākum on January 10th, and it sailed on yesterday with a hundred—Brothers Reardon and A. Gordon being superintendents, and Miss Stoddard, Mr. Doyle, and Dr. Huffton working earnestly.

"The Pūdūpett day-school is a triumph—has reached 150 in attendance. At the grand supper led by Mrs. P. B. Gordon on Saturday, from three to five p.m., the pandal was crowded, and surrounded by hundreds.

"Tāmil preaching established on Mondays at Perambore: began last week with eighty.

"Our translation into Tāmil of choice tracts has commenced. We are on our sixth,—have issued ten thousand. You can say to any other charges that we will send them 4000 pages for five rupees. Brother P. B. Gordon is our translator: he uses words that the common people can read easily. English tracts have been on the move. Our catechism is now studied in each of the four schools.

"Our Sunday School Normal Class and Teachers' Meeting was organized, for weekly meetings of the Sunday School teachers of the charge, on Saturday, Jan. 9, 1875. The workers have begun a course of reading—Sunday School Teachers' Library; one volume per week.

"Pursewākum Chapel was crowded on Monday, at a service of sacred song.

"Brother Haudin is doing finely; and I have freed him for two weeks, to develop some new work. Sister Haudin has put her earrings into the Lord's treasury!

Jewellery is coming into the collection bags, though but once alluded to!"

"MADRAS, *Jan.* 28, 1875.

"DEAR SUPERINTENDENT,—Your welcome letter from 2500 miles away came duly; and then I sent off a letter which had been waiting for your post-office address to Kurrachee. And now I am wondering whether you will stay at Lahore half a year, and repeat the history of the Madras work, or soon find Brother Goodwin on his great field. A trip up the railway last week was a joy: three meetings at Arconum, and five saved; two meetings at Jollarapett, and ten saved—seven being railway men, and two wives; three sermons at Salem Station,—two saved and two seekers. 'Squire Middleton hired the Town Hall at Salem on Monday evening, and sent his carriage. Half the band took bullock-carts, and helped sing and testify. The Salem Station Band is a gem: twenty-eight. They sent twenty rupees towards my moving expenses, five rupees for Tāmil tracts, and five rupees for Berean leaves, as I organized a school for them. Pūdūpett day-school has 180 a day, and still they flock in. The Esplanade is a tough job—can't get out of the 'thirties.'

"Your Son,

"CLARK."

"MADRAS, *Feb.* 1, 1875.

"DEAR SUPERINTENDENT,—May this find you happy, after a hard day's work for Jesus! We were happy here yesterday. I took Brother Chatelier (blessed man of God!) all the trip yesterday, in visiting the following fellowship bands: Pursewākum at eight, Pūdūpett at eleven, Royapetta at two, Gabriel's at four, Esplanade at five. Eight men and women, from twenty-five to sixty years of age, found Jesus yesterday in that trip: four being at

Pūdūpett, one at Chindārapetta, one at Royapetta, and two at the Esplanade (one was a soldier from the Ordnance lines). This fellowship band business—is it not a grand means of preservation?

"In looking into my book, I see that in January, 110 men and women (equally divided) have presented themselves for prayers; sixty have joined on probation.

"It was a scene of glory at Pūdūpett yesterday—baptizing a woman turned from heathenism, then her child, then four or five children whose heathen parents have signed a request that their little boys and girls be baptized in the faith of Jesus. A heathen mother thus stood by her two boys. I went through the whole length of both forms of baptism, prayers and all being interpreted by Brother Peters. He interpreted for me to the parents that we would never baptize any but at the request of their parents or guardians—that the children are to stay at home and be obedient, but not to serve idols—that the religious training of the children in day and Sabbath school is to be in the hands of Brother and Sister Fitzgerald and their helpers. It was an earnest of Pentecost at Jerusalem repeated, from the 'Parthians' to the 'Arabians'—all colours, from white to the blackest! Singing and prayers and Bible reading alternated in English and Tāmil. Then, as Brother Fitzgerald had been crying to me (glorious worker he is!) for more teachers for the day-school, I preached from David's words (Ps. li. 13): '*Then will I teach!*'

"Rev. S. C. Douglas preached in the Esplanade Pandal on Thursday night. We brought in as many seats as we could find, and the rest of the people that did not choose to stand in the crowd about the Pandal drove away. The Revs. Gillings, Barton, and Fitzpatrick, were present. Mr. Douglas tears off the mantles of the formalists—a man of

God! He took occasion before the sermon to express his joy in *this* work in Madras, of which he had heard before leaving England, and now was glad to see; and asked our prayers for those who have to work among the rich—of whom few come to Jesus. I took up our Saturday afternoon appointment, to have our people go to hear him that night at the Fort. He leaves soon. That (Thursday) night two men were saved, and two young ladies sought the Lord.

"Sister Raitt (well) writes from Calcutta, of 1400 in the Theatre, and of 'dear Brother Taylor' going to spend two months there.* The chances of Madras to have you soon grow slim. We will try to be brave.

"With much love,

"Your Son,

"CLARK."

To this letter is appended the following summary:—

"During the month of January, in the Madras Circuit, there has been this work done (as a part):

"Sermons preached by pastor . .	34
" " by helpers . .	46
Total sermons . .	80
Prayer-meetings (regular sessions) .	70
Fellowship Band sessions . . .	80
Sunday Schools organized . .	2
Seekers	110
Received on probation . . .	60
Value of Books sold . . .	200 rupees.

* That plan has been superseded by my trip to England.—W. T.

"Tāmil Sermons (besides the above) every day; two day-schools and five Sunday Schools; 60,000 pages of tracts translated and printed."

I clip the following from the *Bombay Guardian*:—

"TĀMIL TRACTS AT MADRAS.

"SIR,—The translation of a selection of very excellent tracts from the New York Methodist Tract Society's List was undertaken in January by P. B. Gordon, Esq., who is a local preacher in the Madras Circuit. A man of fifty years of age, brought into a glorious experience of salvation during the past twelve months, and a thorough student of the languages of India for many years, is now being utilized; as he has charge of the Tāmil preachers and preaching in the Circuit. He was impressed with the power of the tracts placed in his hands by his pastor, and was moved by the Holy Spirit to begin their translation in terms which the common people will read gladly. They lead to a present salvation—Jesus 'mighty to save now.'

"Sixty thousand pages have been printed in January. The list thus far is as follows:

"No. 1.—'A Plain Question,'—leading the enquirer to Christ.

"No. 2.—'Come to Jesus.' By Dr. T. L. Cuyler.

"No. 3.—'The Value of Christ's Precious Blood.'

"No. 4.—'Faith and Good Works'—a tract putting aside the latter as a ground of salvation, and explaining the former.

"No. 5.—'A Voice from One in Heaven.'

"No. 6.—'The Supreme Deity of Christ proved'—a sermon by Rev. Elijah Hedding, D.D., Bishop of the

Methodist Episcopal Church. This is a pamphlet of forty-eight pages, with a Tāmil glossary of four pages added by the translator.*

"The printing of these has been obtained much more cheaply than is usual, because of the constancy of employment given to a special printer. New editions will be struck off as required. The work is well done. The translator is recognized as one of the finest Tāmil scholars in Southern India. Four thousand pages may be obtained for five rupees, of the Secretary of the Methodist Tract Society of Madras—viz., Mr. H. Wallace, Anderson Street, Madras."

Rev. Brother Hard, in a letter dated April 9th, 1875, gives many further interesting details of the work of God in Madras. I will clip but one incident from it:—

"A stranger came here about the middle of March, and introduced himself to me as Robert B—— (Superintendent of the Lithographing Department of Government); saying he had heard that I could persuade men to do right.

* In a letter from Brother Gordon, dated May 28th, 1875, he says: "I look upon this as a very precious and timely tract. Just imagine, one morning about seven o'clock, when I was putting the finishing stroke to the translation, who should walk into my house but a Mr. T——, who announced himself as a clergyman of the Unitarian persuasion, handing me a tract which he had translated into Tāmil, from a Mr. Priestley's work on Unitarianism! I never was more astonished in my life. I had spent a fortnight in the translation of Hedding's sermon; and all the time thoughts kept popping into my mind—'You are wasting your time; this will never be of any use to the Native Church in India.' How glad I was then, that in spite of such thoughts, I persevered and got the tract through the press! We have struck off 2000, and it is being circulated widely. It is a thorough answer to all Unitarians, and a perfect antidote to their poisons."

'Come and see my brother Charles; he is in a drunken spree: we can do nothing,—perhaps you can save him.' I got in his carriage,—midday—hot,—and he took me to Poonamalee Road. As we drove into the compound, Charles was roaming about in the scorching heat without a hat, leading his little son by the hand. We entered the house: a beautiful home of the two brothers and their families. The wife of the drunken man was lying on the bed of sickness, having given birth to her third child three days previously, and was in consequent weakness. Charles was invited in, but would not come. I was left alone with him in the back verandah, and talked—then sang; at times he leered, and staggered up to me, and then again slunk off by the wall. At last he was melted, as much as a very drunken man could be, and consented to go in, and took me to his room. We knelt down by his couch. At times I encouraged him that he could be saved, then sang to him, and at last got him to say words of prayer after me. As soon as prayer was done, he cried out, 'Give me my liquor; you can't save me.' In the room where his wife was, he sat on the edge of the bed, said with threatening looks, pointing his finger at Mrs. B——, while she was weeping, 'You have taken away my liquor: I will have it.' He hurled against the wall some helping drink which the apothecary had prepared for her. At last, that day, toward evening, he was taken to the hospital, because he could not be managed at home. Two days later, by written request of his wife, I went to the hospital. He was sober, but weak and nervous; he was sorry for what had taken place, and resolved to be right, but felt his utter weakness in every way. He wrote to me afterwards, stating that he was passing Pūdūpett Pandal one evening, soon after he left the hospital, and was induced to go in. He heard Lawyer Gordon just then relating one of Dr. Condon's statements concerning a man who resolved often not to drink, but at last, in his drunken delirium, shot himself; and that God's help is necessary.

"B—— sought the Lord, and wrote to me the next day that he wanted to join our flock. Now he is in meeting almost every evening, at the Esplanade, or Pūdūpett, or Perambore, or Pursewākum: a splendid man in appearance, fine in bearing, bright in face, of beautiful penmanship, of good education, drawing a good salary. His wife—a beautiful woman, once a Roman Catholic—is now happy indeed. They signed the pledge on Wednesday night of this week (as did others), and are going on to Mount Zion, glad in Jesus.

"C. P. HARD."

I have also received full minutes of the second Quarterly Meeting of the Madras Circuit for this year (1875), which was held April 1st.

The preacher in charge, and each of his thirty-three official helpers, handed in to the secretary of the Quarterly Conference a written report containing a statement regarding their religious experience and their work in its variety.

These reports have been forwarded to me, and would, with numerous welcome letters from sisters and brothers besides, fill a volume; but this one is so full already, as to preclude their insertion, except the following summary report, and a few illustrative specimens.

"QUARTERLY REPORT OF THE METHODIST EPISCOPAL CHURCH OF MADRAS.

"From the written reports received by the Secretary

of the Quarterly Conference the following items are gathered, giving some information as to the work of the first quarter of 1875 :—

"One hundred and ten preaching services have been held by Rev. C. P. Hard, the pastor, and 123 by his assistants in the English work; who have also conducted 142 meetings appointed in the Circuit Plan for exhortation and prayer. Two hundred men and women have sought an interest in the prayers of the Church, of whom over 100 have joined it on probation. A religious book depository has been opened at Messrs. De Beaux's Dispensary, Esplanade. New branches of church work have been commenced; and on the first day of the endeavour to obtain subscriptions for a church building, 2000 rupees were offered,—and the fund is advancing under the care of trustees. The pastor has officiated at ten baptisms, two funerals, and one marriage. The tract distributors are active, under the direction of a secretary and seven superintendents of tract districts. The fellowship bands along the railway have been prospering.

"The present work of this Church in the city of Madras is partially stated thus: During each week eleven sermons are preached, in the appointments of the four Sabbath morning, three Sabbath evening, and three week-evening congregations. Four Sabbath Schools meet each Sabbath at half-past seven a.m. Eighteen fellowship bands, and seventeen meetings for prayer and exhortation, have regular weekly sessions in thirteen sections of the city. Over fifty religious assemblies are in this manner gathered every week, using the English tongue. Beyond this, half a dozen sermons in Tāmil are usually delivered in the pandals and streets daily. Three day-schools are in operation. A Sabbath School Teachers' Normal Class has weekly sessions in each of two places;

and a Theological Training Class, for thirty of the men who had meetings appointed in the Circuit Plan, meets twice a month. The pastor preaches Saturday evenings at the Esplanade Pandal, and Sabbath evenings at the Chapel in Pursewākum.

"H. WALLACE, SECRETARY."

The following is the pastor's own personal report for the quarter :—

"I will limit my report to my own experience as an individual of the company making their statements to-night. To the *Quarterly Conference Record* I may give a summary of the quarter's items reported this evening.

"For myself, with regard to religious experience, I can say I am trying to 'perfect holiness in the fear of the Lord'; and almost every hour I 'joy in God through our Lord Jesus Christ.' I read that the name of our Jehovah-Jesus is 'Wonderful,' and I find that the salvation which He gives is like His name.

"As to my work, I love it. As to my surroundings, I am happy in a home where every possible kind attention is extended to me, and all my wants are anticipated. To the sisters and brothers in the Circuit, how can I render sufficient thanks, that by their words and deeds they endear the place to me every day! Thank God that He makes me very happy in the love of that saved membership!—which is rapidly increasing, there having been during these three months some two hundred seekers of salvation in our meetings, of whom over half have become probationers.

"My home in India is also made pleasant by the fraternal letters which I have received from the brethren in our Conference in Northern India, and by frequent communication with Brother Taylor and his assistants.

"My thoughts go still further; and I have reason to thank my Heavenly Father that I have received three letters from my parents, stating that their health is good, as also that of my brother (a pastor) and his family, and that of my boy, whose new picture—taken on the first of February, when he was two years ten months and twenty-two days old—reached me this morning.

"My mother, who in her old age has this Benjamin, writes me: 'He is a care, but no trouble, and we love him plenty enough; and your father says that he never saw a better, more cheerful, and happy boy than Frank; and he thinks that he never loved either of his own children as well as he loves him. Frank tells people that his "papa has gone to Bombay, to peach mans be goog," and that his "papa will come home when meetin's out." I am trying to be cheerful and happy, and to take care of the darling boy the best I know how; but *oh how I miss you!* But it is all for Jesus!' *

"My father writes from the midst of glorious revivals, in which he is leading hundreds to Jesus: 'I don't pretend to tell what it costs me to give you to this work. It seems as though a part of myself was gone. I try to be resigned, and to say but little; but oh, the depth of my loss God only knows! No words can tell our love to you. Much prayer is offered everywhere for you.'

"I am thankful to the Lord for good health, which has permitted me this quarter to engage in that work of which the public services are but a portion; yet I find that my daily-record book reports me this quarter in this respect thus:

---

* I have since learned that the dear little boy has gone to his mother in heaven. He will there wait for his papa "to come home when the meetin's out."—W. T.

"Eighty-three sermons: eighteen evenings, beyond this, have been devoted to leading prayer or praise and exhortation meetings. Three evenings this quarter I have not been engaged in religious meetings. On one of these I was occupied with church work; another I spent abroad; and one evening I rested at home.

"C. P. HARD, PASTOR."

By the stewards' report, I see the income for the quarter, not including subscriptions for new chapel, was 512 rupees 8 annas 4 pice; disbursements, 484 rupees 5 annas 7 pice: leaving balance-in-hand of 28 rupees 2 annas 9 pice.

The Esplanade day and Sunday School reports may be summed up as follows:—Officers and teachers, 11; boys 53; girls, 45: total average attendance, 81. The day-school there numbers about 40.

Pūdūpet Sunday School has an average attendance of 120. The Pursewākum Sunday School has on the roll 75, and an average attendance of 67. Perambore Sunday School has 33, and a free day-school of 32 scholars. As the report of the Banner day-school at Pūdūpet—Lawyer Gordon, superintendent—is short, and contains facts illustrative of our new school system, I will crowd it in at this point.

"REPORT OF THE METHODIST EPISCOPAL CHURCH (No. 2 PANDAL) DAY SCHOOL, ENDING FIRST QUARTER.

"The school began in August, 1874, with fifty scholars of both sexes—natives and East Indians. It now musters, on an average, 130.

"The course of studies pursued is the elements of

the English and Tāmil languages. The progress has been very satisfactory. Four children of the school, from eight to twelve years of age, and a parent (mother), were, during this quarter, brought to the knowledge of the Lord, and baptized.

"The teachers who have come forward to teach have done it cheerfully, and without any remuneration; but latterly, the number of scholars having considerably increased, the staff of teachers is inadequate to meet the demand. I feel it my duty to bring this prominently to notice, that our sisters and brothers, who may have an hour hanging heavily on their hands in the morning, may be induced to devote it for this grand work of the Lord. Brother Taylor kindly inaugurated a plan, that should any sister or brother be unable to attend themselves, they might either send or pay for a substitute, to carry on the work. In this manner three teachers are sent, and are now assisting.

"P. B. GORDON, SUPERINTENDENT."

As reports and statistics in full are not very interesting to general readers, I have not inserted them in regard to any part of this Mission; but I should remark that in every place all our records are carefully kept by competent business laymen; and in illustration of this statement, I will insert the following resolution passed by this Quarterly Conference:—

"Our thanks are due, and are hereby tendered, to Brother H. Wallace for the services which he has rendered as recording steward for the year past—the first year of our existence as a church. The journal is a model record of such a body as ours. The penmanship is superb, and the index made by him will be very valuable, rendering it easy to refer to any item required.

"Signed on behalf of Quarterly Conference,

"C. P. HARD, CHAIRMAN."

I will also insert part of the reports of one or two of our native preachers. Brother Benjamin Peters, who was converted to God at our services in the Memorial Hall last year, says :—

"I am thankful to the Lord to say that I am getting on very well indeed,—daily growing in light, power, and knowledge. 'For me to live is Christ,' and death will be a gain. The ambition of my heart is the salvation of the heathen. 'O Lord! how long?' is the cry of my heart day and night. I beg the church to pray for this work. During the past quarter I have preached sixty-five times in the streets, and assisted Brother Gordon at Pūdūpett and Perambore. I am very glad to inform you that the heathen are becoming thoughtful and attentive listeners; in fact, many of them withstand those who attempt to disturb our preaching. They say, 'Why do you disturb them?—they are preaching nothing but the truth,' and so on. They themselves get into arguments, one portion for the Gospel, and the other against it. Sometimes their debates are so boisterous, that we are obliged to leave them to themselves, and quit the ground and go to another, for the sake of preserving order."

In a letter to me, dated April 11th, he says :—

"The Tāmil work has been steadily progressing since you left us. Three have been saved from heathenism, and four more will be very soon. The Lord is most wonderfully drawing my heart towards my perishing countrymen. The subject of my thought moment by moment, and the ambition of my heart, is the *salvation of my country*. I am so much taken up with preaching, that my wife says that I keep preaching in my sleep. Oh, my dear father, will you please pray for me and this great work? Ask the brethren in London to pray for India: I know that the dear people in America are now praying for me and India. If India is to be saved, it must be saved now, and that mainly through our agency. The Hindūs are becoming very attentive listeners. Soon the floodgates of salvation will be opened. The apostles added by three and five thousands, but we will add by tens of thousands. I believe it, and am daily looking out for that result. Why may I not look for it? We have the promise of the Father to that effect."

The next is an extract from the report of a young native, brought to God since I left:—

"I was converted at watch-meeting three months ago, and called into the Tāmil work in connexion with the Methodist Episcopal Church of Madras on Friday, the 15th day of January, 1875. From this date to the 11th of March I exhorted forty-six times, besides being with Brother Gordon at No. 2 Pandal. Since March 11th I have taken part in fifty Tāmil meetings in co-operation with others. It has been mine to conduct Sunday meetings for the servants at Brother Reardon's, and also to preach to the heathen at the fountain opposite Doveton College, and by the side of the Pursewākum Post-office.

"As to my spiritual progress, I desire to say that during these months I have had times of weeping and times of rejoicing. I am happy to declare that I have drawn nearer to God and He to me. I am sure that He has prepared a mansion for me. God be praised for His loving-kindness! J. GLORIA."

I will add a specimen report of one of our class-leaders :—

"I am happy to say that God's work has been going on in my own soul during the past quarter. I have often felt so exceedingly happy that I really cannot describe what I have felt. I feel more than ever God's claims upon me as one of His children. I realize the truth that I am not my own, but that I am the purchase of Christ's blood, and therefore I should glorify Him in my body and my spirit, which are His.

"During the past quarter I have endeavoured to do something for the promotion of God's glory, and He has blessed me personally, and has also blessed my feeble efforts for the extension of His kingdom. I think, or rather I should say I am sure, that God has blessed our infant church wonderfully, and is still blessing us, and we should return our heartfelt acknowledgments to Him for all His goodness. When our beloved pastor, Rev. W. Taylor, began to work, how small and feeble it looked: but look at it this day! And what will it not be when our dear brother returns, if he is spared to see us again! And what will it not be a few years hence, when you and I are mouldering in the dust! Brothers and sisters, thank God and take courage. Come up yourselves to the help of the Lord, to the help of the Lord against the mighty :—

"'When He first the work begun,
Small and feeble was His day :
Now the word doth swiftly run,
Now it wins its widening way ;
More and more it spreads and grows,
Ever mighty to prevail,
Sin's strongholds it now o'erthrows,
Shakes the trembling gates of hell.'

"With regard to the work in the circuit plan, our dear Brother Hard had kindly given me only seven preaching appointments and six for prayer. In addition to these, I have taken up a great many more appointments for both; and I am happy to say to-night that I have seen sinners weep over their sins and cry to God for mercy. Oh, how encouraging this has been to me! It has sent a thrill through my soul that I cannot describe! You must experience it for yourself.

"In addition to the English work, I have commenced Tāmil street-preaching in my neighbourhood; and I would, brothers and sisters, ask your prayers that God would bless His Word proclaimed in the highways and hedges. Do beseech God that He will bless the heathen, no matter of what caste, with His salvation!

"'Hasten, Lord, the glorious time,
When beneath Messiah's sway,
Every nation, every clime,
Shall the Gospel call obey.'

"I should like to say something with regard to my fellowship band. It has been a glorious means of grace to us. I have been personally greatly blessed, as I have from week to week listened to the rich experience of God's dear children. How it has encouraged me to go on my way rejoicing, and to prepare for that glorious meeting when all of God's children will be together to talk of His love, and to cause the courts of heaven to ring with praise!

"'Yet onward I haste
To the heavenly feast;
That—that is the fulness,
But this is the taste.'

"There is yet one other thing that I wish to allude to, and that is our Sabbath School at Pursewākum—the fourth of our Church in this city, organized recently by our pastor.

God is blessing us in this branch of His vineyard. We meet every Sabbath morning from a quarter-past seven to half-past eight, endeavouring, by the aid of the Almighty, to sow the seed of eternal life in the hearts of nearly 100. Pray for all the teachers, that God may bless their efforts, —that He may water their own souls with the dew of heaven, so that they may water the souls entrusted to them.

"Sisters and brothers, is not all this very encouraging? I have said nothing as to how anxious people are to hear the Word of God as we go from house to house, reading and praying with them. And does not God speak to one and all of you? Has He no message for you? Yes, He has. I tell you sincerely, He has. And will you listen to it? He says to one and all of you who have tasted of His love, 'Go, work in my vineyard.' Will you obey the call from this hour, and live to His glory, and say,—

"''Tis to my Saviour I would live—
To Him who for my ransom died;
Nor could all worldly honour give
Such bliss as crowns me at His side.
His work my hoary age shall bless
When youthful vigour is no more,
And my last hour of life confess
His saving love, His glorious power'?

God grant it, for His name's sake.

"J. J. REARDON, LEADER, No. 7."

I will close the present review of God's work in Madras by inserting the Circuit Plan (overleaf) for the second quarter of 1875.

The work in Bangalore is on the advance steadily; and Brother Shaw, with improved health, is in fine spirits. Brother Gordon gives me an account of Brother Shaw's great success in Her Majesty's 18th

Huzzars there, and adds that "the people of the world stand aghast, not knowing what to make of it."

By late report, Madras Circuit has 51 full members and 94 probationers: total 145, with one day and two Sunday Schools.

Secunderabad, too, is moving onward. Brother Robinson writes to Brother Hard as follows:—

"[Motto for 1875—'OMNI JESU'].

"SECUNDERABAD, *Saturday*, *Jan.* 2, 1875.

"DEAR BROTHER CLARK,—The happiest of happy New Years, with 'grace, mercy, and peace from God our Father and Jesus Christ our Lord,' to my own dear brother in the faith! Your letter has been just handed me; and oh, how welcome it is! These ten days have indeed been delightful. Never has work for the Master been so blessed. Like you, I have had plenty of it, but strength and grace have been vouchsafed me. Secunderabad is a pleasant place, so far as climate is concerned. My quarters and the worshipping place are a little outside the town proper, in a very pleasant locality.

"Never have I had a deeper sense of the Father's love and care than since I arrived. The warmth of reception, the comfortable surroundings, etc., all combined with the amount of work on hand, which is my native element, fill my soul with gratitude. I board with a good, kind widow lady, Sister Summers—whose family comprises one little granddaughter. My surroundings are not perhaps just as comfortable and inviting as yours, but I am so happy and thankful.

"Last Sabbath was a delightful day. I led a prayer-meeting, preached twice, and organized the Sunday School. We had twenty-seven children to organize with, and plenty of available teachers. I shall go to work on the newest

METHODIST EPISCOPAL CHURCH,

SECOND QUARTER, 1875.]

Public Preaching.			April.				May.				
Esplanade Pandal	Saturday	6·30 p.m.	3- 1	10- 1	17- 1	24- 1	1- 1	8- 1	15- 1	22- 1	29-
Pursewâkum	Sabbath	11 a.m.	4- 1	11- 6	18- 3	25-15	2- 1	9- 6	16-13	23-10	30-
Esplanade Pandal	Sabbath	8·30 a.m.	4- 6	11- 1	18-18	25-17	2- 7	9- 1	16- 9	23- 8	30-
Pūdūpett	Sabbath	9 a.m.	4- 3	11-17	18- 1	25- 3	2-15	9- 9	16- 1	23- 6	30-1
Perambore	Sabbath	9 a.m.	4- 9	11-10	18- 7	25- 1	2- 4	9-11	16-17	23- 1	30-
Pursewâkum	Sabbath	6·30 p.m.	4- V	11- 1	18- 1	25- 1	2- 3	9- 1	16- 1	23- 1	30-
Esplanade Pandal	Sabbath	6·30 p.m.	4- 1	11- 3	18- 4	25- 3	2- 1	9- 3	16- 7	23- 3	30- 1
Perambore	Sabbath	6·30 p.m.	4- 9	11- 4	18- 3	25- 6	2- 4	9- 7	16- 3	23- 4	30- 7
Pursewâkum	Tuesday	6·30 p.m.	6- 3	13- 4	20- 6	27- 1	4- 3	11- 4	18- 6	25- 1	*June* 1 -
Pūdūpett	Wednesday	6·30 p.m.	7- 1	14- 3	21- 4	28- 1	5- 3	12- 4	19- 1	26- 3	2- 4
Perambore	Friday	6·30 p.m.	2- 1	9- 6	16- 1	23- 4	*Apr.* 30- 1	7-17	14- 1	21- 4	*May* 28- 1

Madras Harbour . . . . Rev. O. A. Kramer preaches Sabbath mornings on board the Shipping.

The Mount . . . .
Palaveram . . . . } The Pastor and others will preach at these places from time to time, sending notice; while the Band and Prayer-meetings are in care of persons residing there.

Arconum . . . .
Jollarapett . . . .
Salem Station . . . .
Erode . . . .
Pothanoor . . . . } Rev. C. J. Haudin is continuously devoted this quarter to the appointments on the Railway, having Pothanoor for head-quarters. The Pastor will announce his own work on the line by letters.

Prayer Meetings.								*May*				
Narasingapoorum	Mrs. Cranston's	M.	6·30 p.m.	5-22	12- 1	19-27	26-25	3-26	10- 1	17-25	24-22	31-24
New Town	Mrs. Jones's	Tu.	6·30 p.m.	6- 1	13- 6	20-10	27- 4	4- 1	11- 8	18-10	25- 4	*June* 1- 1
Perambore	The Pandal	Tu.	6·30 p.m.	6-18	13-19	20- 1	27-20	4-21	11-18	18- 4	25-19	1-20
Royapettah	Serjt. Ballantyne's	W.	6·30 p.m.	7- 1	14 -1	21-23	28-15	5- 1	12-24	19-17	26- 7	2- 1
Otary	T. Crosbie's	W.	6·30 p.m.	7-20	14-21	21-11	28- 6	5-12	12-19	19- 7	26- 1	2-20
Big Parcherry	J. Smaller's	W.	6·30 p.m.	7-12	14-28	21 -6	28-15	5-28	12- 1	19- 8	26-12	2- 8
Esplanade Pandal		Th.	6·30 p.m.	8- 1	15- 1	22- 1	29- 1	6- 1	13- 1	20- 1	27- 1	3- 1
Pūdūpett	G. Purvis's	Th.	6·30 p.m.	8- 3	15-14	22-22	29-24	6- 3	13-14	20-26	27-25	3- 3
Black Town	A. Chatelier's, Anderson Street,	F.	6·30 p.m.	2-13	9- 4	16-22	23- 9	*Apr.* 30-24	7-13	14-18	21-15	*May* 28-23
	Mrs. De Beaux's, Esplanade,	F.	6·39 p.m.	2- 6	9-15	16-10	23- 7	30-13	7- 9	14- 8	21-12	28-20
Pursewâkum	J. Reardon's	F.	6·30 p.m.	2-17	9- 1	16-11	23-18	30- 6	7- 4	14-13	21-19	28- 8
	D. Stevens's	alt. F.	6·30 p.m.	2- 8	..	16- 8	..	30- 8	..	14-8	..	28- 8
Egmore	J. C. Fitzgerald's	alt. F.	6·30 p.m.	..	9-14	..	23-14	..	7-14	..	21-14	..
Chintadrepettah	Mrs. Swain's	F.	6·30 p.m.	2-22	9-23	16- 4	23-17	30-25	7-26	14-10	21-27	28-17
Park Town	C. De Weltz's	F.	6.30 p.m.	2- 9	9- 9	16- 9	23- 9	30-27	7- 8	14-15	21-13	28-22
Royapoorum	C. Huntley's, 166, Church Street,	F.	6·30 p.m.	2-12	9-28	16- 6	23-13	30-12	7- 1	14- 4	21- 6	28-13
Otary	T. Crosbie's	F.	6·30 p.m.	2- 4	9-22	16-15	23- 1	30- 4	7-20	14-11	21- 1	28- 4

The double figures in the columns indicate—the first the date, the second the number of the Leader.

PLAN OF MADRAS CIRCUIT.

June.			
4- 1	12- 1	19- 1	26- 1
6-12	13- 8	20-14	27- 1
6- 1	13- 6	20- 4	27- 7
6- 3	13- 1	20- 3	27- 8
6- 8	13- 7	20- 1	27-17
6- 1	13- 1	20- 1	27- 3
6- 7	13- 3	20- 6	27- 1
6- 8	13- 9	20- 4	27- 6
8- 4	15- 6	22- 1	29- 1
9- 1	16- 3	22- 4	30- 3
9 1	11- 6	18- 1	25- 4

V = Dr. W. J. Vansomeren, who will preach as often in the Plan on Sabbath evenings as his official duties will permit.

Rev. W. Taylor, *Supt.*
Rev. C. P. Hard, *Pastor* . . . 1
C. J. Haudin . . . 2
P. B. Gordon . . . 3
O. A. Kramer . . . 4
B. Peters 5
B. Aitken. 6
J. Reardon 7
H. Wallace 8
J. O'Hara 9
O. W. Jones 10
A. W. Gordon . . . 11
W. H. Titnuss . . . 12
J. Boyle 13
J. C. Fitzgerald . . 14
A. Chatelier. . . . 15
E. Grant 16
H. H. Lynsdale . . 17
P. W. Curtis. . . . 18
J. Bain 19
C. A. Taylor. . . . 20
J. W. Douglas . . . 21
J. Gabriel. 22
T. E. Morton. . . . 23
C. Moore 24
R. Stanley 25
D. Michael 26
T. Conquest 27
C. Huntley 28
J. Huggins 29
S. T. Fisher 30
J. Marsh 31
J. James 32
J. Hyde 33
W. Mersh. 34

Fellowship Bands.

Tuesday	6·30 p.m.	C. Huntley's	12
Wednesday	7 a.m.	Swain's	17
,,	5·30 p.m.	Pŭdŭpett Pandal	14
,,	6·30 p.m.	Mrs. De Beaux's	13
Thursday	6·30 p.m.	J. Brown's	18
,,	6·30 p.m.	J. Bain's	19
Friday	7·30 a.m.	Serjeant Ballantyne's	23
,,	5 p.m.	J. C. Fitzgerald's (Youths)	14
,,	6 p.m.	C. De Weltz's	8
Saturday	7·30 a.m.	J. O'Hara's	9
,,	7·30 a.m.	A. Chatelier's	15
Sabbath	4 p.m.	Pŭdŭpett Pandal (Tamil)	5
,,	4·30 p.m.	Mrs. Matthews'	22
,,	4·30 p.m.	Mrs. Wallace's	10
,,	4·30 p.m.	J. Burr's	16
,,	5 p.m.	J. Reardon's	7
,,	5 p.m.	Mrs. Inglebright's	11

Band at St. Thomas's Mount, at C. J. Haudin's . . . 2
,, Palaveram 2
,, Arconum. . . . . 29 and 30
,, Jollarapett 31
,, Salem Station 32
,, Erode 33
,, Pothanoor 34

7- 5	14-27	21-26	28-24
8-17	15-10	22- 4	29-10
8-21	15- 1	22-18	..
9-23	16- 7	23-25	30- 1
9-21	16- 8	23-18	30-19
9-22	16- 1	23-12	30-15
10- 1	17- 1	24- 1	..
10-14	17-27	24-22	..
11- 4	11-19	18-20	25-21
4- 9	11-21	18- 6	25-13
4-20	11-11	18-21	25- 7
..	11- S	..	25- S
4-14	..	18-14	..
4-13	11- 1	18-23	25-17
4- 1	11- 4	18- 9	25- 8
4-15	11-12	18-28	26- 6
4-11	11-21	18- 4	25- 1

S = D. Stephens.

Preaching in Tamil.

P. B. Gordon, in charge; Benjamin Peters and J. E. Gloria, Assistants.

Sabbath, 11 a.m., at W. H. Titnuss'.
,, 4 p.m., at J. H. Reardon's.
,, 5 p.m., at Pŭdŭpett Pandal.

Monday, 4 p.m., at Perambore.
,, 5 p.m. Pursewăkum High Road.

Tuesday and Wednesday, 5 p.m., in open air, at John Pereira's.
Tuesday, Thursday, and Friday, 6·30 p.m., at Pŭdŭpett Pandal.
Thursday and Saturday, 5 p.m., at Esplanade Pandal.

Day Schools.

At Esplanade Pandal, 7 to 9 a.m. | At Pŭdŭpett Pandal, 7 to 9 a.m.

Sunday Schools.

At L. M. Chapel, Pursewăkum, 7.30 a.m.; J. Reardon and A. Gordon, Supts.
,, Esplanade Pandal, 7·30 a.m.; Henry Wallace and B. Aitken, Supts.
,, Pŭdŭpett Pandal, 7·30 a.m.; P. B. Gordon and J. C. Fitzgerald, Supts.
,, Perambore Pandal, 7·30 a.m.; Charles A. Taylor, Supt.
,, Salem Station, 7·30 a.m.; T. Schell, Supt.

Week Evening Bible Class.

At R. Thomas', Semboodos Street, Monday, 6·30 p.m.

Ladies' Meetings.

Tuesday, from 5 to 6 p.m., at Mrs. Inglebright's, Pursewăkum.
,, ,, ,, Wallace's, Anderson Street.

Circuit Meetings.

Sunday School Teachers' Normal Class, at Esplanade Pandal, Saturday, 5·30 p.m.

Monthly Financial Meeting of Leaders at the Esplanade Pandal, at 7·30, Saturday, May 1, and June 5; at Pursewăkum, at 7·30 p.m., Tuesday, June 29.

Monthly Meeting of persons named in this Plan in a Theological Training Class, at Esplanade Pandal, at 7·30 p.m., Saturday, April 17, May 15, and June 12.

Quarterly Love Feast, at Esplanade Pandal, Saturday, July 3, at 6·30 p.m., to be followed by the Quarterly Conference.

and most approved American plan,—senior, intermediate, and primary. I shall have to fight to get the adults to join; but I intend to.

"The Lord is giving me power in my work. I have three preaching-places besides Secunderabad (Chudderghaut, Trimulgherry, and Bolarum); but they are of minor importance, for the reason that they are within reach of the town, and the people come to our principal meetings regularly. Yet they must be attended to. Thank God for a band of good earnest workers, many of them sisters, who stand by me, willing to do anything for the Lord!

"Instead of a magnificent equipage like yours, I am the proud and happy owner of a 'bandy,'—modest, but substantial. For an animal of the equine species, my people have provided me with a pair of the bovine. My Jehu can't speak a word of English, and I have quite a time with him.

"Our 'Methodist Hall' is a comfortable, but by no means an elegant one. Many precious souls have been born in it, however; and that beautifies any place. Last Wednesday evening we had a glorious time. It was the occasion of our Sacrament service. The glory of the Lord did fill the house. It was a memorable hour in my history. For the first time I administered the Holy Communion, and for the first time I welcomed members—my members—into the fold. Our holiness meetings are very precious. We had a grand rally for the watchnight of all our stations. We had three half-hour addresses, by two of my local preachers and Captain Wodehouse, a Plymouth Brother. I brought up the rear; and God helped me wonderfully. I have reason to believe that great good was done. We had Europeans, Eurasians, Hindūs, Mohamedans, Presbyterians, Episcopalians, and Roman Catholics present. One of the latter was a woman who three weeks ago turned one of our sisters out of her house because she distributed tracts in it. She was deeply moved. Let me say very gratefully, very thankfully, that I am getting a hold on some of the natives. There were four (one a Mohamedan) at our Monday evening prayer-meeting; and under a special inspiration from God, I presented to them some plain truths about Christ and the happy effects of embracing His religion. The Lord wonderfully supplied me with thoughts and utterance. The whole four, in response to a clearly presented suggestion of mine, rose to publicly testify their belief that Jesus Christ was the Son of God. I re-echo your anthem —'Glory to God for this field, and that we are here!' I wouldn't exchange my humble appointment for any American pastorate. I shouldn't care if I didn't receive a rupee salary. I have asked not a single question in reference to it: the Lord will provide. We hope to have our chapel ready for dedication by June."

An extract from another of Brother Robinson's letters to Brother Hard—dated Secunderabad, March 6th—will give us a further peep into their work :—

"Our people love Brother Hard, 'whom they have not seen,' and are longing to set eyes on the little man: for one or two, who have been to Madras and back, report you as small of stature but great of soul.

"Glad of the Bangalore dedication. I am driving the matter of *our* church; but it's hard work, for several reasons,—hard to get an eligible site in cantonment limits, and hard to get the people stirring. The Sunday School gets on nicely, notwithstanding heavy losses by removal,—ten this week alone. Sunday-school letter-writers must be scarce in India when my poor hasty scribble was deemed worthy of a place in the *Guardian*. There's lots of Sunday-school work to be done in India, brother. God has given us success here in drawing the unconverted to our services, saving some of them, and reclaiming several backsliders.

"One reclaimed brother, Donohoe, goes on to Madras to-day, with his battery, and will probably seek you. It's a hard fight against all the odds, but there's no use in complaining or despairing. Our hope and trust are firmly placed in God, and we are determined

> "'To watch, and fight, and pray,
> And the battle ne'er give o'er.'

"A tea-meeting under the auspices of our ladies came off last Thursday evening. It was a grand success. I made the acquaintance of several whom I never saw before, and I am sure good will come out of it to souls. Our programme was a pretty good one, though I say it. Opened with 'Praise God,' and prayer; four anthems from 'The Victory,' very well rendered indeed, by a choir of thirteen or fourteen; three songs by your humble servant, which went home to hearts, as I intended they should,—'A hundred years to come,' 'My ain Countrie,' and 'While the days are going by'; four or five choice readings and recitations interspersed, closing with 'God save the Queen,' and the Doxology. These exercises, occupying from seven to a quarter-past eight p.m., made a very enjoyable affair; and every one was greatly pleased. It will help to create a more favourable impression regarding the poor despised Methodists.

"I start for Shahabad (D.V.) on Monday,—my third visit to that benighted spot; but God is blessing us there. Last time I organized a class of seven, and started a weekly prayer-meeting.

"I started bazār preaching in Secunderabad two weeks ago. Every day, except Sunday, there is preaching in at least two of the three tongues spoken here. The Mohamedans are bitterly opposed, but we are determined to *preach* down their bitterness. They beat a tum-tum once in a while, and resort to other kindred devices." [I may add that we have a Brother Cornelius, who has since successfully opened a free day-school in Shahabad.]

III. *Bombay Progress.*

THE work in Bombay, which has been noted up to the beginning of 1875, is progressing beautifully. Our official workers are daily pushing the battle with patient faith and zeal, and not a doubt of ultimate success in saving the Hindūs, Parsees, and Mohamedans, whom they love with Christ-like sympathy. Our non-official workers, also commissioned by the Holy Spirit to witness for Jesus and win souls to Him, manifest great zeal and skill in their glorious high calling. Among these we have many sisters whom God is honouring in this work: Miss Matilda Miles, Mrs. George Miles, the Misses Emily and Alice Miles, Mrs. James Morris, Mrs. George Ainsworth, Mrs. Waller, Mrs. Page, Miss Grace Page, Miss Rebecca Christian, and a host of others. As our Mission develops from month to month, under the fostering care of the Holy Spirit, it is very interesting to see how all other churches and their ministers are led to appreciate it as a great work of God with a glorious future; and hence a blessed blending spirit of union is growing daily.

A year ago the general spirit of distrust and opposition to me and my work may be indicated by the following editorial of the *Bombay Guardian*, May 31, 1874:—

"THE REV. MR. TAYLOR.

"THERE never has been, to our knowledge, a man so abused in Bombay as this evangelist has been. All sorts of calumnies have been uttered against a man who came to this country at his own charge, pays all his own expenses, is ready to share what he has with any poor man, takes nothing from any; a man devotedly attached to his family, yet who has foregone their society for six years that he may proclaim the Gospel of God to those that are 'far off'; a man whom God has acknowledged by saving and blessing multitudes through his ministry; who has borne the calumnies and insults addressed to him with the meekness that becomes his mission,—not replying again. And when a sense of justice leads some one else to point out the wrongfulness of such attacks, immediately there is an outcry about our glorification of Mr. Taylor. There has never been anything of the kind on our part. If Mr. Taylor had been solicitous of the honour that cometh from man, he would have pursued a very different course from that which he has followed; in fact, the Lord would not have used him. Our contemporaries sometimes favour us with articles explanatory of what they call the failure of Missions, the powerlessness of the pulpit, etc.,—referring in terms by no means flattering to the love of money, comfort, position, in those who preach the Gospel. From the strain of their remarks one would infer that they would be enraptured to see a man against whom no trace of this feeling can be alleged. When a man comes whose life in all particulars embodies a complete disdain of these things, they are more bitter against him than they ever were against any. 'But wisdom is justified of her children.'"

Now compare that with the following notice of an all-day meeting in the principal Methodist preaching-hall in that city, as given by the same editor in the issue of April 3rd, 1875:—

"THE All-day Meeting on Friday, March 26th, at Falkland Road Hall, was very well attended, and was an occasion of much blessing. After the hymn 'I am so glad that our Father in Heaven,' and prayer, Psalm xxxiv. 1-10 was read, with comments, and the meeting was then thrown open for thanksgiving or the acknowledgment of mercies. Some twenty-five or thirty testified to the goodness of the Lord—some in general terms, others by mentioning special blessings bestowed, answers to prayer in behalf of others, etc. This, with prayer and singing, carried us into the second hour. A Bible reading followed: subject, Faith. Texts showing what faith is, its objects, in whom, its fruits, its necessity, its preciousness, and other particulars about it, were read out by individuals in the congregation, as called for—slips indicating the texts having been distributed beforehand; and brief remarks on each text were made by the leader. More than fifty passages of God's Word thus passed in review. The third hour was devoted to a prayer-meeting. Many special requests were presented. Much prayer was offered for a blessing upon the labours of the Rev. Mr. Douglas and Rev. Mr. Somerville in Bombay. One brother testified that God had graciously turned the hearts of four of his relatives to love and serve Him within the last eighteen months, in answer to prayer; and requested prayer for the remaining members of his family. Prayer was requested, among others, for the Bishop of Bombay—obliged to leave India by a serious illness. At one p.m. the sixty-seventh Psalm was read, and remarks were made on the connexion between fulness of spiritual life in the Christian and the awakening of the unconverted:

'God be merciful unto us and bless us; and cause His face to shine upon us ; that Thy way may be known upon earth, Thy saving health among all nations.' There is a condition of the body that denotes health. Anything short of this creates uneasiness and anxiety, and efforts are made to reach again the state of entire health. There is a corresponding health of the soul, for the obtainment of which an adequate provision is made in Christ; and anything short of this should awaken solicitude and stimulate effort. God's saving health is that condition of soul-health to which the Gospel brings those who fully submit to it. When this bright and shining way of God is shown in the consecrated, loving, and self-denying lives of His people, the world will be attracted to it, the multitudes around us will become painfully sensible of their need, and will ask to become our fellow-pilgrims in the journey of life. Upon this general theme a number spoke. There were present in the course of the day the following ministers: Dr. Wilson, Mr. Stothert, and Mr. McKichen, of the Free Church Mission ; Mr. Macpherson and Mr. Ross, of the Established Church of Scotland; Mr. Harding, of the American Mission; Mr. Somerville, the evangelist, and Messrs. Robbins and Bowen of the Methodist Episcopal Church. The entrance of Mr. Somerville was an agreeable surprise, as it was not thought he could attend. Informed of the subject that was before the meeting, and invited to speak upon it, he gave a very beautiful and impressive address, that will long remain in the memories of those who heard it. With reference to our Lord's words, 'If any man thirst, let him come unto me and drink . . . and forth from him shall flow rivers of living water,' he described a beautiful Scotch lake embowered in hills, having besides its own loveliness the reflected beauty of the heavens and of the green hills: we follow the lake till it finds a narrower channel and flows forth as a river, upon whose banks are many factories, which receive their impulses from the stream; fertility and enterprise mark its onward course; the great city is reached and passed; finally the river pours itself into the ocean. He dwelt upon the fact that the Christian can only give as he receives. The stream of vivifying influence that issues from him must first descend into him. Men plunge into the heart of Africa to try if they can discover the rise of great rivers; but there are great rivers of hallowed influence issuing from the individual believer. Words of earnest appeal followed. Mr. Stothert bore unhesitating testimony to the work that had been inaugurated by Mr. Taylor in Bombay; made mention of the joy with which he had heard in Scotland of blessings that came upon many in whom he was interested, and of the satisfaction with which he had seen for himself, since returning, the evidence of the genuineness of this work. Dr. Wilson spoke very earnestly and impressively on Enoch's walking with God (literally, 'walking God'), and Paul's 'to live is Christ.' Mr. Harding spoke with great feeling of the responsibility upon all professing Christians to co-operate heartily in the evangelistic work now being prosecuted in this city. Besides the ministers, a number of others spoke. The last hour was chiefly given to prayer. An opportunity having been given for any who wished to seek the Lord to manifest their desire for prayer by rising, a young man arose with much feeling. Prayer was offered and instruction given; he made a full surrender of himself, and in the course of the day found peace. Many continued in the meeting all the six hours, and did not find them long; many speak of it as a day of extraordinary blessing to their souls."

Similar fruits are seen in *Poona* also :—

"In Poona, on the same day, an all-day meeting was held in the Methodist Hall, from eleven a.m. to four p.m., and again in the evening. The Rev. Mr. Dhanjībhāī, of the Free Church, the Rev. Messrs. Hormusjee and Francis, of the Baptist Church, and Rev. Mr. Fox, of the Methodist Episcopal Church, took part with others in the meeting. It was a time of great blessing."

The work in *Baroda* has suffered some interruption by the disturbances in the trial and removal of the late Guikwar; and Brother Gilder, our preacher there, has been obliged to leave for a time.

The work in *Jubbulpore* (Brother Curties, preacher) is struggling on with brightening prospects, both in soul-saving and a native school.

Khandwa, also, under Brother Metta, gives promise of success.

Egutpoora has an established and growing cause. Brother Pearcey, a local deacon, is its mainstay. Brother Seale, now a railway guard, is giving him help.

An extract from a letter from Brother Robbins, now the preacher in charge of Bombay Circuit, dated March 29th, 1875, will give us a few facts of interest :—

"In Bombay the work is encouraging. Mr. Somerville and Mr. Douglas arrived here and began work the same day; and there is now considerable interest. Mr. Somerville's lecture to the educated natives last Saturday night, on the Introduction of Christianity into Europe—founded on Acts xvi. 6-33—was very excellent, and well received. He preached in Falkland Road Hall yesterday morning to a large congregation. The Scotch people are very backward, but I hope he will be able to reach them. His services in the week are at Frâmjī Cawāsjī Hall. There were four seekers at Falkland Road last night.

"The work at Egutpoora is prospering very well. They have good attendance. A short time ago they had a remarkable case of conversion,—an engine-driver, an old chum of Brother Geering's, who promises to be as earnest as he. His previous opposition, too, was almost as great as that of Brother Catley.

"You remember that when Brother Shaw two years ago went to Egutpoora, Sister Catley was afraid to go home from the fellowship band until he and Brother Pearcey accompanied her. When they arrived at the house, they found him half drunk, with his sword drawn, determined to kill her, and, as he said afterwards, to kill himself. After much persuading and a little scuffle, they got him quiet and on his knees; and he prayed, and submitted to the Lord, and has ever since been a faithful follower of Jesus.

"Dr. and Mrs. Condon left yesterday, and hope to be in London in about a month. They are fine Christian people: God bless them!

"We all sympathize with you in the loss of your mother, of which we hear in the *Advocate*.

"Three weeks ago, one of the famous 'six hundred,' who survived the dreadful charge at Balaklava, sought the Lord at Forbes Street. May he be as loyal to his God as he has been to his Queen and country! His name is Holland,—now in the Post-office Department."

Brother Goodwin is having a hard pull in *Kurrachee;* but having Brother Coen, Civil engineer and local preacher in Hydrabad, from Bombay, and a band of valiant young converts to help him, by the power of Jesus he is bound to succeed. He is delighted with his new field, and is raising funds to erect a chapel.

CHAPTER XXVIII.

THE OUTLOOK.

IT is asked, "Do you expect to carry on all your India Mission-work without appropriations from the Missionary Society?"

Should our India resources fail to keep up with the growing demands of the widening sweep of our advance, and should the Holy Spirit make it plain to us that we cannot get on without Missionary money, then we will ask the Society to help us; though they require ten times the amount of their present receipts to enable them to man the fields God has opened to us in our day, where no such available resources as we are utilizing in India are at command.

"Would not that be a departure from the principles of self-support, on which your Mission is avowedly founded?"

Not at all; but in accordance with them. Our ground from the first covers two simple principles, deduced from an admitted fact—viz.: Self-support is a sound, safe principle, and the only permanently reliable foundation, to which all Missions aspire and hope to attain; if, therefore, it be a good thing to aim at in the future, it is a good thing to begin with, where resources are available. If not adequate to the growing demands of the work, then our second principle is to develop the indigenous resources available, before we begin to subsidize them by foreign funds; as such appropriations in advance will in most cases supersede them. Our Mission is composed almost exclusively of the middle labouring classes—most of whom, on account of fast-living excesses, were in debt when we got them converted to God. When they obtain salvation, and become Methodists, their ambition and pride to rise in the world, and keep up appearances beyond their means, are cut off, and their heavy expenses for wine and spirits precluded. The reduction of this item from Major Raitt's table expenses was equal to the board and lodging of two men; and he begged us to allow him, by that saving, to keep two missionaries at his own expense.

When our people get their proper bearings in the Church of God, they act promptly on two bits of advice which we give them: "Get out of debt as soon as you can; and when you get out, take care you don't get in again."

So our Mission is supported almost entirely from resources, in men and money, which have hitherto been monopolized by Satan and hence antagonized to the work of God in India, but now utilized for the advancement of Christ's kingdom. Thus far these have been adequate for our work, and we believe will be adequate—so far, especially, as the food, raiment, and homes of all our workers are concerned—to the end.

The following statistics of receipts and expenditure may serve to illustrate my statement:—

BOMBAY AND BENGAL MISSION,

BOMBAY

Receipts and Disbursements from

RECEIPTS.	1872. From Jan. to Oct. 13. R.	AN.	P.	1872-3. Oct. 13, 1872 to Dec. 31, 1873. R.	AN.	P.	1874. Jan. 1 to Dec. 31. R.	AN.	P.	TOTAL. R.	AN.	P.
Collected in Fellowship Bands...	2708	10	1...	4148	0	11...	3291	15	2...	10148	10	2
Ordinary Collections	1222	7	3...	1276	5	8...	560	0	6...	3058	13	5
Donations and Subscriptions ...	...	...	...	1289	12	0...	1012	10	0...	2302	6	0
Poor Fund Collection...	...	...	...	569	6	8..	633	14	0...	1203	4	8
Missionary Collection...	111	9	0...	...	...	...	490	9	3...	602	2	3
Bengal Famine Fund...	...	...	...	...	...	...	166	12	3...	166	12	3
Sunday School	...	...	...	...	...	...	380	12	0...	380	12	0
Egutpoora Church	...	...	...	...	...	...	260	0	6...	260	0	6
Miscellaneous	...	...	...	17	11	0...	246	1	6...	263	12	6
Interest on Circuit Fund, from Jan. 1872 to Dec. 1873	...	...	...	44	2	3...	...	...	...	44	2	3
Interest on Building Fund, from Jan. 1872 to Dec. 1873	...	...	...	71	14	10...	24	10	4...	96	9	2

TOTAL RUPEES—18,527 5 2

J. MORRIS,

METHODIST EPISCOPAL CHURCH.

CIRCUIT.

January 1872 *to* December 31, 1874.

DISBURSEMENTS.	1872. From Jan. to Oct. 13.			1872-3. Oct. 13, 1872 to Dec. 31, 1873.			1874. Jan. 1 to Dec. 31.			Total.		
	R.	AN.	P.	R.	AN.	P.	R.	AN.	P.	R.	AN.	P.
Rent, Lighting, etc.	893	12	1	1519	9	2	1455	1	2	3868	6	5
Preachers' Personal Expenses,—Bombay, Baroda, and Jubbulpore				1574	10	2	2079	10	1	3653	12	0
Native Preachers' Expenses				140	0	0	508	0	0	648	0	0
Preacher's Travelling Expenses	62	0	0	394	2	6	924	10	0	1380	12	6
Circuit Conveyance	567	6	0							567	6	0
Keep of Horse, etc.	260	9	0	577	11	6				838	4	6
Poor Fund				718	12	6	583	4	5	1302	0	11
Printing	52	4	0	119	8	0	123	11	0	295	7	0
Books Purchased				73	6	9	83	6	0	156	12	9
Church Fittings, Furniture, etc.	445	8	0	380	8	6	58	0	0	884	0	6
Sunday School	210	0	0	10	0	0	276	8	0	496	8	0
Donation to Cawnpore Methodist Church	111	9	0							111	9	0
Donation to Lanowlī Methodist Church							200	0	0	200	0	0
Donation to Egutpoora Methodist Church, for Fence							185	1	0	185	1	0
Bengal Famine Fund							166	12	3	166	12	3
Missionary Societies							490	9	3	490	9	3
Expenses of Egutpoora Church							260	0	6	260	0	6
Miscellaneous	236	14	5	339	7	0	339	11	0	916	0	5
Balance in Hand—												
Circuit Fund, on 31st December, 1874										806	9	2
Building Fund, placed as a fixed deposit in the Bombay Bank										1299	5	0
Total Rupees—										18,527	5	2

Secretary, Bombay Circuit.

REPORT OF FINANCES FOR POONA CIRCUIT.

	R.	R.
Total Receipts in 1873	3046	
Disbursements in 1873	3046	
Total Receipts in 1874	3860	
Disbursements in 1874	3810	
Balance in hand	——	50
Receipts for the First Quarter in 1875, ending March 31st	998	
Balance in hand		50
Total Balance in hand		100

The receipts for the first quarter of this year, taken as an average for the year, will show an increase over the past year.

	R.
Missionary Money collected in 1874	39
Collected by Sunday School Missionary Society for the year ending May 1875	60
Chapel built and paid for at Lanowli	3000

CALCUTTA.

Aggregate Memorandum of Cash Collected and Paid, covering about a year and a half.

	R.
Two Chapels—Probable Value	17000
Paid to Pastor's Fund in 1874	1200
New Building Fund—Paid	4500
Current Expenses	1200
Poor Fund	500

MADRAS CIRCUIT FUND.

(Its existence does not cover a year, and hence the months are put in.)

RECEIPTS.

	R.	A.	P.
1874.			
First Quarter, up to July 6	805	3	4
July	301	2	1
August and September	187	8	0
October	159	13	9
November	210	13	9
December	122	5	4
1875.			
January	210	4	6
February	154	10	3
March	147	9	7
April	277	1	11
TOTAL RUPEES	2576	8	6

DISBURSEMENTS.

	R.	A.	P.
1874.			
First Quarter up to July 6	746	15	0
July	281	13	0
August and September	237	13	0
October	176	1	6
November	160	15	0
December	183	5	5
1875.			
January	173	7	8
February	174	11	0
March	136	2	0
April	264	8	3
Balance in hand, May 1, 1875	40	12	5
TOTAL RUPEES	2576	8	6

THE PASTOR'S FUND (*Extra*).—RECEIPTS, from January to April 30, 1875, 145 rup.; DISBURSEMENTS, from January to April 30, 1875, 157 rup. 7 an. 9 p.; DEFICIT, 12 rup. 7 an. 9 p. This deficit was made good out of the Circuit Fund.

The cost of the places of worship built amounts to an aggregate of 1840 rupees; and a subscription additional towards a chapel of 3000 rupees.

FINANCIAL STATEMENT OF THE SECUNDERABAD CIRCUIT OF THE METHODIST EPISCOPAL CHURCH.

For the Year ending December 31, 1874.

RECEIPTS.	R.	A.	P.	DISBURSEMENTS.	R.	A.	P.
Fellowship Band Collections	706	12	0	Church Fittings, Furniture, Lamps, etc.	492	6	1
Ordinary Collections	768	0	3	Servants, and Miscellaneous Expenses	289	9	0
Extraordinary Collections	87	8	0	Preacher's Personal and Travelling Expenses	532	0	0
				Rent of Hall for Third and Fourth Quarters	178	0	0
				Balance in Treasury, Dec. 31, 1874 ...	70	5	0
TOTAL RUPEES—	1562	4	3	TOTAL RUPEES—	1562	4	3

For Quarter ending March 31, 1875.

RECEIPTS.	R.	A.	P.	DISBURSEMENTS.	R.	A.	P.
Balance in hand, Jan. 1st, 1875 ...	70	5	0	Rent of Hall	96	0	0
Fellowship Band Collections	382	4	0	Preacher's Personal, Travelling, and Moving Expenses	455	12	0
Ordinary Collections	214	15	0	Servants, and Miscellaneous Expenses	105	11	0
				Balance in hand, March 31	10	1	0
TOTAL RUPEES—	667	8	0	TOTAL RUPEES —	667	8	0

SUBSCRIPTIONS FOR CHURCH BUILDING.

	R.	A.	P.
Total Amount Subscribed up to May 1, 1875 ...	2869	6	0
,, Collected ,, ,, ...	2000	0	0
Balance to be Collected	869	6	0

Bangalore cash account, from September 25th, 1874, to end of April 1875 :—Total receipts, 1964 rup. 12 an. 11 p.; disbursements, 1903 rup. 12 an. 11 p.: balance in hand, 61 rup. *Scinde* cash account, from August 18th, 1874, to June 1st, 1875 :—Total receipts, 1489 rup. 14 an. 8 p.; disbursements, 1464 rup. 11 an.: balance in hand, 25 rup. 3 an. 8 p.

The work is now divided into three districts :—

Bombay District,	GEORGE BOWEN,	*Presiding Elder.*
Bengal ,,	J. M. THOBURN	,,
Madras ,,	C. P. HARD	,,

Our working force consists of twelve ordained and twelve other preachers, devoted wholly to evangelistic and pastoral work, and a membership of 1300 workers.

Having no Conference organization, our presiding elders have not been appointed in the regular way; but I have deputed them to superintend the work in my absence, and Bishop Harris has endorsed and approved my action.

Such being our financial position, we hope to make no drafts on the Missionary Society for our present Mission, nor for the Conferences to be developed out of it; but we do not propose to debar God's people of other countries the privilege of helping us in the stupendous work we have undertaken. What I have pledged our India people for specially, is the support of all their ministerial workers—first for the sake of a simple standard of economy suitable for an indigenous native church on fraternal equality; and secondly, to preclude hireling workers, and to remove all ground for the deep, damaging suspicion of it on the minds of the native masses whom we are seeking to save. This spirit of suspicion was so rife in Corinth that when Paul explained God's ordinance "that they which preach the Gospel should live by the Gospel," he adds, "I have used none of these things; neither have I written these things that it should be so done unto me: for it would be better for me to die, than that any man should make my glorying void." Paul thankfully accepted support from the church in Philippi (Phil. iv. 10-20).

Selfishness and covetousness are so dominant in the carnal world, that this obstructive suspicion that God's ambassadors are hirelings is to be found in every country, but was especially so in Corinth of old, and is so in India at the present day.

The first thought and question of Hindūs, Mohamedans, or Parsees, on hearing the voice of God's heralds, is, "How many rupees per month do you get for all that?" If a native preacher, they will curse him as a traitor bought with foreign money, and hired to oppose the religion of his fathers. So the position of our preachers is worth a hundred times more than it costs in the way of self-denial, in being able to say, "Not a worker in the Bombay, Bengal, and Madras Mission gets an anna from any foreign source." The mass of them work with their own hands and support themselves, and preach daily besides; and those devoted wholly to evangelistic and pastoral work receive simply subsistence allowance from "circuit stewards" by the voluntary gifts of the people. But in a work of such vast proportions—without a single church edifice or school-house to begin with—it was presumed and stated from the first that we should probably require assistance, not for the support of any of our workers, but to help our people in buying sites and in building preaching-halls and school-houses. To receive such assistance, therefore, would not infringe our principles, and, properly used, would not interfere with the independent standing of our workers as before described. As yet we have not asked for a penny outside of India, for any purpose; but I am showing what our principles are, and how well they are adapted to any emergency that may arise. It becomes the more necessary to re-state them, because some good people, it seems, cannot readily understand them.

My friend, the editor of the *New York Advocate*, for example, philosophizing on the principles of my Mission, intimated that the missionaries of all Missions should conform to them, and if not entirely resign their salary, bring it down to a wholesome starvation point; then a correspondent replied, and recommended the editor to resign his salary, and set a good example for the poor missionaries. Such reasoning involves a fallacious stretch of our principles, specially applicable to Corinth in Paul's day, and to India in ours. In regard to other countries, so far as practical experience and personal knowledge can determine their applicability, they should at once be applied by the men on the ground, and not by the dictation of any speculative generalization. No missionary authorities, nor circuit stewards, have any right to put missionaries on a lower grade of support than that of regular pastors at home. Our principles can only be reached by the voluntary self-sacrifice of the missionaries themselves.

"Well: in what way can Christian philanthropists outside of India help *you* financially in your great work?"

First,—in regard to myself a circular recently published in London, containing synoptically what has been written, will answer that question. It is as follows:—

"MR. TAYLOR'S WORK.

"REV. WILLIAM TAYLOR, of California, has been for many years labouring as a missionary evangelist in most of the Mission fields of the globe, and among agents of all the principal Missionary Societies of all churches. Within a few years past, God has founded a self-supporting Mission in India, composed of newly-converted European residents, East Indians, Parsees, Hindūs, and Mohamedans. These resources in men and their money, which in the main have hitherto been monopolized by Satan, and used against the advance of Christ's kingdom in India, are now utilized for the support of a live missionary force in the midst of the heathen. Its object, in conjunction with other organizations, is the conquest of India for Christ. It does not draw a penny from any Missionary Society, except the funds required to send missionaries to them. This Mission is now firmly planted in Bombay, Poona, Kurrachee (west of the Indus), Calcutta, Madras, Bangalore, Secunderabad, and more than a score of smaller places. It requires more than 5000 miles of travel to visit all the organized, self-supporting centres of this work. It is called 'The Bombay, Bengal, and Madras Mission,'—these being the three great centres of its operations; but it is not limited to these.

"Mr. Taylor, under God, is the founder and the superintendent of this Mission. Its present working force comprises 12 ordained and 12 lay preachers, devoted wholly to evangelistic and pastoral work, and 1300 members and workers, who support their own ministers, and pay all running expenses of their work, except their pioneer superintendent, who refuses to take a penny from them. For many years, in addition to his preaching, God has been using his pen for the spread of His Gospel. By the proceeds of his books he supports his family, pays his own sea travelling expenses, and bears the expense of planting Missions and developing resources for their support—after which he turns them over to the care of faithful ministers whom God appoints as his coadjutors in this great work. Mr. Taylor's funds are very low now. He will not receive gifts; he has three sons to educate, and needs help. The only way open to help him is to buy his books.

"He maintains firmly the Bible doctrine that the labourer is worthy of his hire, and that as a rule all ministers and missionaries should be supported by the voluntary funds of the people; but Paul, as a pioneer, chose to forego his rights, and built tents, so Mr. Taylor sees it best for him, in his world-wide range as an evangelist, to proceed on St. Paul's principle, using books instead of tents."

This circular became necessary for the information of the people, and to prevent an influx of gifts. Soon after my recent return to London, a cheque for £100 was sent me, which I respectfully declined. But I require a Missionary Transit Fund, of a few hundred pounds only, to assist in paying the passage of my new missionaries from London to India. Any one wishing to help can correspond with Mr. M. H.

HODDER, 27, Paternoster Row, or remit directly to the treasurer of the said fund, Mr. Wm. MCARTHUR, M.P., 83, Coleman Street, London, E.C. The said cheque for £100 has been paid into that fund.

Secondly,—I would recommend Rev. Dr. Thoburn's church enterprise in Calcutta to merchants and shippers who are interested in seamen, and to all who desire the salvation of the Bengālīs. (See p. 349.)

Brother Thoburn has not asked for help outside of India, and hopes not to require it; but the need is too heavy for our people and friends there, and the danger is, that without help they will be obliged to build on a narrow, cheap gauge, inadequate to the demand.

Any person wishing to put a few bricks into that building can remit direct to Rev. J. M. THOBURN, care of Lawyer Leslie, North Road Entally, Calcutta; or to Mr. Wm. MCARTHUR, M.P., 83, Coleman Street, London, E.C.; or to Messrs. NELSON and PHILLIPS, 805, Broadway, New York.

Thirdly,—the Cawnpore Memorial High School, under the auspices of the India Mission Conference, is an institution of vast importance in affording facilities for a sound education for the English-speaking youth of India. The Government and the Missionary Societies have been very liberal—and justly so—in providing institutions of learning for the Hindūs and Mohamedans, but neither have done much for the rising generation of the Europeans and East Indians; and some good schools for such, with sound religious teaching, where they may be brought to God and prepared to help in evangelizing the nations of India, are greatly needed. The Cawnpore

Memorial High School, under the care of Rev. H. Jackson and wife, and Mr. Annet, is a self-sustaining success in regard to tuition, but is greatly in need of buildings. (See p. 46.)

Any one wishing to take stock in that enterprise can correspond with the agent of the said institution, Rev. T. J. SCOTT, Zanesville, Ohio, or remit funds direct to Dr. James CONDON, M.D., Civil Surgeon, Cawnpore, India ; or to Mr. Wm. MCARTHUR, M.P., 83, Coleman Street, London, E.C.; or to Messrs. NELSON and PHILLIPS, 805, Broadway, New York.

Our District Conference in Bombay, last December, passed resolutions for the establishment of a Western India Academy in Poona, to provide for the education of our young people in Western and Southern India. We are negotiating for a good teacher and his wife to be sent from America this year, and hope soon to have the enterprise in prosperous operation. The building now used for public worship in Poona, for which we are paying about 150 rupees per month, will afford accommodation for the school till buildings can be erected, which will require more funds than our people can raise for a long time to come.

Any one interested in this movement can correspond with Dr. FRASER, Col. George EVEZARD, or Rev. D. O. FOX, Poona, India.

And if any friends will start for us a Church Extension Fund, for the purchase of good sites for places of worship, residence of ministers, and our schools, —with an arrangement to pay to any of our duly constituted boards of trustees an amount equal to what they will raise on the ground, it will be a good thing.

The receipt of funds by any of the afore-named treasurers, for any of the purposes indicated, will be duly acknowledged at once to the parties remitting the funds.

We want it distinctly understood that we do not wish any one to give us a penny, for any of these purposes, which they would otherwise give to some Missionary Society. I am not out begging for any of these good enterprises, and have not been asked to refer to them in this work; but I do it to show that our principles are not so narrow as to preclude the privilege of such co-operation, if need be, and the more cheerfully because these are all deserving.

Thus far, there is only one man out of India who has invested a shilling in the Bombay, Bengal, and Madras Mission—my friend and brother, Henry Reed, Esq. He once offered me a cheque for £100, which I respectfully refused to receive as a gift—preferring to depend entirely on the proceeds of my books, on the principle of business equivalents; so that all my preaching labours should be given, like the Gospel, without money or price. He then requested me to give him an open order on my binder for books, without any limit as to time or quantity. I have never yet learned how many books he has circulated; but on my expensive voyages, and my long pull in India, whenever I found myself straitened for funds, I soon after received, unasked, a cheque from Brother Reed "on book account." In that way he has managed to get stock in our India Mission. He also sent a small amount to help us in building preaching-halls.

The said 10,000 rupees, which was such a godsend to our work in Calcutta, was made and given in India; but in my recent three weeks' work in Colston Hall, Bristol, I incidentally learned a fact which goes to illustrate God's compensative laws, under which even a cup of cold water given to Jesus, in the person of any of His disciples, shall not lose its reward. The Bombay donor did not wish to have his name mentioned; but I am sure he will excuse the liberty I now take in recording the illustration. My kind host in Bristol, Brother Charles B. Ker, who spent twenty years in India as a Civil engineer, learned so to appreciate the self-sacrificing labours of my dear Brother B——, that he wanted to settle on him a small endowment. He knew that if he put money into the hands of the said good man, he would give it away to the first deserving object that might come under his notice; so he deposited £1000 in the bank, with instructions that the interest should be paid to the said man of God annually, but that the principal should be kept for five years, when it should be subject to the said good man's order. So our Calcutta need came at the expiration of the five years, and the £1000 supplied it.

Brother Ker, the Honorary Secretary of the Union Evangelical Committee in Bristol, under which we have just had a glorious work of God, was delighted to know that he had thus become a shareholder in our India Mission. He sees the compensative providence of God in bringing me to Bristol, and is more joyous over the conversion of so many souls in that city than he could be by the gain of ten times the amount of his Bombay investment.

"Do you not require a resident Bishop in India?"

The visit of an itinerant Bishop in India is an occasion of great joy to us all. I would not in any way underrate its importance, both on the work in India, and its representation by such a high official authority to the Church at home. The three Bishops who have presided at the India Mission Conference are grand men of God, and did good service for the Mission, and two of them have finished their course and obtained a crown of righteousness; but a Bishop on a hasty excursion round the globe can learn but little about such a vast and complicated work, except what he learns from the missionaries; they are therefore the teachers, and he is the learner. Hence his difficulty in giving counsel from a broad, matured judgment, and of imparting the full tide of sympathy and moral support to be expected from him; and hence the necessity of his "being made like unto his brethren," and personally grappling with the difficulties which they encounter in such an empire of heathenish darkness. Mr. Wesley saw the situation in America, when it had a population of but about 3,000,000, and ordained Dr. Coke, not to visit that wilderness once in four years simply, but to ordain Mr. Asbury to remain with the pioneer veterans, and be foremost among them in privations, sufferings, labours, and successes. So it will be seen that India, with her 240,000,000, and China with her 400,000,000 of population, will each require an

Asbury to lead the van, and Bishops from the soil, as the advancing legions shall proceed, under God, in their grand mission of giving "the heathen to Jesus for His inheritance, and the uttermost parts of the earth for His possession."

The Church of England has three Bishops in India, and one in Ceylon; all other Missions have simple presbyterian ordination; but we, who are so well up in everything else, can't authorize a soul-saving preacher, whom God has called and used in bringing Hindūs into His kingdom, to baptize a convert, except by waiting for the quadrennial tour of a Bishop round the world. The election of such Bishops will require much prayer and fasting, and great wisdom on the part of those on whom that responsibility may devolve. I can't speak for China; but India, with a self-supporting Mission covering most of the empire, will require a man of Asburian simplicity and self-denial—not forfeiting, but cheerfully foregoing his rights, for the sake of establishing a healthy, homogeneous native church, on the principles of Gospel fraternity and equality.

The principle in America, when I was there thirteen years ago, was, that the Conference within whose bounds a Bishop resided should fix the amount of his salary—with the design, I believe, of harmonizing it with that of his brethren residing within a city involving equal cost of living.

That principle will do for our Mission in India. Our ministers get food and raiment, and are "therewith content"; but to place over them a Bishop, drawing what is supposed to be but a reasonable amount in New York—10,000 rupees per annum—would soon attract a swarm of worshippers, each with his "salāms to my Lord Bishop," and he would find his 10,000 rupees a year quite inadequate to the Eastern style of "saluting men by the way." It would be better for us to forego for ever the advantages of having an Indian Bishop, than to cripple our young cause in that way.

"But a Bishop for India means a change of our itinerant to diocesan episcopacy."

Not at all. We have had a missionary Bishop in Africa for years; and the last General Conference established episcopal districts, and designated the Bishops to reside in them. Compare any one of those districts with India or China, and see if the same rule will not apply to them, with an occasional alternation, if need be.

These two new districts would bring an addition of 640,000,000 of souls under more direct episcopal supervision.

"But where, in these vast empires, are the churches and the Conferences over which a Bishop could preside?"

The Bishops required for such fields should be such as were Paul, and Titus, and Timotheus,—to be the pioneer founders of churches and Conferences.

"That looks as though you would like to be Bishop yourself."

The Lord gave me the highest appointment He had to confer upon man years ago, as a world-wide evangelist; and nothing short of an unmistakable order from Him could induce me to risk the freedom of action under my Divine commission, which episcopal official routine trammels might involve.

"What about 'a charter for the organization of a Bombay Conference'?"

The result of my petition for it to the last General Conference is known. The reasons on which that petition was based have not the same force now, the Captain of our salvation having run us through the straits into the broad ocean; and our present connexion with the India Mission Conference enables us to receive and graduate our candidates for our itinerant ministry. There would be some important advantages gained by the organization of our Mission into one great India Conference; and the day is not far distant (probably by the General Conference of 1880) when we shall, by the all-conquering advance of Jesus Christ, our King, add the Bombay, Bengal, Madras, and "North West" Conferences to our list. "He shall not fail nor be discouraged, till He have set judgment in the earth: and the isles shall wait for His law." "Hallelujah! the Lord God Omnipotent reigneth!"

THE END.